AS PE for AQA

Nesta Wiggins-James

Rob James

Graham Thompson

Selected text used by permission of Sarah van Wely

www.heinemann.co.uk
✓ Free online support
✓ Useful weblinks
✓ 24 hour online ordering

01865 888058

Heinemann

Inspiring generations

Heinemann Educational Publishers
Halley Court, Jordan Hill, Oxford OX2 8EJ
Part of Harcourt Education

Heinemann is the registered trademark of
Harcourt Education Limited

© Harcourt Education Ltd, 2005

First published 2005

10 09 08 07 06
10 9 8 7 6 5 4 3

British Library Cataloguing in Publication Data is available
from the British Library on request.

ISBN 0 435 499300 / 978 0 435499 30 3

Typeset by 🌂 Tek-Art, Croydon, Surrey

Original illustrations © Harcourt Education Limited, 2005

Printed and bound in China through Phoenix Offset

Cover photo: © Corbis

Nesta and Rob would like to thank Ffion, Ellie, Rees and Cai for their support and patience during
the writing of this book.

Acknowledgements
Every effort has been made to contact copyright holders of material reproduced in this book.
Any omissions will be rectified in subsequent printings if notice is given to the publishers.

Photo credits:
Figure 2.07 pp32 Action Plus; Figure 4.03 p72 Science Photo Library BSIP, LAURENT
H.AMERICAN/SCIENCE PHOTO LIBRARY; Figure 4.04 pp74 Action Plus; Figure 4.06 p;78 supplied by the
author; Figure 5.01 pp94 Action Plus; Figure 5.02 pp94 Action Plus; Figure 5.05 pp97 Getty
Images/Photodisc; Figure 5.06 pp97 Action Plus; Figure 5.07 pp98 Action Plus; Figure 5.08 Action
Plus; Figure 5.09 pp99 Action Plus; Figure 6.01 pp106 Action Plus; Figure 6.02 pp107 Empics;
Figure 6.03 pp108 Action Plus; Figure 6.09 pp112 Corbis; Figure 6.11 pp115 Empics; Figure 7.01
pp120 Action Plus; Figure 7.02 pp120 Action Plus; Figure 7.03 pp122 Empics; Figure 7.04 pp123
Empics; Figure 7.06 pp126 Corbis; Figure 8.04 pp141 Empics/Tony Marshall; Figure 9.04 pp151
Action Plus; Figure 9.06 pp151 Empics; Figure 9.07 pp154 Action Plus/Glyn Kirk/Tony Marshall;
Peter Morris; Figure 10.2 pp168 Corbis; Figure 13.08 pp234 Action Plus; Figure 13.09 pp234
Action Plus

Text in artworks 10.1, 11.01, 11.02, 11.03, 11.04, 11.05, 11.06, 11.07, 11.08, 12.02, 13.01 used by
permission of Sarah van Wely.

AQA examination questions are reproduced courtesy of the Assessment and Qualifications Alliance.

Contents

Introduction

This book has been specifically designed for students following the AQA AS sport and physical education course. For maximal benefit this book should be used in conjunction with the **student workbook** written alongside this text, which provides a much greater range of tasks and past paper questions.

This text will support and reinforce the teaching that you receive in your centre and attempts to help you apply your understanding of theory to practical performance. The content of the book is presented in a form that is identical to the AQA specification and is arranged under the same sections and sub-headings.

Organization of the book

The book is divided into 3 sections – one for each module of your study.
- Unit 1 (PED1) – Physiological and psychological factors which improve performance
- Unit 2 (PED2) – Socio-cultural and historical effects on participation in physical activity and their influence on performance
- Unit 3 (PE3P or PE3C) – Analysis and improvement of performance

Each section is divided into chapters, which begin with a list of **learning objectives**. These are invaluable when it comes to preparing for your examination. Make sure that you can achieve each learning objective stated before you sit your examination.

Throughout each chapter you will find a series of **TASKS**, which are designed to help you understand and apply your knowledge in a way required by the final examination. Look out also in the margins for:
- HOT TIPS – helpful exam advice
- APPLICATION – how to put relevant application of theory into practice.

These have been specifically written to help improve your examination performance. At the end of each chapter is a short activity 'Revise as you go' list to help you assess what you have learnt so far.

At the end of each Unit, there are practice examination questions on some of the topics covered to help you prepare for the written exam.

Some essential guidance for the successful completion of your **Personal Exercise Programme** and your **Project coursework** (*optional*) is also contained in Unit 3. Do use this: if you follow the advice carefully you can't fail to do well!

How you will be examined

There are three units you must complete in order to gain your AS in Sport and Physical Education. PED1 and PED2 are assessed by written examination, whilst PE3P/C (your coursework) is assessed by your teachers in the first instance and then subject to moderation by the examination board.

UNIT 1 (PED1) Physiological and psychological factors which improve performance	UNIT 2 (PED2) Socio-cultural and historical effects on participation in physical activity and their influence on performance	UNIT 3 (PE3P or PE3C) Analysis and improvement of performance
$1\frac{1}{2}$ hours written examination	$1\frac{1}{4}$ hours written examination	Personal Exercise programme (12%)
4 from 5 × 18 mark questions + 3 marks QWC	3 from 4 × 18 mark questions + 3 marks QWC	Practical demonstration Or Written project (18%)
40% of total AS mark	30% of total AS mark	30% of total AS mark

Exam tips

1. Read the questions thoroughly so that you understand what they are asking you and what you have to do.
2. Relate your answer to the number of marks available for that question. Remember that you usually have to make one point in your answer for each mark that is available.
3. Wherever possible, apply theory to a practical activity and make sure that you name that activity.
4. Make sure that in your anatomy and physiology, and skill answers you use the appropriate technical terms.
5. In the contemporary studies questions make sure that your spelling, grammar and punctuation are correct, and that you write in sentences. Use paragraphs where appropriate.
6. In the contemporary studies questions make sure that you plan your answers – particularly in the questions that have 5–8 marks available.
7. Make sure that you plan the use of your time properly.
8. In the exam you will write your answers on the question paper. The number of lines available gives you an indication of the length of answer required.
9. Make sure that you revise all aspects of each area. Do not think that just because a topic was in a previous exam it will not be in yours.

Unit 1: Physiological and psychological factors which improve performance

Section 1: Physiological factors which affect participation, performance and improvement in performance

Chapter 1: Joints, muscles and mechanics – a study of human movement

Learning outcomes

By the end of this chapter you should be able to:
- name the major bones and muscles of the body
- explain the role of joints in the body and describe the structure of a synovial joint
- explain the term 'antagonistic muscle action' using an example from the human body
- describe the different types of muscle contraction: isotonic (concentric and eccentric) and isometric
- undertake a complete movement analysis of the following movements in relation to planes and axes of the body:
  a) leg action in running/sprinting
  b) movement at the shoulder in over-arm throwing and racket strokes
  c) leg action in squats
  d) arm action in push-ups
  e) leg action in kicking
  f) leg action in jumping
- identify the three classes of lever system, giving examples of each from the human body
- explain how an understanding of lever systems can aid effective performance in sport with reference to mechanical disadvantage, and range and speed of movement.

Introduction

The human body is an amazing machine. At the heart of its operations is movement, which occurs due to two of its systems working together: the skeletal and muscular systems. The muscles are the engines of movement that power the levers or bones of the body and enable us to move. This chapter will investigate the structure and function of each of these systems and look at how they interact to produce co-ordinated movements from a smooth sprinting action to a powerful tennis serve. The main focus of this chapter is movement analysis, and the knowledge you acquire from this chapter will help you describe and explain your sporting performances.

The skeletal system

 KEY WORDS

Ligament

A tough fibrous connective tissue that attaches one bone to another.

The skeletal system is made up of approximately 206 bones, which are joined together by **ligaments** to provide a framework of support for our muscles. The skeleton ensures the body can stand erect and maintain posture as well as providing protection for our vital organs. Bones also store essential minerals as well as being a centre for blood production. Another important function of the skeleton is that bones act as a system of levers that muscles can put into action to enable movement. Figure 1.01 identifies the names of those bones of the skeleton that are required for your study. Familiarize yourself with the names and location of these bones and then attempt Task 1 overleaf.

The skeleton can be divided into two basic sections known as the **axial** and **appendicular** skeletons. The axial skeleton consists of the bones that form

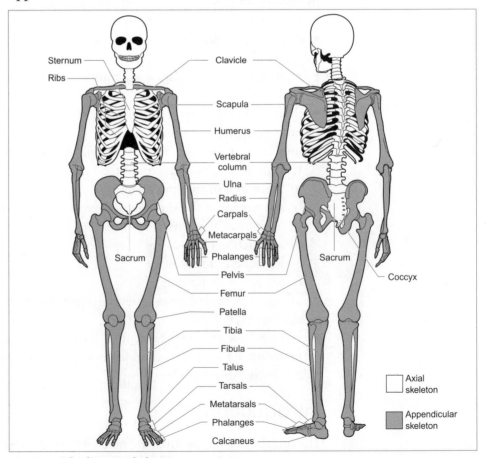

Fig. 1.01 The human skeleton

HOT TIPS

Make sure you use the appropriate technical terminology in your written exam.

the head, neck and trunk, and houses the vertebral column, ribcage and sternum. These bones are unshaded in Figure 1.01. The bones that form the axial skeleton form the main support and stabilizing structure of the body. The appendicular skeleton consists of the shoulder girdle (including the scapula and clavicle) together with the bones of the arms and hands as well as the hip girdle with the bones of the legs and feet. These bones are shaded in Figure 1.01. The majority of sporting movements are a result of moving the bones of the appendicular skeleton.

TASK 1

Using a partner's body as a model, correctly locate and label as many bones of their skeleton as possible. Use a stopwatch to time each other to see who can name the most bones in the quickest time.

TASK 2

Summarize the main functions of the skeleton.

The articular system: joints

Joints are formed wherever two or more bones meet and are the only places in the body where movement can take place. The site at which bones move against one another is sometimes called an articulation, but this term can only really be used of joints that allow movement. These are called **synovial** or freely movable joints and enable us to perform a wide range of movements. Fixed or immovable joints are called **fibrous joints**. Their role is to prevent any movement at the point at which two bones meet. A good example of this is where the bony plates of the skull meet. **Cartilaginous** or slightly movable joints are so called because they only allow a small degree of movement. The best examples of these in the human body are between the adjacent vertebrae of the spinal column. However, it is synovial joints that you must mainly focus on for your examination.

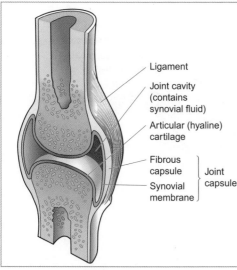

Ligament

Joint cavity (contains synovial fluid)

Articular (hyaline) cartilage

Fibrous capsule }
Synovial membrane } Joint capsule

Fig. 1.02 A typical synovial joint

Synovial joints

Synovial joints are categorized according to the range of movement possible at each joint. This is largely determined by the shapes of the articulating surfaces of the bones within the joint capsule, and the position and number of ligaments that surround the joint. All synovial joints possess several defining features (Figure 1.02). These include:

- **a joint capsule** – a tough connective tissue that surrounds and encases the bones of the joint
- **a joint cavity** – filled with synovial fluid, which helps to lubricate the joint
- **a synovial membrane** – this lines the inside of the joint capsule and secretes the synovial fluid

KEY WORDS

Bursae

Small sacs of synovial fluid located at points of friction in and around the joint capsule.

Meniscus (pl. menisci)

Discs of cartilage found between the articulating surfaces of the bones in the knee joint. They prevent wear and tear of the bones and help in shock absorption.

Pads of fat

Fatty tissue located in the joints to give added protection.

• **articular (hyaline) cartilage** – a smooth, slippery cartilage that covers the ends of the articulating bones, preventing friction and general wear and tear.

TASK 3

1 Figure 1.03 illustrates a typical synovial joint. Name the structures 1–5.

2 State whether the functions of these features are to increase protection, stability or mobility.

3 Several other features of a synovial joint include **ligaments, bursae, menisci** and **pads of fat**. Find out the role of each in the joint. For each feature, state whether they are there to increase protection, stability or mobility.

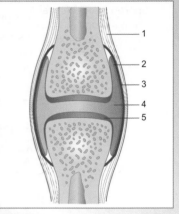

Fig. 1.03

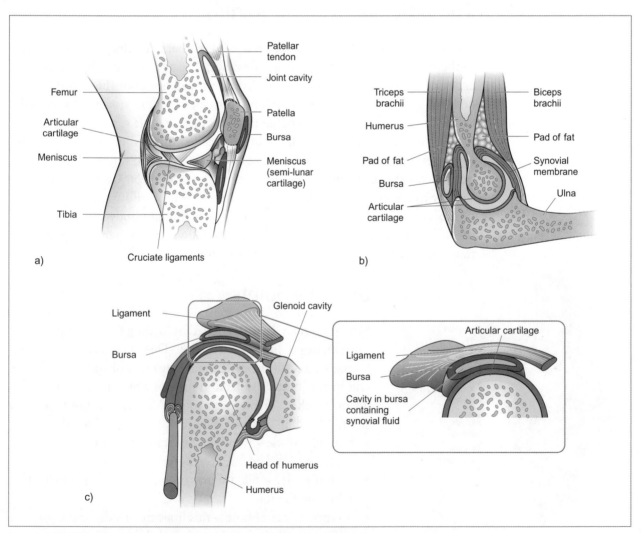

Fig. 1.04 a) The knee joint; b) the elbow joint; c) the shoulder joint

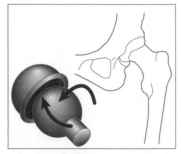

Fig. 1.05 Ball and socket joint

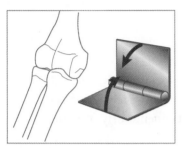

Fig. 1.06 Hinge joint

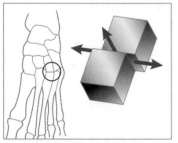

Fig. 1.08 Gliding joint

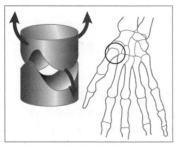

Fig. 1.09 Saddle joint

Types of synovial joint

The shapes of articulating surfaces at a joint can vary tremendously and can determine the range of movement that occurs (Figure 1.04). Synovial joints are therefore categorized according to the shape of these articulating surfaces. There are six types of synovial joint. These are outlined and illustrated below.

Ball and socket joint: these joints offer the widest range of movement. The head of one bone fits snugly into the cup-shaped cavity of another. Movement at these joints occurs in all three planes, allowing side-to-side, back and forth, and rotational movements. Examples include the shoulder and hip joints.

Hinge joint: these joints offer back and forth movement only in one plane. Here, bony protrusions called condyles articulate in depressions of a second articulating bone. Hinge joints also possess an intricate network of ligaments that restrict movement but make the joint very stable. Examples include the knee and elbow joints.

Pivot joint: pivot joints allow rotational movement only in one plane. Typically, the structure of a pivot joint includes the head or 'peg' of one bone articulating in a deep depression or socket of a second bone. Examples include the radio-ulnar joint and between the atlas and axis vertebrae.

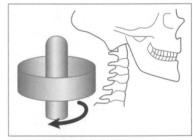

Fig. 1.07 Pivot joint

Gliding joint: these joints offer movement in two planes, back and forth and side-to-side movement. Typically, they occur where the articulating bones have flat surfaces that can slide past each other. Movement at these joints is limited by the action of ligaments. Examples include between the carpal bones of the wrist and between the ribs and thoracic vertebrae.

Saddle joint: a saddle joint permits side-to-side and back and forth, but no rotational movement. Two saddle-shaped articulating surfaces of adjacent bones (either concave or convex) 'fit' together at right angles to allow movement in these two planes. A good example can be found in the thumb at the site where the carpal and metacarpal meet.

Condyloid joint (ellipsoid): this is very similar to a hinge joint but instead of having movement restricted to one plane, side-to-side movement can also take place. The bony projections (condyles) of one bone articulate with hollow depressions of another. A good example is the radio-carpal joint where the radius articulates with the carpals at the wrist.

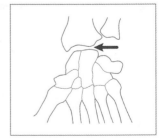

Fig. 1.10 Condyloid joint

TASK 4

1 Name the bones that articulate at the following joints:
   a) the shoulder joint   b) the elbow joint
   c) the hip joint   d) the knee joint
   e) the ankle joint.
2 When performing the butterfly stroke in swimming, the knee joint and shoulder joint are central to the performance. Briefly outline the structure of each joint and suggest how this structure suits the particular function of each joint in this activity.

Terms of movement

APPLICATION

To work out in which plane a particular movement takes place, think of a pane of glass splitting the body in two, running parallel to the movement occurring. This will give you the correct body plane.

In order to describe the movements of the body, special terms are used to explain the movements that are taking place. Using these terms correctly when studying movement analysis will help you tremendously in your examination. This language falls into three main areas:
- planes of the body
- terms of movement or 'movement patterns'
- axes of the body.

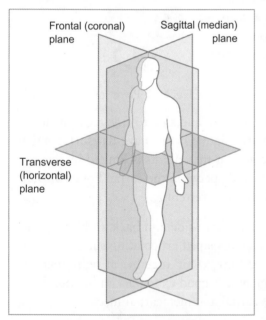

Fig. 1.11 Planes of the human body

Frontal (coronal) plane

Sagittal (median) plane

Transverse (horizontal) plane

Planes of the body

To aid our understanding of movement, it is useful to describe the body as having a series of 'planes' or imaginary flat surfaces (for example, panes of glass) running through the body within which different types of movement take place (Figure 1.11). There are three such planes:

1 **the sagittal (median) plane** divides the body vertically into left and right sides
2 **the frontal (coronal) plane** divides the body vertically into front and back sections
3 **the transverse (horizontal) plane** divides the body into top and bottom halves and runs horizontally parallel to the ground.

Terms of movement or 'movement patterns'

There are many different types of movement possible at synovial joints. You may remember that the movements permitted at any particular joint are largely determined by the joint structure. Some joints (the ball and socket joints) are designed to allow a wide range of movement, whilst others (hinge joints) are designed more for stability, which limits the amount of movement possible. Movements at synovial joints can be classified according to how the movement relates to the anatomical position.

APPLICATION

The anatomical position refers to a person standing upright, facing forwards, with the head erect, feet slightly apart, arms to the side and the palms of the hands facing forwards.

Movement patterns typically occur in pairs since if we can perform a movement at a joint in one direction, we must be able to return the body part to its original starting position, which requires movement in the opposite direction.

For your AS course, it is important that you can identify movement patterns and the planes in which each movement occurs. For ease, therefore, each pair of movement patterns has been categorized according to the relevant plane of movement.

Movements in the sagittal (median) plane

The sagittal plane divides the body down the middle into left and right halves. The following movements are parallel to this plane and are therefore said to take place within it.

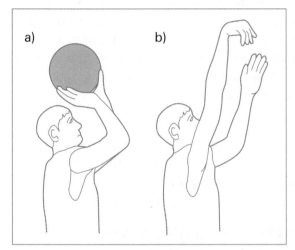

Fig. 1.12 a) Flexion and b) extension at the elbow during a set shot in basketball

- **Flexion and extension**

Flexion and extension (Figure 1.12) are distinctive to the sagittal plane. Flexion typically occurs when there is a decrease in angle between the articulating bones of a joint and there is a movement forward from the anatomical position. For example, bending the arm at the elbow during the upward phase of a bicep curl or bringing the arm forward at the shoulder joint. There are, however, one or two exceptions where flexion occurs with a movement backwards from the anatomical position, including bending the leg at the knee. Extension is usually any straightening movement that brings a body part backwards from its anatomical position. Extension will cause an increase in angle between the articulating bones at a joint, for example at the elbow when lowering the barbell during a bicep curl. Once again, extension at the knee is an exception, where extension brings the body part forward from the anatomical position. A continuation of extension beyond the anatomical position is sometimes referred to as hyperextension.

- **Plantar flexion and dorsiflexion**

Plantar flexion is unique to the ankle joint and is characterized by the pointing of the toes. More simply, it is extension at the ankle joint. Plantar flexion occurs at the ankle when performing a handstand, ensuring a neat bodyline. Flexion at the ankle joint is termed 'dorsiflexion' and occurs when there is a decrease in angle between the tibia and the foot, for example if you walk on your heels.

Movements in the frontal (coronal) plane

The frontal plane divides the body down the middle into front and back halves. The following movements are parallel to this plane and are therefore said to take place within it.

KEY WORDS

Abduction/adduction

Muscles that cause abduction are called abductors. Muscles that cause adduction are called adductors.

- **Abduction** and **adduction**

Abduction and adduction are distinctive to the frontal plane. Abduction is any movement that takes a body part *away* from the midline of the body, for example when raising the arm out sideways at the shoulder when performing 'the crucifix' on the rings apparatus in gymnastics. Adduction involves the movement of a body part *towards* the midline of the body. Taking our earlier example, adduction will occur when lowering the arm back to the sides of the body.

- **Lateral flexion**

The movement of the head or bending of the trunk sideways away from the midline of the body is termed lateral flexion.

- **Inversion and eversion**

Abduction and adduction of the foot are termed 'eversion' and 'inversion' respectively. Eversion of the foot is characterized by turning the sole of the foot laterally outwards, for example during the 'kicking' phase of a breaststroke leg kick. Inversion takes place when the sole of the foot is turned towards the midline of the body. This might happen when placing spin on a ball by kicking it with the outside of the foot.

- **Elevation and depression**

Movement of the scapula upwards, for example when shrugging the shoulders, is termed 'elevation'. This can be seen in the sporting arena when shooting in netball or basketball. When the scapulae are lowered back down, depression occurs.

Movements in the transverse (horizontal) plane

The transverse plane divides the body across the middle into upper and lower halves. The following movements are parallel to this plane and are therefore said to take place within it.

- **Lateral and medial rotation**

Rotation of a joint occurs when a bone moves about its longitudinal axis. Medial rotation is rotation that occurs towards the midline of the body from the anatomical position. When swimming butterfly, for example, medial rotation at the shoulder takes place when the arms enter the water. Lateral rotation, on the other hand, occurs when there is rotation of a body part towards the outside of the body from the anatomical position. For example, when preparing to put topspin on a tennis ball, lateral rotation must first take place at the shoulder joint.

- **Pronation and supination**

Rotation at the radio-ulnar joint is uniquely termed 'pronation' or 'supination'. Pronation is a form of medial rotation characterized by the turning of the palm of the hand to face downwards or backwards. Pronation will take place when placing topspin on a tennis ball. Supination of the radio-ulnar joint involves lateral rotation and will typically have occurred when the palm is facing upwards or forwards. When performing a 'dig' in volleyball, the forearms and palms of the hands will be facing upwards – supination has occurred.

- **Horizontal abduction and adduction (Horizontal flexion extension)**
Abduction and adduction in the horizontal plane are termed 'horizontal abduction' and 'horizontal adduction'. These movements can be demonstrated by raising your arm out in front of you so that your arm is parallel to the ground: this is flexion of the shoulder. Now move your arm towards the outside of the body, keeping it parallel to the ground: this is horizontal abduction. From here, move your arm towards the midline of your body: you have just performed horizontal adduction of the shoulder. Perhaps the best example of horizontal abduction and horizontal adduction is during the preparation and execution phases, respectively, of a discus throw.

There are several other movement patterns that take place in the body. One in particular that is necessary for your study is circumduction. **Circumduction** is said to occur when the distal end of a body part can describe a circle. Essentially, circumduction is a combination of flexion, extension, abduction and adduction, but can only truly happen at the ball and socket joints of the shoulder and hip. Circumduction occurs in two planes of movement: the sagittal and frontal planes. Circumduction occurs at the shoulder during the execution of a cricket bowl.

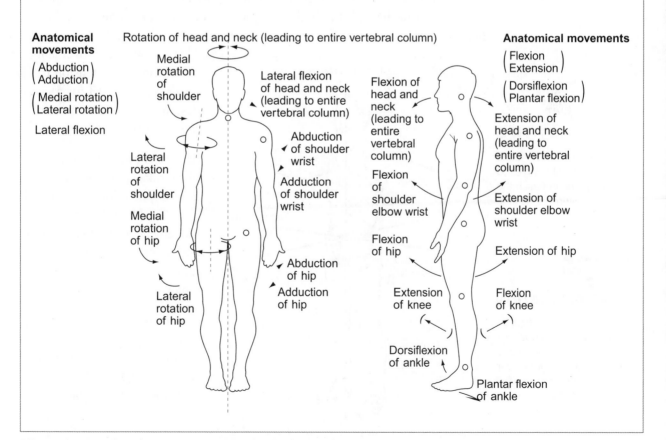

Fig. 1.13 Examples of movement patterns in the human body

TASK 5

Working with a partner, identify the movement patterns that occur at each of the joints outlined in Table 1.01. Once you have worked out these movements, complete the table in your student workbook. For each movement pattern identified, think of a relevant sporting example and write it in the third column of the table. An example for the hip has been started to help you.

Table 1.01

Joint	Movement patterns	Relevant sporting example
Hip	Flexion	During the downward phase of a leg squat
	Extension	When driving out of the blocks during a sprint start
	Abduction	
	Adduction	
	Medial rotation	
	Lateral rotation	
	Circumduction	
Knee		
Ankle		
Shoulder		
Elbow		
Radio-ulnar		
Wrist		

Axes of the body

Just as the earth rotates about its axis, articulating bones at the joints must rotate about one of three body axes (Figure 1.14). Like the body planes, these can once again be viewed as a series of imaginary lines (for example, poles) that run through the body. For movement to occur in the sagittal plane, rotation about the horizontal axis (transverse axis) must take place.

This enables the movements of flexion and extension to occur (see page 13 for a description of these types of movement).

Movement in the frontal plane takes place about the anterio-posterior axis (frontal axis), enabling the movements of abduction and adduction as well as some other associated movements, which are outlined below.

Finally, movement in the transverse plane takes place about the longitudinal axis, enabling rotational movement to take place.

HOT TIPS

The axis of rotation is always at right angles to the plane in which the movement occurs.

APPLICATION

Movement can take place about more than one axis and in more than one plane. Think of a high diver performing a full twisting dive.

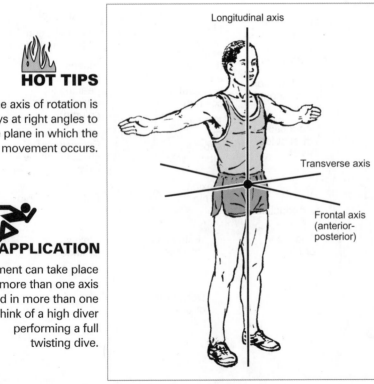

Fig. 1.14 The axes of the body

TASK 6

For each of the actions in Table 1.02, state the axis and plane in which the movement takes place.

Table 1.02

Movement	Plane	Axis of rotation
A cartwheel		
A backward somersault		
An ice skater spinning		
A full twisting somersault		

TASK 7

Write out the following statements, stating clearly beside them whether they are **true** or **false**.
1 The cruciate ligaments help to stabilize the knee joint.
2 The radio-ulnar joint is just another name for the elbow joint.
3 A front somersault takes place in the sagittal plane.
4 Horizontal abduction is also known as horizontal flexion.
5 The movements of flexion and extension take place about the horizontal axis.

Muscles – the engines of movement

The body possesses three types of muscle tissue: **skeletal muscle, cardiac muscle and smooth muscle.** Cardiac and smooth muscle are involuntary, working outside our conscious control, and are to be found in the heart and blood vessels respectively (smooth muscle is also found in the intestines and bladder). Skeletal muscle, however, is attached to the skeleton and is under our voluntary control. Consequently, it enables voluntary movement to take place. In addition to movement, skeletal muscle also helps to support and maintain the posture of the body through **muscle tone**, and produces heat, keeping the body warm through contraction. Since the focus of this chapter is an analysis of human movement, we will only be considering skeletal muscle in the following discussion.

At the end of this section, you should be able to locate some of the major skeletal muscles in the body, explain the function of each and apply this to a range of sporting performances.

Skeletal muscle

The human body contains in excess of 600 skeletal muscles, which contain contractile units that are able to convert chemical energy into mechanical energy and facilitate movement. Skeletal muscle is attached to the skeleton via **tendons**, which transmit the muscular 'pull' to the bones, causing them to move. Typically, a muscle will have two or more attachments onto the skeleton (via tendons). The attachment of the muscle on a bone nearer the midline of the body (the proximal end) is known as an **origin**. This is normally a flat, relatively stable bone. The attachment at the distal end of the bone, furthest away from the midline of the body, is known as the **insertion** and is typically attached to the bone that the muscle puts into action. Figure 1.15 shows the origin and insertion of the biceps brachii and triceps brachii muscles.

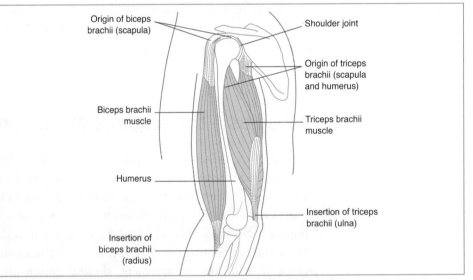

Fig. 1.15 The origin and insertion of the biceps brachii and triceps brachii muscles

Figure 1.16 illustrates the locations and functions of the major muscles that you are required to know for this AS course. Learning them all may seem a bit daunting, but by reading over them regularly, you will be surprised at how quickly you will be able to recall them.

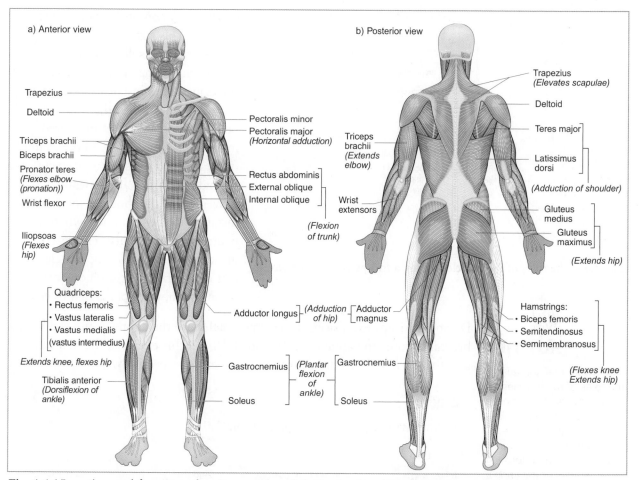

Fig. 1.16 Location and function of major muscles of the body, showing an anterior and posterior view

The co-ordination of movement – antagonistic muscle action

For smooth co-ordinated movements to occur, skeletal muscles need to co-operate and work together. Because muscles can only pull and not push, they will generally work in pairs with the help of several other muscles to ensure that the desired movements take place as effectively as possible. For any particular movement, muscles will take up one of several roles. The muscle that is directly responsible for the desired movement at a joint will typically shorten and is known as the **agonist** or **prime mover**. To assist this movement, the other muscle of the pair will lengthen and act as an **antagonist**. During the upward phase of a bicep curl, for example, flexion occurs at the elbow joint; the biceps brachii are the muscles directly responsible for this movement and shorten. They are the agonists. The triceps brachii are the antagonists and lengthen. However, several other muscles will ensure that this movement occurs smoothly. The trapezius will stabilize the scapula upon

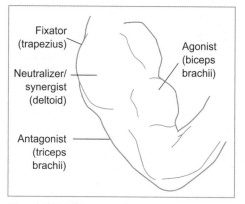

Fig. 1.17 A bicep curl

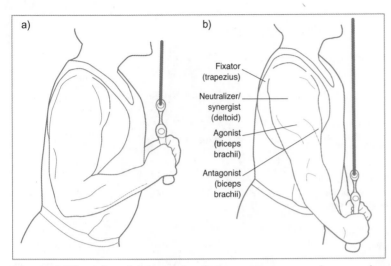

Fig. 1.18 The roles of the muscles during a triceps extension exercise

which the origin of the biceps brachii attaches. This ensures that the biceps have something solid to pull against when contracting. The role of the trapezius in this instance is as a **fixator** muscle. Meanwhile, other muscles will be preventing any other undesired movements in the body. In the example of the upward phase of a bicep curl, the deltoid neutralizes any unwanted movement at the shoulder joint. In this instance, the deltoid is known as a **neutralizer** or **synergist**. Figure 1.17 illustrates the antagonistic muscle action occurring at the elbow joint during the upward phase of a bicep curl.

During a triceps extension, the triceps brachii are the agonists and the biceps brachii become the antagonist (Figure 1.18). In this exercise, the neutralizer and fixator remain as the deltoid and trapezius respectively.

HOT TIPS

Be aware that sometimes the roles of the muscles do not reverse for opposite movements – this is especially true for downward movements such as when performing squats or lowering a barbell.

APPLICATION

During the downward phase of a bicep curl, the bicep remains as the agonist but lengthens as it contracts. In doing so, it acts like a brake to control the forearm as it lowers.

APPLICATION

Similarly, during the downward phase of a leg squat, the quadricep group is the agonist even though flexion is occurring at the knee. This controls the movement and prevents the body from collapsing to the floor.

TASK 8

Working with a partner, complete Table 1.03.

Table 1.03

Joint	Movement pattern	Agonist	Antagonist
Elbow	Flexion		
Elbow	Extension		
Radio-ulnar	Pronation		
Radio-ulnar	Supination		
Shoulder	Flexion		
Shoulder	Extension		
Shoulder	Abduction		
Shoulder	Adduction		
Trunk (lumbar)	Flexion		
Trunk (lumbar)	Extension		
Trunk (lumbar)	Lateral flexion		
Hip	Flexion		
Hip	Extension		
Hip	Abduction		
Hip	Adduction		
Knee	Flexion		
Knee	Extension		
Ankle	Plantar flexion		
Ankle	Dorsiflexion		

KEY WORDS

Types of muscular contraction

Isotonic contraction

An isotonic contraction involves some visible movement of the muscle. This can be either shortening (concentric) or lengthening (eccentric).

Isometric contraction

An isometric contraction occurs when a muscle is contracting but there is no visible movement of the main bulk of the muscle or muscle belly.

Muscles have different contraction capacities depending upon the role they are playing in the movement (Figure 1.19).

- The agonist muscle will generally shorten and fatten whilst contracting, drawing the insertion of the muscle towards the origin. This is **isotonic** concentric contraction. The triceps brachii undergo concentric contraction during the upward phase of a press-up.
- Sometimes muscles will contract whilst lengthening, acting like a brake to control the movement. When a muscle contracts whilst lengthening, isotonic eccentric contraction is taking place. The triceps brachii will undergo eccentric contraction during the downward phase of a press-up.
- A third type of muscle contraction occurs when there is an increase in muscle tension but no visible movement of the muscle. This is **isometric** muscle contraction and will invariably occur when a muscle is acting as a fixator or neutralizer. In the example of a press-up, the deltoids will work isometrically. We may also see isometric contraction taking place if the muscle is exerting a force against a resistance that it cannot overcome, for example when pushing against a wall or remaining stationary in the press-up position.

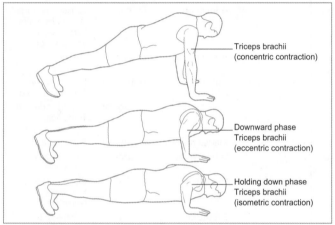

Fig. 1.19 Concentric, eccentric and isometric muscle contraction during a press-up

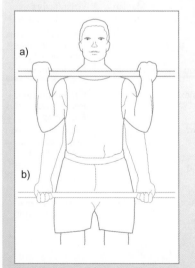

Fig. 1.20 A bicep curl being performed: a) upward phase and b) downward phase

TASK 9

1. Perform a bicep curl. Observe the movement occurring in the biceps brachii and triceps brachii during both the upward and downward phases of the curl.
2. Hold the barbell so that your elbows are held at 90°. Note the action of the triceps and biceps.
3. Complete Table 1.04 in your student workbook.

Table 1.04

Phase of bicep curl	Action of biceps brachii	Action of triceps brachii
Upward		
Downward		
Elbow at 90°		

Muscle functions

Flexors/extensors

Muscles that cause flexion are known as flexors. Muscles that cause extension are called extensors.

Table 1.05 summarizes the major functions of the muscles that surround each joint. You will need to study this so that you have a good understanding of these muscle functions.

Table 1.05 The major functions of the muscles

Joint	Action	Plane	Muscles used	Joint	Action	Plane	Muscles used
Hip	Flexion	Median	Psoas } Iliopsoas Iliacus Rectus femoris	Shoulder	Flexion	Median	Anterior deltoid Pectoralis major
	Extension	Median	Gluteus maximus Biceps femoris Semimembranosus Semitendinosus Gluteus medius		Extension	Median	Posterior deltoid Latissimus dorsi Teres major
					Adduction	Frontal	Latissimus dorsi Pectoralis major Teres major Teres minor
	Abduction	Frontal	Gluteus medius Gluteus minimus Tensor fasciae latae		Abduction	Frontal	Medial deltoid Supraspinatus
	Adduction	Frontal	Adductor magnus Adductor brevis Adductor longus gracilis		Horizontal adduction	Horizontal	Pectoralis major Anterior deltoid
					Horizontal abduction	Horizontal	Posterior deltoid Trapezius Latissimus dorsi
	Medial rotation	Horizontal	Gluteus medius Gluteus minimus Tensor fasciae latae		Medial rotation	Horizontal	Subscapularis
	Lateral rotation	Horizontal	Gluteus maximus Adductors		Lateral rotation	Horizontal	Infraspinatus Teres minor
Knee	Flexion	Median	Hamstrings (semitendinosus, semimembranosus, biceps femoris) Gastrocnemius	Elbow	Flexion	Median	Biceps brachii Brachialis Brachioradialis
					Extension	Median	Triceps brachii
	Extension	Median	Quadriceps (rectus femoris, vastus medialis, vastus lateralis, vastus intermedius) Tensor fasciae latae	Radio-ulnar	Pronation	Horizontal	Pronator teres Brachioradialis
					Supination	Horizontal	Biceps brachii Supinator
				Wrist	Flexion	Median	Wrist **flexors**
					Extension	Median	Wrist **extensors**
Ankle	Dorsiflexion	Median	Tibialis anterior Extensor digitorum longus	Movement of the trunk	Flexion	Median	Rectus abdominus Internal obliques External obliques
					Extension	Median	Erector spinae Spinalis
	Plantar flexion	Median	Gastrocnemius Soleus Flexor digitorum longus		Lateral flexion	Frontal	Internal obliques Rectus abdominus Erector spinae
	Inversion	Frontal	Tibialis anterior Flexor digitorum longus		Rotation		External obliques Rectus abdominus Erector spinae
	Eversion	Frontal	Peroneus longus Peroneus brevis Extensor digitorum longus	Movement of the scapulae	Elevation	Frontal	Levator scapulae Trapezius Rhomboids
					Depression	Frontal	Lower trapezius Pectoralis minor

Levers of the body

We established earlier in this chapter that in order for us to perform sporting movements, from kicking a rugby ball to serving in tennis, the bones of the skeleton act as a series of levers against which the muscles can pull. Levers are relatively simple mechanisms that involve a rigid bar rotating about a fixed point when a force or effort is applied to overcome a resistance.

Levers in the body can help us to:
- maintain balance
- give greater speed to an object by throwing it or kicking it
- overcome a heavy resistance with little effort
- give a wider range of movement.

There are three components to every lever system.
1 **An effort point (E).** In the human body, this will be the point at which the force supplied by a contracting muscle is applied, that is, the insertion of the muscle.
2 **A pivot point or fulcrum (F).** In the human body, this will be the joint itself.
3 **A resistance point or load (L).** This may simply be the weight of the lever or body part, or an object that we are trying to move.

There are three types (classes) of lever system found in the human body: first, second and third. Each has a particular function, whether it is to increase the amount of resistance that can be overcome by a given force or to increase the speed of an object. A lever system is classified according to the relative positions of the effort, fulcrum and load (the three components listed above). Look at the information in the following table, which explains the function of each class of lever.

HOT TIPS

If you are having difficulty in working out what class of lever is operating at a particular joint, try to work out the middle component. Once you have this, you will be able to determine the lever system working. Use the following rhyme: 'For 1, 2, 3, think F, L, E.' Whereby F is the middle component of a first class lever, L for a second class lever and E for a third class lever system.

Table 1.06 Classes of levers in the body

Class of lever	Positions of components	Example in the human body	Function
First class lever	Fig. 1.21	When throwing the javelin (L), the triceps brachii provides the effort to extend the arm at the elbow (F) Fig. 1.22	Can be used to increase speed of an object

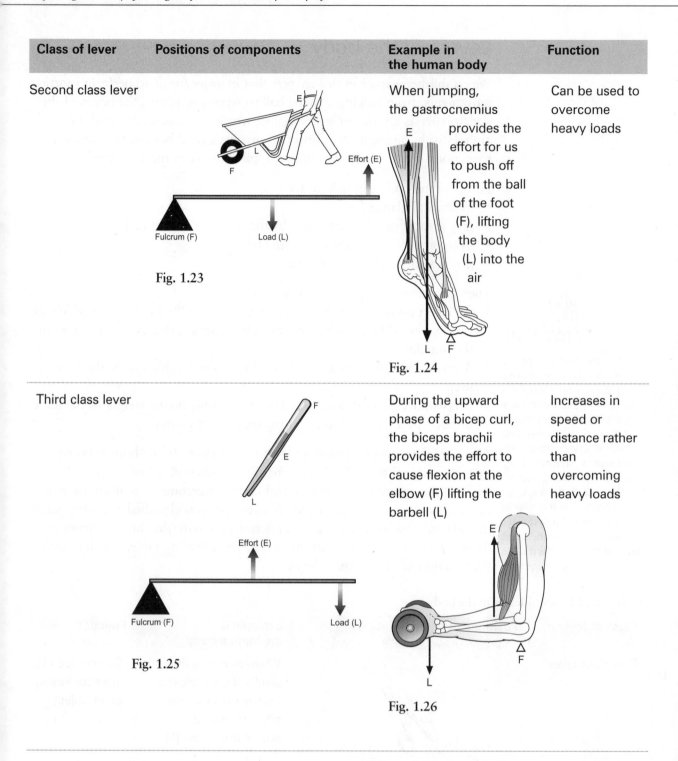

Class of lever	Positions of components	Example in the human body	Function
Second class lever	Fig. 1.23	When jumping, the gastrocnemius provides the effort for us to push off from the ball of the foot (F), lifting the body (L) into the air Fig. 1.24	Can be used to overcome heavy loads
Third class lever	Fig. 1.25	During the upward phase of a bicep curl, the biceps brachii provides the effort to cause flexion at the elbow (F) lifting the barbell (L) Fig. 1.26	Increases in speed or distance rather than overcoming heavy loads

HOT TIPS

Most lever systems used in the human body are third class lever systems!

Two other important features of lever systems are the **force arm** and the **resistance arm**. The force arm (also known as the effort arm) is the name given to the shortest perpendicular distance between the fulcrum and the application of the force, whilst the resistance arm refers to the shortest perpendicular distance between the fulcrum and the resistance. Figure 1.22 illustrates a first class lever system operating at the elbow. Here, the longer resistance arm cannot move as heavy a load but gives greater speed to the

KEY WORDS

Mechanical disadvantage

Mechanical disadvantage occurs in a lever system when the resistance arm is longer than the force arm. This means that the lever system cannot move as heavy a load but can do it faster.

Mechanical advantage

Mechanical advantage occurs in a lever system when the force arm is longer than the resistance arm. This means that the lever system can move a large load over a short distance.

system. When the resistance arm is greater than the force arm, the lever system is at a **mechanical disadvantage**. A longer force arm allows for more force to be developed and a large load can be moved over a short distance. This is known as **mechanical advantage**.

TASK 10

Draw a simple second class lever system from the human body. On your diagram, label the force arm and the resistance arm. Which is longer? What does this tell you about the function of second class lever systems?

The vast majority of levers in the human body are third class levers, which are better suited to increasing the body's ability to move quickly than to improving its ability to move heavy loads. This is because in third class levers the resistance arm is always greater than the effort arm, and therefore mechanical disadvantage exists.

The body's levers can be made even more effective by using implements such as rackets, oars and ski poles. In essence, striking implements such as rackets and clubs are extensions of the body's third class levers, increasing the length of the resistance arm of the lever and consequently the speed at the end of it. Keeping the arm extended when bowling a cricket ball or during a tennis serve will maximize the length of the resistance arm and allow more force to be exerted. Tall tennis players have an advantage on the serve as they have very long levers and can impart a great deal of speed onto the tennis ball.

TASK 11

Name and sketch the lever system that is in operation in each of the following examples:
a) at the ankle during the take-off phase of a long jump
b) at the elbow when throwing the javelin
c) at the knee when kicking a football.

TASK 12

Write out the following statements, stating clearly beside them whether they are **true** or **false**.
1 The tibialis anterior causes plantar flexion at the ankle.
2 The gluteus maximus causes extension at the hip.
3 The origin of the gastrocnemius muscle is on the femur.
4 When performing a leg squat, the quadriceps muscle group are the agonist in both the downward and upward phases of the movement.
5 When performing a press-up, the triceps brachii are the agonists in both the downward and upward phases of the movement.
6 When jumping, a first class lever system operates at the ankle joint.

Putting it all together – movement analysis

You now have all the information that you need to comprehensively complete a full movement analysis of a wide range of skills. To help you remember the key features of a movement analysis, ask yourself the questions outlined below.

- What bones are articulating?
- At what type of joint is the movement taking place?
- What movement pattern or joint action is happening?
- In which plane and about what axis is the movement taking place?
- What are the name and function of the muscle contracting?
- How is the muscle contracting?
- Which lever system is operating?

The following section investigates a range of skills from a variety of sporting activities. For each skill, a complete movement analysis has been undertaken. Your task is to study each completed skill and then complete a full analysis for:

a) leg action in jumping

b) arm action in throwing

c) leg action in kicking

d) the arm action during a tennis serve.

For the AQA specification, you must be able to perform a movement analysis for each of the skills listed below:

- leg action in running/sprinting
- leg action in squats
- leg action in kicking
- leg action in jumping
- arm/shoulder action in throwing
- shoulder/arm action in racket strokes
- arm action in press-ups.

Leg action in running/sprinting

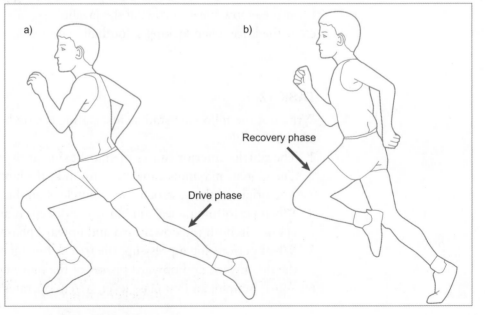

Fig. 1.27 A running action: a) drive phase and b) recovery phase

HOT TIPS

In your examination, it may be easier to draw up a movement analysis table to help your explanation and description of movement taking place.

Table 1.07 Analysis of leg action in running/sprinting

Joint	Phase of movement	Plane	Axis	Movement pattern	Muscles responsible	Role of muscle	Type of contraction	Lever system
Hip	Drive	Sagittal	Transverse	Extension/ hyperextension	Gluteal muscles Hamstring group	Agonist	Concentric	Third
	Recovery	Sagittal	Transverse	Flexion	Hip flexors (quadriceps and iliopsoas)	Agonist	Concentric	Third
Knee	Drive	Sagittal	Transverse	Extension	Quadriceps group	Agonist	Concentric	Third
	Recovery	Sagittal	Transverse	Flexion	Hamstring group	Agonist	Concentric	Third
Ankle	Drive	Sagittal	Transverse	Plantar flexion	Gastrocnemius	Agonist	Concentric	Second
	Recovery	Sagittal	Transverse	Dorsiflexion	Tibialis anterior	Agonist	Concentric	Second

Table 1.08 Analysis of leg action in a squat

Joint	Phase of movement	Plane	Axis	Movement pattern	Muscles responsible	Role of muscle	Type of contraction	Lever system
Hip	Downward	Sagittal	Transverse	Flexion	Gluteal muscles	Agonist	Eccentric	Third
	Upward	Sagittal	Transverse	Extension	Gluteal muscles	Agonist	Concentric	Third
Knee	Downward	Sagittal	Transverse	Flexion	Quadriceps group	Agonist	Eccentric	Third
	Upward	Sagittal	Transverse	Extension	Quadriceps group	Agonist	Concentric	Third
Ankle	Downward	Sagittal	Transverse	Dorsiflexion	Gastrocnemius	Agonist	Eccentric	Second
	Upward	Sagittal	Transverse	Plantar flexion	Gastrocnemius	Agonist	Plantar flexion	Second

Table 1.09 Analysis of arm action in a press-up

Joint	Phase of movement	Plane	Axis	Movement pattern	Muscles responsible	Role of muscle	Type of contraction	Lever system
Elbow (triceps press)	Downward	Sagittal	Transverse	Flexion	Triceps brachii	Agonist	Eccentric	First
	Upward	Sagittal	Transverse	Extension	Triceps brachii	Agonist	Concentric	First
Shoulder ('pec' press)	Downward	Transverse	Longitudinal	Horizontal abduction	Pectoralis major	Agonist	Eccentric	Third
	Upward	Transverse	Longitudinal	Horizontal adduction	Pectoralis major	Agonist	Concentric	Third

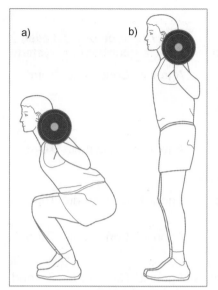

Fig. 1.28 Leg squats: a) downward phase and b) upward phase

Leg action in squats

You will note from Table 1.08 that the same muscle is responsible for both flexion and extension at each of the joints. This is because the action of a squat is in a downward direction with the added force of gravity. In order to stop the body collapsing to the floor during this downward movement, the agonist muscle lengthens, undergoing an eccentric contraction, which controls the movement and acts as a brake. A similar situation occurs in the arms during a press-up (Figure 1.29 and Table 1.09).

Arm action in a press-up

Note that there are two different ways a press-up can be performed:
- a triceps press is where hands are placed shoulder width apart and predominantly works the triceps brachii
- a 'pec' press is where hands are placed wider than shoulder width apart and predominantly works the pectoralis major.

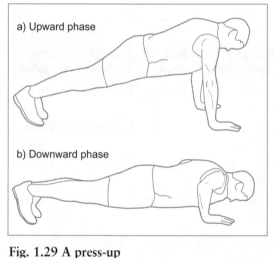

Fig. 1.29 A press-up

TASK 13

Draw a blank movement analysis table and complete a full movement analysis for each of the following:
a) the leg action in jumping
b) the arm action in throwing
c) the leg action in kicking
d) the arm action during a tennis serve.

Revise as you go!

1 Identify the bones that articulate at: a) the shoulder joint
b) the knee joint
c) the ankle joint.

2 Which plane of movement: a) divides the body into left and right sections
b) divides the body into front and back sections
c) divides the body into top and bottom?

3 During the action of a press-up, state the function of the triceps brachii in both the upward and downward phases.

4 State the three components of a lever system.

Chapter 2: The cardiovascular system – the maintenance and control of blood supply

Learning outcomes

By the end of this chapter you should be able to:
- describe how the heart is structured in relation to its function as a dual action pump
- explain the events of the cardiac cycle in relation to the conduction system of the heart
- define heart rate, stroke volume and cardiac output, giving typical resting values and describing the effects of varying workloads upon them
- draw and label the expected heart rate curves for sub-maximal and maximal workloads
- differentiate between pulmonary and systemic circulation
- name and describe the structure of the blood vessels, identifying their main features in relation to their respective functions
- explain the importance of blood pressure in relation to the redistribution of blood during exercise
- describe the mechanisms of venous return
- explain the regulation and control of the heart rate through neural and hormonal means
- describe the effects of training on cardiac functioning
- explain what is meant by the terms 'bradycardia' and 'cardiac hypertrophy'.

Introduction

The body has its own unique plumbing system that ensures that all parts of the body receive an adequate supply of blood. At the centre of this operation is the heart, an efficient muscular pump made out of specialist cardiac tissue that works continuously. The blood vessels act as an extensive network of pipes, which extend into and reach all parts of the body to feed the living tissues with blood.

The blood nourishes these tissues, feeding them with the oxygen and nutrients they require as well as removing any waste products that have been produced. Together the heart, blood vessels and the blood form the cardiovascular system, and this works in conjunction with the respiratory system (see Chapter 3) to maintain a constant supply of oxygen to the muscles both at rest and during exercise. In this chapter you will see how the maintenance and control of the blood supply is the major determining factor in the effective and successful performance of **aerobic** or endurance-based exercise.

KEY WORDS

Aerobic exercise
Exercise that is sub-maximal and requires oxygen.

The structure of the heart

You will recall from your previous study that the heart is structured as a dual purpose pump. The left side of the heart (on the right as you look at it) is responsible for pumping oxygen-rich blood around the whole of the body, whilst the right side pumps blood that is low in oxygen around to the lungs where it can be re-oxygenated and returned to the left side of the heart. To ensure this process functions as effectively as possible, there are many anatomical structures of the heart, which are illustrated in Figure 2.01.

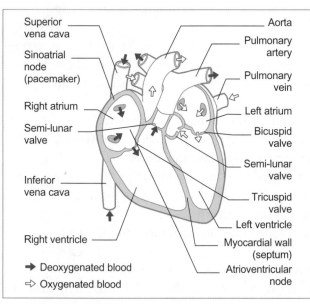

Fig. 2.01 The anatomical structure of the heart

To help understand the anatomy of the heart you will now be taken on a journey through it. Make a note of the key structures and their functions as you go.

Blood low in oxygen returns from the body to the right atrium via the superior (upper body) and inferior (lower body) vena cava. At the same time, oxygen-rich blood returns to the left atrium from the lungs via the pulmonary veins. The **atria** are the top two chambers of the heart. You will see from Figure 2.01 that they are separated by a thick muscular wall that runs through the middle of the heart, known as the **septum**. This enables the two pumps to function separately – thus enabling the heart to be dual purpose (Figure 2.02).

Blood will eventually start to enter the larger lower chambers of the heart, called the right and left **ventricles**. In doing so, it passes the **atrioventricular** (AV) valves. The right AV valve is the **tricuspid valve** and the left AV valve is the **bicuspid valve**. The purpose of these valves is not merely to separate the atria from the ventricles but also to ensure that the blood can only flow in one direction through the heart. When the ventricles contract, blood on the right side of the heart is forced through the semi-lunar pulmonary valve into the pulmonary artery from where it travels towards the lungs. Meanwhile, blood from the left ventricle enters the aorta via the semi-lunar aortic valve. The aorta branches into many different arteries, which then transport the blood around the whole body. Once again, the semi-lunar valves ensure the unidirectional flow of blood, preventing backflow of blood into the heart.

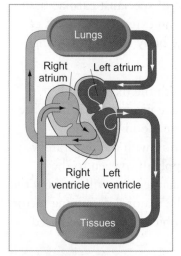

Fig. 2.02 The heart as a dual action pump

KEY WORDS

Myocardium

Cardiac muscle that makes up the heart.

HOT TIPS

Remember that the heart requires its own blood supply. It achieves this via the coronary arteries, which feed the myocardium with oxygen and other nutrients to keep it pumping continuously.

As the left side of the heart is responsible for pumping blood around the whole body, the wall of cardiac tissue (**myocardium**) surrounding the left ventricle is much thicker than that on the right side of the heart.

TASK 1

Table 2.01

Structure of the heart	Function
Aorta	
AV bicuspid valve	
Right ventricle	
Pulmonary vein	
Septum	

Copy and complete Table 2.01, identifying the relevant function for the anatomical structure of the heart identified.

KEY WORDS

Myogenic

The ability of the heart to produce its own impulses.

The conduction system of the heart

Cardiac tissue is extremely specialized. To start with, it is '**myogenic**', which means that it can generate its own electrical impulses and does not require stimulation by the brain. It also possesses an intricate network of nerves. Together, these two factors ensure an efficient flow of blood through the heart and around the body.

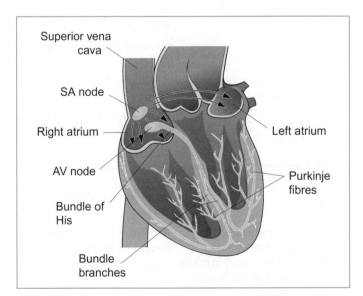

Fig. 2.03 The spread of a cardiac impulse through the heart

The cardiac impulse originates from the **sinoatrial node** (SA node). This is a specialized area of cardiac muscle fibres located in the muscular wall of the right atrium and acts as the heart's intrinsic pacemaker. Once the SA node has emitted the electrical impulse, it rapidly spreads throughout both atria, creating a wave of excitation and causing them both to contract. The impulse then arrives at and activates another specialized area of cardiac tissue known as the **atrioventricular node** (AV node). The AV node initially delays the transmission of the cardiac impulse from spreading to the ventricles (for approx 0.1 seconds). This enables the atria to contract fully before ventricular contraction begins.

After this short delay, the impulse is sent down the septum of the heart via the bundle of His and throughout the muscular walls of the ventricles via Purkinje fibres. Both ventricles now contract, forcing the blood out of the

HOT TIPS

The SA node emits a cardiac impulse approximately 72 times per minute for the average person.

heart and around the body. Figure 2.03 traces the journey of an impulse through the heart's conduction system. Take a few minutes to familiarize yourself with the components of this system.

The cardiac cycle

The cardiac cycle refers to the electrical and mechanical events that take place in the heart during one complete heartbeat. Typically, at rest, one complete heartbeat will occur every 0.8 seconds and occurs approximately 72 times per minute. During this time, the heart will at first relax and fill with blood – known as the **diastolic phase** – and then contract, forcing blood from one part of the heart to another or forcing blood out of the heart altogether – this is referred to as the **systolic phase**.

It is possible to summarize the cardiac cycle into four stages:

Stage 1 Atrial diastole   } 0.5 seconds
Stage 2 Ventricular diastole

Stage 3 Atrial systole   } 0.3 seconds
Stage 4 Ventricular systole

Table 2.02 A summary of the events of the cardiac cycle

HOT TIPS

It is very important that you can link the events of the cardiac cycle to the conduction system of the heart. The flow diagram in Figure 2.04 should help you do this.

Stage of cardiac cycle	Description	Action of valves
Atrial diastole (relaxation)	Atria fill with blood	Atrioventricular valves are closed Semi-lunar valves are open
Ventricular diastole (relaxation)	Rising pressure in the atria causes the AV valves to open and the ventricles to fill with blood	Atrioventricular valves open Semi-lunar valves are closed
Atrial systole (contraction)	Atria contract, forcing blood into the ventricles	Atrioventricular valves open Semi-lunar valves are closed
Ventricular systole (contraction)	Ventricles contract, increasing pressure in the ventricles, and forcing blood into the aorta and pulmonary artery	Atrioventricular valves are forced to close

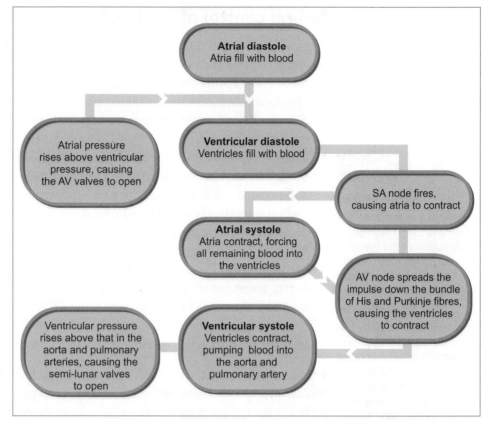

Fig. 2.04 The events of the cardiac cycle linked to the conduction system of the heart

The control of the heart rate

It was stated earlier that the heart is myogenic – it generates its own impulses from its own intrinsic pacemaker, the sinoatrial node (SA node). However, the rate at which cardiac impulses are fired can be altered and controlled by mechanisms external to the heart. During exercise, for example, the heart rate must increase and the SA node must fire impulses more rapidly in order to meet the body's demands for oxygen. It is able to do this through two main regulatory mechanisms:

- **neural control mechanism**
- **hormonal control mechanism.**

Central to the regulation of the heart rate is the **cardiac control centre (CCC)** (see Figure 2.05), situated in the **medulla oblongata**. Forming part of the **autonomic nervous system,** the CCC is under involuntary control and is made up of two components:

1 **the sympathetic nervous system** or cardio-acceleratory centre, which, as the name suggests, is responsible for increasing heart rate
2 **the parasympathetic nervous system** or cardio-inhibitory centre, which is the heart's braking system, returning heart rate back to normal resting levels.

Both the sympathetic and parasympathetic systems act upon the SA node and will cause the heart rate to increase or decrease, respectively, depending upon the requirements of the body.

KEY WORDS

Medulla oblongata

Part of the brain that controls such functions as heart and respiratory rate.

Autonomic nervous system

The self-governing or involuntary component of the nervous system. It transmits nerve impulses from the central nervous system to the heart, lungs and smooth muscle without our conscious control.

Neural control of the heart

The cardiac control centre receives information from different sensory receptors around the body which include:

- **mechanoreceptors and proprioceptors.** These inform the CCC of the extent of movement that is taking place within the muscles and tendons. Exercise brings about an increase in muscular activity, which requires an increase in heart rate
- **chemoreceptors.** These are specialized cells that detect changes in the pH of the blood. They are located in the aorta and carotid arteries of the neck and provide information to the CCC concerning the concentration of carbon dioxide, lactic acid and oxygen in the blood. Increases in carbon dioxide and lactic acid that accompany exercise will cause the pH of the blood to fall and cause the heart rate to increase
- **baroreceptors.** These are stretch receptors that exist in the walls of the aorta, venae cavae and carotid arteries. They detect increases in blood flow and therefore blood pressure within these vessels. If these stretch receptors within the venae cavae are stimulated, then the CCC causes an increase in heart rate, which in turn causes an increase in cardiac output.

During strenuous exercise, the CCC responds to information from the mechanoreceptors, chemoreceptors and baroreceptors by stimulating the SA node via the sympathetic or cardiac acceleratory nerve, which causes the heart rate and stroke volume to increase. Once exercise stops, the stimulation of the SA node by the sympathetic nerve reduces and allows the parasympathetic vagus nerve to take over, causing a decrease in the heart rate. The more stimulation of the SA node by the vagus nerve, the quicker the heart rate will return to normal resting levels.

Hormonal control of heart rate

You may have experienced the feeling of 'butterflies' together with an increase in your heart rate prior to an important competition. This 'anticipatory' response or rise is largely due to the hormone **adrenaline**, which is released by the adrenal glands into the bloodstream during times of stress. It prepares the body for the impending exercise by increasing heart rate and strength of ventricular contraction, and consequently forms part of the sympathetic system. During exercise, adrenaline (and its close relative noradrenaline) can aid the body's response to exercise by:

- increasing heart rate and rate of respiration
- constricting blood vessels, which increases blood pressure, helping blood to reach the active muscles
- increasing blood glucose levels by stimulating the breakdown of glycogen in the liver. This helps to fuel muscular contraction.

KEY WORDS

Chemoreceptors

Receptors in the body that are sensitive to changes in the acidity of the blood. In particular, they monitor levels of carbon dioxide and lactic acid in the blood.

Baroreceptors

Receptors in the body that monitor the degree of stretch of various blood vessels (carotid arteries, aorta, venae cavae). The level of stretch can give an indication of blood pressure.

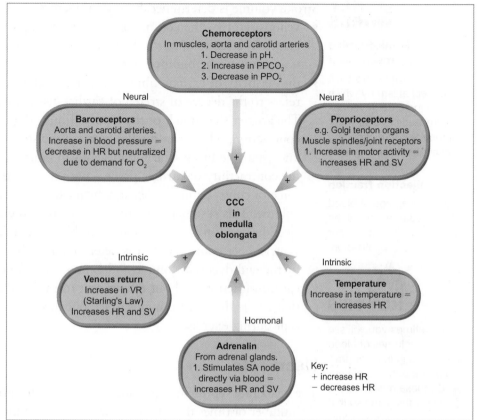

Fig. 2.05 A summary of factors affecting the cardiac control centre (CCC)

It was established earlier that following exercise, stimulation of the SA node by the sympathetic nerve decreases, which allows the parasympathetic nerve to take over, causing the heart rate to fall. It is the action of another hormone, acetylcholine, released by parasympathetic nerves, that in fact causes this decrease in heart rate.

TASK 2

In your own words, explain the antagonistic action of the sympathetic and parasympathetic nerves in the regulation of heart rate during and following exercise.

Cardiac dynamics and performance

The performance of the heart is largely dependent upon two variables that work together to optimize cardiac functioning. These two variables are:
- stroke volume (SV)
- heart rate (HR).

Stroke volume

Stroke volume is 'the volume of blood pumped out of the heart per beat'. It usually refers to the blood ejected from the left ventricle and is measured in millilitres (ml) or cm^3. A typical resting value of stroke volume at rest is about 75ml, but this can increase significantly in a trained athlete.

Stroke volume is determined by several factors:

- **venous return** – the volume of blood returning to the right atrium. The greater the venous return, the greater the stroke volume since more blood is available to be pumped out
- **the elasticity of cardiac fibres** (sometimes referred to as pre-load) – this refers to the degree of stretch of cardiac tissue just prior to contraction. The greater the stretch of the cardiac fibres, the greater the force of contraction, which can further increase the stroke volume. This is also known as the **Frank-Starling mechanism** (Starling's Law).
- **the contractility of cardiac tissue** – with increased contractility, a greater force of contraction can occur, which can cause an increase in stroke volume. This results partly due to an increased **ejection fraction**. The ejection fraction is the percentage of blood actually pumped out of the left ventricle per contraction. It is determined by dividing the stroke volume by the end-diastolic volume and expressed as a percentage. At rest, the ejection fraction is about 60 per cent (meaning that 40 per cent of blood that enters the heart remains in it), but this can increase to over 85 per cent during exercise.

Heart rate

The heart rate represents the number of complete cardiac cycles and therefore the number of times the left ventricle ejects blood into the aorta per minute. The average resting heart rate of a human is 72 beats per minute, but this can vary tremendously depending upon levels of fitness. We might expect, for example, an elite endurance athlete to have a resting heart rate of below 60 beats per minute. When this happens, **bradycardia** is said to have taken place.

It is possible to measure your heart rate by palpating your radial or carotid arteries. This is referred to as your **pulse rate**.

Cardiac output

Cardiac output reflects the relationship between stroke volume and heart rate. It is defined as the volume of blood ejected by the heart per minute and measured in litres per minute (l/min) or dm^3. It is the product of stroke volume and heart rate and can be expressed as:

cardiac output (Q) = stroke volume (SV) × heart rate (HR).

This relationship shows that if there is an increase in either stroke volume or heart rate (or both), then cardiac output will increase. This will be discussed further in the following section when we will investigate the response of the heart to exercise. Table 2.03 gives expected values for cardiac output, stroke volume and heart rate.

Table 2.03 Typical values for cardiac output, stroke volume and heart rate at rest

	Cardiac output =	stroke volume ×	heart rate
Definition	The volume of blood ejected from the heart per minute	The volume of blood ejected from the heart per beat	The number of cardiac cycles per minute
Untrained subject	Five litres or dm³ per minute	70ml or cm³	72bpm
Trained subject	Five litres or dm³ per minute	85ml or cm³	60bpm

Cardiac dynamics during exercise

During exercise, the body's muscles demand more oxygen. Consequently, the heart must work harder in order to ensure that sufficient oxygen is delivered by the blood to the working muscles, and that waste products such as carbon dioxide and lactic acid are removed. You will recall that:

cardiac output (Q) = stroke volume (SV) x heart rate (HR).

It is now necessary to consider what happens to each of these variables during exercise.

Heart rate response to exercise

KEY WORDS

Sub-maximal exercise

Exercise that is of low intensity and well within the capabilities of the performer. It is significantly below their maximum effort.

Anticipatory rise

The pre-exercise response of the heart to the release of adrenaline, which results in an elevated heart rate.

You are aware that when we exercise, heart rate increases, but the extent of the increase is largely dependent upon exercise intensity. Typically, heart rate increases linearly in direct proportion to exercise intensity so that the harder you are working, the higher your heart rate will be. This proportional increase in heart rate will continue until you approach your maximum heart rate (this can be calculated by subtracting your age from 220). However, we do not always perform exercise of increasing intensity. During **sub-maximal exercise**, where exercise is performed at constant intensity over a prolonged period of time such as a 1500m swim, you might expect heart rate to plateau into a **steady state** for much of the swim. This steady state represents the point where oxygen demand is being met by oxygen supply and the exercise should therefore be relatively comfortable. Figure 2.06 illustrates typical heart rate curves for maximal and sub-maximal exercise. Make sure that you are able to draw and label these curves.

You will note that just prior to exercise, heart rate increases even though the exercise is yet to commence. This phenomenon is known as the **anticipatory rise** and represents the heart's preparation for the forthcoming activity. It results from the release of hormones such as adrenaline, which causes the SA node to increase the heart rate. You will also note that following exercise, the heart rate takes a while to return to its resting level; this represents the body's recovery period. During this phase, the heart rate must remain slightly elevated in order to rid the body of waste products such as lactic acid.

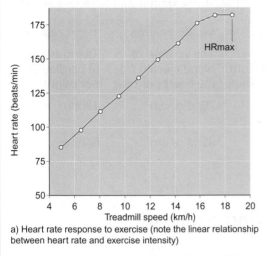
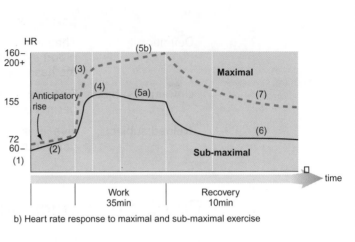

a) Heart rate response to exercise (note the linear relationship between heart rate and exercise intensity)

b) Heart rate response to maximal and sub-maximal exercise

Fig. 2.06 The response of the heart to exercise

TASK 3

HOT TIPS

If you are asked to *plot* a graph in your examination, make sure you ask for graph paper. If you are asked to *sketch* a graph, then you can usually do this just in your answer booklet.

Fig. 2.07
World class rowers are exceptionally fit. They are able to push themselves almost to their maximum during competition and can reach heart rates that the average human will never get near

Table 2.04 Heart rate of Olympic rowers

Matthew Pinsent	Heart rate	James Cracknell	Heart rate
Resting HR	45	Resting HR	40
Just prior to the start	55	Just prior to the start	50
500m into race	160	500m into race	155
1000m into the race	160	1000m into race	155
1500m into the race	160	1500m into the race	155
1750m into the race	190	1750m into the race	185
2000m–the finish	190	2000m–the finish	185

Table 2.05 Heart rate values at rest and during exercise for trained and untrained subjects

	Resting heart rate	Sub-maximal	Maximal
Trained	40–60bpm	140bpm	180bpm
Untrained	60–80bpm (average 72bpm)	110bpm	220 minus age

1 On a piece of graph paper, plot the data from Table 2.04, which illustrates the pattern of heart rate for rowers Pinsent and Cracknell during the Olympic final. Place heart rate along the y-axis (vertical axis) and distance covered along the x-axis (horizontal axis).

2 Explain the pattern of heart rate response that the graph illustrates.

3 Draw and label the expected heart rate curve for a hockey outfield player during a hockey match. Give a brief explanation of the curve you have drawn.

Stroke volume response to exercise

You will recall that stroke volume is the volume of blood pumped out of the heart with each contraction. As with heart rate, stroke volume increases linearly with increasing intensity, but only up to 40–60 per cent of maximum effort. After this point, stroke volume plateaus (see Figure 2.08). One reason for this is the shorter diastolic phase (ventricular filling) that results from the significantly increased heart rate near maximal effort.

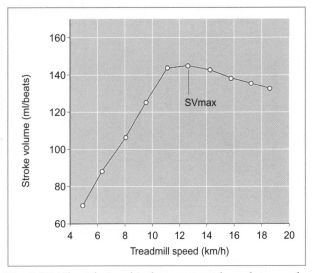

Fig. 2.08 The relationship between stroke volume and exercise intensity

Stroke volume is able to increase during exercise for several reasons:

- **increased venous return** – this is the volume of blood that returns from the body to the right side of the heart. During exercise, the venous return significantly increases due to a mechanism termed the **muscle pump**, where skeletal muscles squeeze blood back towards the heart (this will be explained a little later in this chapter)
- **the Frank-Starling mechanism** – this mechanism basically suggests that when the heart ventricles stretch more, then they can contract with greater force and therefore pump more blood out of the heart. With increased venous return, more blood enters the ventricles during the diastolic phase, which causes them to stretch more and thus contract more forcefully. The reduced heart rate that is experienced by the trained athlete also allows a greater time for the ventricles to fill with blood, increasing the degree of stretch by the cardiac tissue and causing the stroke volume of these trained individuals to increase.

TASK 4

Table 2.06 Stroke volume values at rest and during exercise for trained and untrained subjects

	Resting stroke volume	Sub-maximal exercise	Maximal exercise
Trained	80–110ml	160–200ml	160–200ml
Untrained	60–80ml	100–120ml	100–120ml

Study the data in Table 2.06. Suggest reasons why stroke volume does not change significantly between sub-maximal and maximal exercise.

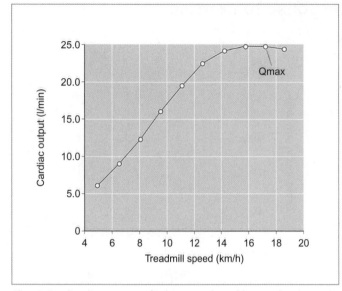

Fig. 2.09 Cardiac output during exercise of increasing intensity

Cardiac output response to exercise

You will recall that cardiac output is the volume of blood pumped out of the heart per minute and is the product of heart rate and stroke volume (cardiac output (Q) = stroke volume (SV) x heart rate (HR)). As such, the response of cardiac output during exercise is easy to predict. You have just discovered that during exercise, both heart rate and stroke volume increase linearly with increasing exercise intensity. Consequently, the pattern of cardiac output during exercise is the same and will continue to increase linearly until maximum exercise capacity, where it will plateau. This is shown in Figure 2.09.

Cardiac output represents the ability of the heart to circulate blood around the body, delivering oxygen to the working muscles. During maximum exercise, cardiac output may reach values of between four to eight times resting values and is therefore a major factor in determining endurance capacity.

TASK 5

Table 2.07 Cardiac output values at rest and during exercise for trained and untrained subjects (approximate values)

	Resting cardiac output	Sub-maximal exercise	Maximal exercise
Trained	5l/min	15–20l/min	30–40l/min
Untrained	5l/min	10–15l/min	20–30l/min

Draw a graph representing the changes in cardiac output that might occur during sub-maximal exercise. Explain the line graph that you have drawn.

Circulation – the vascular system

Blood is transported around the body by a continuous network of blood vessels, which make up the vascular system. Essentially there are two circulatory networks forming a double circuit:

1 **systemic circulation** – oxygenated blood from the left ventricle is transported to the whole of the body's tissues by a network of arteries and arterioles. Oxygen is extracted and deoxygenated blood is returned to the right side of the heart via veins

2 **pulmonary circulation** – deoxygenated blood from the right ventricle is transported to the lungs via the pulmonary artery where it is re-saturated with oxygen and returned to the left side of the heart via the pulmonary vein.

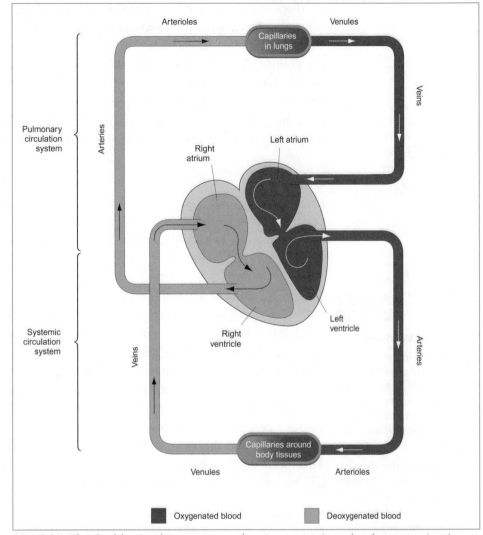

Fig. 2.10 The double circulatory system showing systemic and pulmonary circuits

This double circuit ensures that the blood is continually re-saturated with oxygen and delivered to the working muscles, whilst carbon dioxide can be expelled from the body. Figure 2.10 illustrates the double circulatory system.

Vessels of circulation

There are several different types of blood vessel, each with a specific purpose (Figure 2.11). They include:

- arteries and arterioles
- capillaries
- veins and venules.

- **Arteries and arterioles**

Arteries and arterioles are the vessels that carry blood away from the heart, supplying the body's tissues with oxygenated blood. The main artery of the body is the aorta, which has a very large cross-sectional area, but as arteries get further away from the heart, they branch into smaller vessels, each with a smaller cross-sectional area. The very smallest arteries are known as arterioles. Since arteries and arterioles carry blood at high pressure, their walls are made up of elastic fibres that enable them to stretch and withstand the pumping action of the heart. When the heart contracts, it sends a volume of blood into the aorta, which stretches to accommodate the surge of blood. This stretching and recoiling is repeated along the arterial network, generating a wave of pressure that you can palpate (feel). This is your pulse, which can be felt at several different points in the body.

TASK 6

Practise taking your pulse at the following places: a) radial, b) brachial and c) carotid. Remember, at the first beat, you should start counting from zero. Take your pulse for 30 seconds and multiply by two to give you your heart rate in beats per minute. Record your scores.

KEY WORDS

Vasoconstrict

A reduction in the diameter of artery and arteriole walls. It results in increased blood pressure and helps to speed the flow of blood around the body.

Vasodilate

An increase in the diameter of artery and arteriole walls. It can lead to a decrease in blood pressure.

Vascular shunt

The redistribution of blood around the body so that the working muscles receive an increased proportion. This is achieved through the vasoconstriction and vasodilation of blood vessels.

The elastic walls of arterioles also serve another very important purpose. During exercise, there is competition for blood between the body's muscles and organs. By contracting the elastic fibres within their walls, arterioles can **vasoconstrict**, reducing their diameter and cross-sectional area. This means that they can reduce the amount of blood flowing to various inactive organs of the body. Conversely, arterioles supplying blood to the working muscles of the body can relax the elastic fibres within their walls, causing them to **vasodilate**, increasing the cross-sectional area of the vessel. This means that more blood, and therefore more oxygen, can reach these exercising tissues. This mechanism of blood redistribution is known as the **vascular shunt** (this will be revisited later in this chapter on page 40).

- Capillaries

Blood from the arterioles will eventually enter the extensive network of capillaries that surround all tissues. Capillary walls are just one cell in thickness, which means that the diffusion distance for oxygen and other nutrients is very short. Exchange of gases and other nutrients is further enhanced by the very narrow diameter of the capillaries. Blood cells must travel through the narrow capillaries in single file, which means that blood flow is relatively slow, maximizing the diffusion of nutrients across the cell walls. The vast number of capillaries surrounding the tissues also provides a huge surface area for the exchange of nutrients into and out of the blood.

- Veins and venules

KEY WORDS

Pocket valves

Structures that exist within the veins, which aid the return of the blood to the heart, ensuring that there is no backflow of blood.

Blood from the capillaries is transported back towards the heart via a network of small venules, which join together to form larger vessels called veins. Veins carry deoxygenated blood back to the heart at low pressure. The walls of the veins are less elastic than arteries but do contain a very thin layer of involuntary muscle, which, when stimulated, can help return the blood back to the heart. The return of blood back to the heart (venous return) is aided by **pocket valves** that exist in the veins, ensuring the unidirectional flow of blood towards the heart and preventing backflow. At

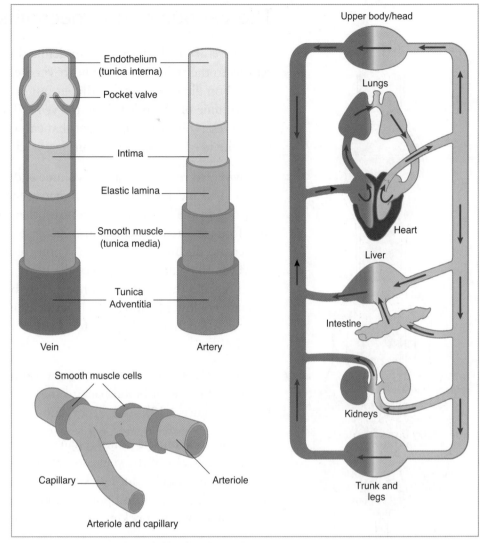

Fig. 2.11 The structure of the blood vessels

rest, the veins act as a reservoir of blood, containing up to 70 per cent of the blood at any one time. This means there is a large reserve to draw upon when we start exercising and accounts partly for the dramatic increase in cardiac output during the first few minutes of activity.

TASK 7

Complete Table 2.08, linking blood vessel structure to its function.

Table 2.08

	Structure	Function
Arteries/arterioles		
Capillaries		
Veins/venules		

The venous return mechanism

Venous return is the term used to define the volume of blood that returns to the right side of the heart via the venules, veins and venae cavae. You discovered earlier that at rest up to 70 per cent of the total volume of blood is held in the veins. This pool of blood acts as a large reservoir or storage depot that can be drawn upon quickly when the need arises, such as during exercise.

You will also recall that stroke volume is dependent upon venous return. This means that if we can increase the volume of blood returning to the heart (venous return), then stroke volume and therefore cardiac output will also increase. Hence, if blood flow is to increase during exercise, then venous return must increase. However, the pumping action of the heart is spent by the time the blood reaches the veins and consequently blood travels in the veins at relatively low pressure, which is sufficient to maintain stroke volume at rest but inadequate for the demands of the body during exercise.

The body has therefore developed several mechanisms to help improve the flow of blood back to the heart and enhance stroke volume (Figure 2.12).

- **The skeletal muscle pump** (Figure 2.12b)
Because the walls of the veins are relatively thin, the contraction and relaxation of muscles during exercise create a massaging effect on them, which squeezes and pumps blood back towards the heart. This is aided by the pocket valves located inside the veins.

- **Pocket valves** (Figure 2.12a)
The pocket valves that exist within the veins snap shut, ensuring that there is no backflow of blood and that the flow is one way back towards the heart.

- **Smooth muscle within veins** (Figure 2.12c)
Located within the walls of the veins is a very thin layer of smooth muscle that can work in conjunction with the muscle pump to squeeze blood back towards the heart.

- **The respiratory pump**
The increased rate and depth of breathing that accompanies exercise creates pressure changes within the thorax and abdomen. On breathing in, increased pressure in the abdomen compresses the veins and squeezes blood into the veins that supply the heart.

- **Gravity**
Gravity assists the flow of blood from the upper extremities of the body into the superior vena cava and then into the right atrium.

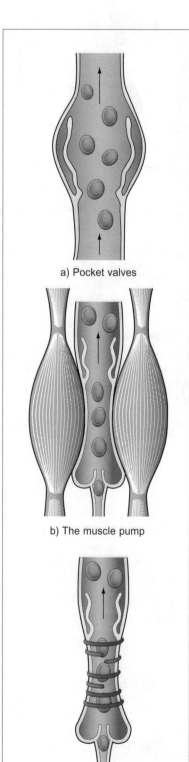

a) Pocket valves

b) The muscle pump

c) Smooth muscle

Fig. 2.12 Venous return mechanisms

The mechanisms of venous return are essential in maintaining cardiac output during exercise. It is important to note, however, that by completing a cool down following exercise, venous return can be maintained, which can prevent the 'pooling' of the blood in the veins. The cool down has the effect of maintaining the muscle pump and cardiac output. A reduced cardiac output following exercise can reduce blood flow to the brain and increase the likelihood of dizziness or even fainting.

The redistribution of blood during exercise

As we begin to exercise, the destination of our blood flow changes dramatically. Through **vasomotor control** and the action of the sympathetic nervous system, blood can be diverted away from non-essential tissues and organs and redirected towards those active during exercise. From Table 2.09 and Figure 2.13, you can see that at rest only about 20 per cent of the total cardiac output is distributed to the muscles, with the majority going to the liver, kidneys and intestines. However, during maximal exercise, the active working muscles may receive as much as 85–90 per cent of the total blood flow, leaving only 10–15 per cent to supply the remaining organs and tissues.

This redistribution of blood flow during exercise results from the **vasoconstriction** or narrowing of arterioles supplying organs such as the intestines, liver and kidneys, and **vasodilation** or opening of the arterioles supplying the more active working muscles. This mechanism is known as the **vascular shunt** and is aided by the presence of a small ring of smooth muscle that exists on the arterioles at the point of entry to the capillary network. These **pre-capillary sphincters** regulate blood flow into the capillaries by either vasoconstricting (narrowing) or vasodilating (opening).

The redirection of blood flow is important to the performer for several reasons:
- it increases oxygen supply to the working muscles
- it provides the working muscles with the necessary fuels to contract (glucose and fatty acids)
- it removes carbon dioxide and lactic acid from the muscles
- it helps maintain body temperature and rids the body of excess heat produced during exercise.

Table 2.09 The distribution of cardiac output during rest and maximal exercise

Destination	Rest	Maximal exercise
Muscle	20%	88%
Brain	15%	3%
Heart	5%	4%
Skin	10%	3%
Liver and intestines	30%	1%
Kidneys	20%	1%

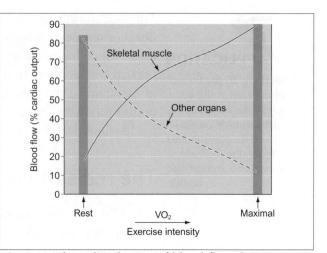

Fig. 2.13 The redistribution of blood flow during exercise

The control of blood redistribution – vasomotor control

The vascular shunt mechanism is regulated by the process of **vasomotor control**. The vasomotor centre is located in the medulla oblongata of the brain. Chemical changes in the blood that result from the onset of exercise (namely increases in carbon dioxide and lactic acid, and low oxygen concentration) are detected by **chemoreceptors**, which inform the vasomotor centre to stimulate the sympathetic nerves located in the smooth muscular walls of the blood vessels. The sympathetic nerves will cause vasoconstriction of those arterioles and pre-capillary sphincters supplying non-essential muscles and organs, decreasing blood flow to these areas. At the same time, vasodilation of arterioles that are supplying the more active working muscles (including the heart) occurs, which will increase blood flow to them. The process of vasomotor control is entirely involuntary and occurs more or less immediately, ensuring that the areas of the body in most need receive the necessary amount of blood and nutrients.

Blood pressure and blood velocity

Blood pressure is the driving force that moves the blood through our circulatory systems and can be defined as '**the force exerted by the blood on the inside walls of the blood vessels**'. As the heart pumps blood around the body, the blood vessels offer resistance to the flow of blood, which generates pressure within the circulatory system. The two main determining factors of blood pressure are:
- blood flow (cardiac output)
- peripheral resistance (resistance offered to the flow of blood due to friction). Resistance is related to three factors:
  1 **blood viscosity** (the relative thickness of the blood)
  2 blood vessel length
  3 blood vessel diameter.

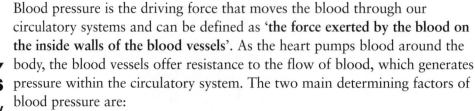

KEY WORDS

Blood viscosity

A term used to describe the relative thickness of the blood. If the blood is very viscous, it has a high amount of blood cells to plasma and consequently does not flow very quickly.

The relationship can be expressed as follows:

blood pressure = cardiac output x peripheral resistance.

The pressure within the system fluctuates in line with the events of the cardiac cycle. The highest blood pressure is seen in arteries close to the heart (aorta) during ventricular systole and is termed 'systolic blood pressure', whilst the lowest is recorded when the ventricles are relaxing (ventricular diastole) and is known as 'diastolic blood pressure'.

Blood pressure reduces the further the blood travels away from the left ventricle. Hence it is greatest in the aorta, lower in the arteries, arterioles and capillaries, lower still in the venules and veins, and at its lowest in the venae cavae as it enters the right atrium of the heart.

As the blood flows away from the heart through the arteries, mean/average blood pressure falls progressively (Figure 2.14). This is partly due to the decreasing effect of the pumping action of the heart but also because there is an increase in the total cross-sectional area of blood vessels as the numbers of arterioles and capillaries increase. This will have the effect of reducing peripheral resistance. Accompanying this increase in total cross-sectional area is a decrease in blood velocity. Thus the velocity of the blood decreases the further away from the heart it gets, so that by the time it reaches the capillaries, the blood is travelling very slowly indeed (Figure 2.15). This slow movement of blood along the capillaries is essential for the effective diffusion of gases and other nutrients into and out of the blood.

However, as the blood enters the venules and veins, blood velocity increases again as the total cross-sectional area of these vessels decreases. The venous return mechanisms outlined earlier also help in increasing the velocity of the blood in the veins.

Measurement of blood pressure

Blood pressure is usually measured in the left brachial artery by a piece of equipment known as a 'sphygmomanometer', although simple readings can be given using a digital blood pressure recorder. A pressure cuff is placed around the arm, which is inflated to the point where it briefly cuts off the circulation. The cuff is then deflated and blood will surge through the artery. At this point, a reading is taken which represents the systolic blood pressure – the force with which blood is pushing against the arterial walls during ventricular contraction. As the cuff deflates fully and the blood fully returns to the arm, a second reading is taken. This reading is the diastolic blood pressure and represents the force of the blood in the arteries during ventricular relaxation. The two readings are expressed as follows:

Systolic pressure
Diastolic pressure

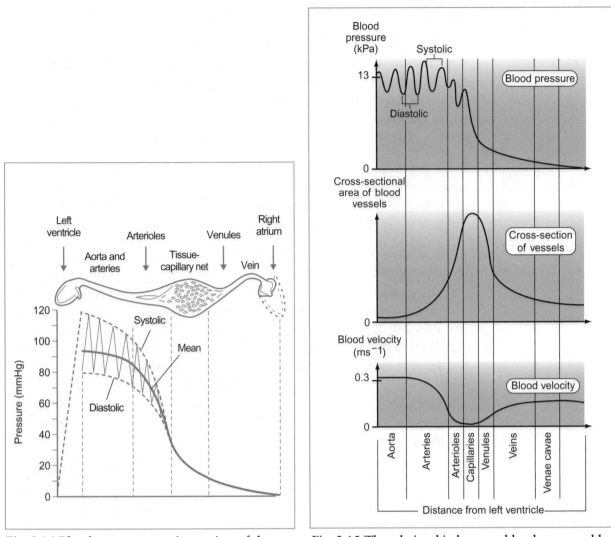

Fig. 2.14 Blood pressure at various points of the circulatory system

Fig. 2.15 The relationship between blood pressure, blood velocity and total cross-sectional area of blood vessels

The blood pressure reading for an average healthy adult is generally regarded as being:

$$\frac{120\text{mmHg}}{80\text{mmHg}}$$

The effects of exercise upon blood pressure

Performing aerobic exercise, such as a long distance run or a distance swim, causes systolic blood pressure to increase (usually in direct proportion to the exercise intensity). Systolic pressure can rise from its resting value of 120mmHg to values approaching 200mmHg. This increase results largely from the increase in cardiac output and the vasoconstriction of arterioles that help the vascular shunting of blood towards the working muscles. However, once steady state is reached, systolic blood pressure may in fact start to gradually decrease due to the arteriole dilation supplying the working muscles. This has the effect of reducing the total peripheral resistance, thereby lowering

KEY WORDS

Mean blood pressure

The average value of systolic and diastolic pressures.

KEY WORDS

Isometric exercise

Exercise that involves static muscle contractions (that is, where the muscle length remains the same during contraction). For example, the abdominal muscles work isometrically when performing a one repetition maximum on the bench press.

mean blood pressure to only just above that of resting levels. The diastolic pressure changes little during this endurance type activity.

During exercise that is more anaerobic or that which involves more **isometric** type muscle contractions such as weightlifting, the changes in blood pressure are very different. In this instance, both systolic and diastolic blood pressures rise significantly, largely due to the performer holding their breath, which increases the pressure within the thorax and abdomen and squeezes on the peripheral blood vessels, increasing overall mean blood pressure.

The control and regulation of blood pressure

The maintenance of blood pressure within a normal range is essential for healthy living. Whereas high blood pressure can damage organs such as the heart and the brain, low pressure can starve the body's tissues of oxygen and other nutrients. It is the role of the vasomotor centre to regulate blood pressure. Pressure receptors or baroreceptors located in the aorta and carotid arteries monitor the blood pressure and feed this sensory information to the vasomotor centre in the medulla oblongata. If blood pressure is too high, then the vasomotor centre will decrease sympathetic stimulation of the arterioles, resulting in vasodilation and a decrease in blood pressure. On the other hand, if blood pressure is too low and an increase in blood pressure is required, then the vasomotor centre will increase sympathetic stimulation, causing vasoconstriction of arterioles.

The vasomotor centre works in conjunction with the cardiac control centre, which will help maintain blood pressure by either increasing or decreasing cardiac output accordingly.

TASK 8

Explain what happens to the systolic pressure of an athlete before, during and following a 10K run. Explain how blood pressure is regulated in each case.

TASK 9

Write out these statements, stating clearly whether they are **true** or **false**.
1   Stroke volume is the difference between end-diastolic and end-systolic volume in the heart.
2   During the cardiac cycle, the semi-lunar valves open because the pressure in the left ventricle is less than the pressure in the aorta.
3   Sympathetic stimulation of the heart causes both the heart rate and force of ventricular contraction to increase.
4   Veins possess larger amounts of elastic fibres than any of the other blood vessels. This helps in the venous return mechanism.
5   Blood pressure is lowest in the capillaries because their total cross-sectional area is much greater than the aorta.

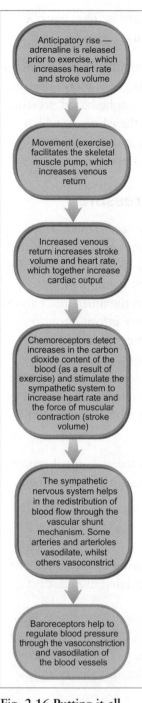

Anticipatory rise — adrenaline is released prior to exercise, which increases heart rate and stroke volume

Movement (exercise) facilitates the skeletal muscle pump, which increases venous return

Increased venous return increases stroke volume and heart rate, which together increase cardiac output

Chemoreceptors detect increases in the carbon dioxide content of the blood (as a result of exercise) and stimulate the sympathetic system to increase heart rate and the force of muscular contraction (stroke volume)

The sympathetic nervous system helps in the redistribution of blood flow through the vascular shunt mechanism. Some arteries and arterioles vasodilate, whilst others vasoconstrict

Baroreceptors help to regulate blood pressure through the vasoconstriction and vasodilation of the blood vessels

Fig. 2.16 Putting it all together – what happens to the cardio-vascular system when we exercise

KEY WORDS

Cardiac hypertrophy
The enlargement of the heart muscle in response to training.

Training effects upon the heart – athlete's heart

Training can induce structural and functional changes to the heart that lead to greater efficiency and improved performance (Figure 2.16). Endurance training, for example, can cause the heart to enlarge, undergoing hypertrophy. This is particularly true of the ventricular cavities, which increase in size, enabling them to fill with more blood during the diastolic phase of the cardiac cycle. This condition leads to a greater stroke volume and a reduced resting heart rate (bradycardia). Resistance or strength training, on the other hand, causes a thickening of the ventricular myocardium (the heart muscle), which increases the force of heart contractions, which in turn increases stroke volume. Both types of athletes will also experience improved contractility of the heart. Consequently, the ejection fraction (the percentage of blood that enters the left ventricle, which is actually pumped out per beat) will increase (from 60 per cent up to 85 per cent).

Cardiac hypertrophy enables the trained heart to beat less frequently both at rest (bradycardia) and during sub-maximal exercise. This is due to increased activity of parasympathetic nerves slowing the heart rate down. This results in a greater filling of the heart during the diastolic phase of the cardiac cycle and therefore, according to Starling's Law, an increase in stroke volume.

There is also increased **capillarization** of the heart (cardiac) muscle itself, which facilitates the diffusion of oxygen into the myocardium.

The adaptations of the heart following a period of training can be summarized as follows:
- cardiac hypertrophy (enlargement of the heart)
- increased contractility (strength of contraction)
- increased stroke volume
- increased maximum cardiac output (although cardiac output at rest and sub-maximal levels remain unchanged)
- increased ejection fraction
- bradycardia (lower resting heart rate)
- greater diastolic filling of the ventricles
- increased capillarization.

Training effects upon the vascular system

Endurance training will also improve the efficiency of the body's vascular system (Figure 2.17). This ensures that when exercising, the working muscles receive the necessary oxygen and other nutrients to sustain the workload, and that any fatiguing waste products can be removed. The primary effect of endurance training on an athlete's vascular system is that there is increased blood flow to the muscles. This results partly from the cardiac adaptations outlined above but also by:
- the increased capillarization of the muscles, enabling a greater surface area for gaseous exchange

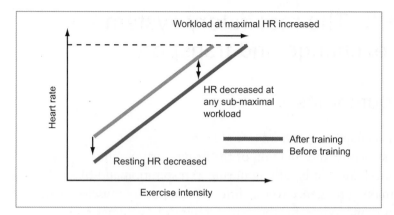

Fig. 2.17 Training effects on the heart rate/workload relationship

🔑 **KEY WORDS**

Buffering

The ability of the body to keep acidity levels (blood pH) within acceptable limits.

- improved ability of arterioles to vasoconstrict and vasodilate, which means that blood redistribution is more effective, ensuring the working muscles receive the greatest supply of blood
- increased blood volume making more blood, and therefore oxygen, available to the working muscles.

Other adaptations of the vascular system that enable a performer to continue exercising for longer include:

- an increase in red blood cell count, and therefore haemoglobin content, which enhances the oxygen-carrying capacity of the blood
- the blood becomes more efficient at removing waste products such as carbon dioxide and lactic acid. This is known as **buffering**
- resting blood pressure can be reduced.

Revise as you go!

1 Which blood vessels carry:
   a) oxygenated blood from the lungs to the heart
   b) deoxygenated blood from the heart to the lungs?
2 Define 'stroke volume', 'heart rate' and 'cardiac output'. State how they are related.
3 Give typical values at rest and during exercise for: a) stroke volume
   b) heart rate
   c) cardiac output.

   How might these differ for a trained athlete?
4 What is the Frank-Starling mechanism?
5 Briefly outline the conduction system of the heart.
6 Explain the events of the cardiac cycle.
7 Sketch the expected heart rate response for: a) sub-maximal exercise
   b) maximal exercise.
8 Explain the function of the sympathetic and parasympathetic nervous systems. How do they regulate the heart rate?
9 Define venous return. Explain the mechanism of venous return.
10 Sketch a graph to show the relationship between blood pressure, blood vessel cross-sectional area and blood velocity.
11 Briefly outline some of the physiological adaptations that we might expect to see as a result of endurance training on: a) the heart
   b) the vascular system.

Chapter 3: The respiratory system – gaseous exchange and transport

Learning outcomes

By the end of this chapter you should be able to:
- describe the structure and function of the respiratory system
- explain the mechanics of breathing during a) inspiration and b) expiration, making reference to the different respiratory muscles involved
- give definitions and values for the major respiratory volumes and capacities at rest and during exercise
- interpret a spirometer trace
- explain the importance of partial pressure in the process of gaseous exchange
- describe the process of gaseous exchange at a) the lungs and b) the tissues and muscles
- state how oxygen and carbon dioxide are transported in the body
- explain the effect of exercise upon the dissociation of oxy-haemoglobin at the tissues
- explain the importance of carbon dioxide in the control of breathing
- explain what is meant by the arterial venous oxygen difference (a-vo$_2$ diff) and state how it differs during exercise from resting values
- describe the effects of training on lung volumes and capacities and gaseous exchange.

Introduction

Successful endurance performance requires the delivery of sufficient oxygen to our muscles to produce the energy which fuels muscle contraction. At the same time, carbon dioxide produced by the muscles must be cleared and removed from the body. The primary function of the respiratory system is therefore to bring oxygen into our bodies so it can be delivered to our muscles and tissues, and to rid us of excess carbon dioxide. It has a dual function of supplying essential nutrients to the working muscles yet also being a waste disposal system.

HOT TIPS

You must be able to show an understanding of the very close relationship and interaction of the cardiovascular and respiratory systems in your examination (Figure 3.01).

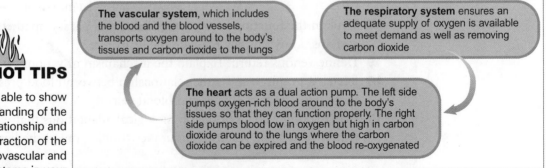

The vascular system, which includes the blood and the blood vessels, transports oxygen around to the body's tissues and carbon dioxide to the lungs

The respiratory system ensures an adequate supply of oxygen is available to meet demand as well as removing carbon dioxide

The heart acts as a dual action pump. The left side pumps oxygen-rich blood around to the body's tissues so that they can function properly. The right side pumps blood low in oxygen but high in carbon dioxide around to the lungs where the carbon dioxide can be expired and the blood re-oxygenated

Fig. 3.01 The interaction of the cardiovascular and respiratory systems

The structure of the respiratory system

Figure 3.02 outlines the main structures of the respiratory system.

Nasal passages
The nasal passages or nostrils are lined with a mucus membrane and tiny hairs (cilia), which moistens, warms and filters the inspired air before it enters the main airways

Oral pharynx and larynx
The oral pharynx or throat is a common passageway for air and food. The larynx or voice box is attached to the epiglottis, which ensures that food is diverted into the digestive tract and air into the trachea

Trachea
The main airway of the respiratory system that extends from the larynx and divides into the right and left bronchus

Alveoli sac

Alveolus

Pulmonary capillaries

Nasal cavity

Oral cavity

Pharynx

Larynx

Trachea

Primary bronchii

Bronchiole

Lung

Capillary network on surface of alveolus

Bronchi and bronchioles
The bronchi are airways that feed directly into each lobe of the lung (three lobes on the right, two on the left). The bronchi then subdivide into bronchioles, which further divide, getting smaller and smaller until they form terminal bronchioles

Alveoli
The alveoli are tiny air sacs and the site of gaseous exchange. They are made up of a single layer of epithelial cells and surrounded by an extensive capillary network, which facilitates the exchange of gases

Fig. 3.02 The structure of the respiratory system

TASK 1

1 Describe how the structure of the lungs is adapted to absorb oxygen.
2 Describe the pathway taken by a molecule of oxygen as it passes from the atmosphere to the blood in the lungs.

The mechanics of breathing

Inspiration

Inspiration or breathing in is an active process that requires the contraction of certain muscles. The **external intercostal muscles,** which lie between each pair of ribs, contract during inspiration, causing the ribcage to move upwards and outwards. At the same time, the **diaphragm**, which forms the floor of the thoracic cavity, contracts downwards and flattens. These actions together cause an overall increase in the size of the thoracic cavity and therefore a decrease in the pressure within the lungs (since the pressure of a given volume of gas is created by the number of molecules of gas present and the size of the area they occupy). In fact, the pressure within the lungs during inspiration falls below the external or atmospheric pressure, and since gases will always move from areas of high pressure to areas of low pressure, air is drawn into the lungs.

During exercise, when the rate and depth of breathing increase, inspiration is aided by certain accessory muscles, which include the **sternocleidomastoid**, the **scalenes and the pectoralis minor**.

Expiration

Expiration or breathing out during normal quiet breathing is a passive process since no muscular contractions are involved. It depends upon two factors:
1 the elastic recoil of the lungs and thoracic tissues
2 the relaxation of the inspiratory muscles, that is, the external intercostal muscles and the diaphragm.

As the external intercostal muscles relax, the ribcage moves downwards and inwards, taking up its original position, whilst the diaphragm relaxes into its resting dome shape. These movements decrease the size of the thoracic cavity, increasing the pressure within the lungs so that it becomes greater than external or atmospheric pressure. Once again, because gases will move from an area of high pressure to an area of low pressure, air is forced out of the lungs.

Expiration becomes active, however, during exercise, when breathing rates are increased. In this instance, expiration is aided by the **internal intercostal** muscles and the abdominal muscles, which pull the ribcage down more quickly and with greater force. Table 3.01 summarizes the respiratory muscles used at rest and during exercise (Figures 3.03 and 3.04).

Table 3.01 Respiratory muscles used at rest and during exercise

	Rest	Exercise
Inspiration	Contraction of external intercostal muscles and diaphragm	Contraction of external intercostal muscles, diaphragm, sternocleidomastoid, scalenes and pectoralis minor
Expiration	Relaxation of external intercostal muscles and diaphragm	Contraction of internal intercostal muscles and abdominals

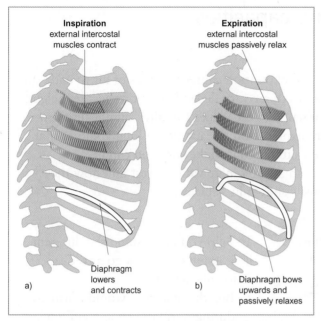

Fig. 3.03 The muscles of a) inspiration and
b) expiration at rest

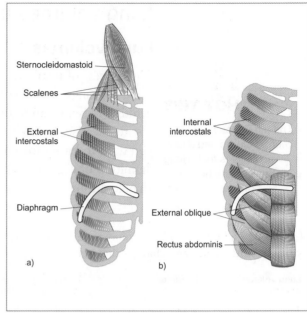

Fig. 3.04 The muscles of a) inspiration and
b) expiration during exercise

TASK 2

1 Place the following stages in the correct order to describe the mechanics
   of inspiration.
   - Thoracic cavity volume increases.
   - Diaphragm and external intercostal muscles contract.
   - Air rushes into the lungs.
   - Pressure within the lungs becomes lower than atmospheric air outside
     the body.
   - Diaphragm flattens whilst the ribcage moves upwards and outwards.

2 Place the following stages in the correct order to describe the mechanics
   of expiration during exercise.
   - Diaphragm pushed upwards whilst the ribcage moves inwards and
     downwards.
   - Air is forced out of the lungs.
   - Thoracic cavity volume decreases.
   - Pressure inside the lungs increases above that of atmospheric pressure
     outside the lungs.
   - Internal intercostal muscles contract along with the abdominals.

Lung volumes and capacities

Lung volumes

HOT TIPS

The difference between a lung volume and a lung capacity is that a lung capacity is made up of two or more volumes.

The process of inspiration and expiration causes volumes of air to enter and leave the lungs. These volumes of air vary depending upon the size, height, health and sex of an individual, and the values can alter significantly from rest to exercise. Below is an explanation of each of the lung volumes that you need to know for your examination. Make sure you can give a definition of each as well as an approximate value at rest and how they change during exercise. This is shown in Table 3.02.

Table 3.02 Definitions of lung volumes and capacities, showing typical resting values and changes that occur during exercise

Lung volume or capacity	Definition	Typical value at rest	Change during exercise
Tidal volume (TV)	Volume inspired **or** expired per breath	500ml	Increase
Inspiratory reserve volume (IRV)	Maximal volume inspired following end of resting inspiration	3100ml	Decrease
Expiratory reserve volume (ERV)	Maximal volume expired following end of resting expiration	1200ml	Decrease
Residual volume (RV) TLC – VC	Volume of air remaining in the lungs at the end of maximal expiration	1200ml	Remains the same
Inspiratory capacity (IC) TV + IRV	Maximum volume of air inspired from resting expiratory levels	3600ml	Increase
Vital capacity (VC) IRV + TV + ERV	The maximum volume forcibly expired following maximal inspiration	5000ml	Slight decrease
Total lung capacity (TLC) VC + RV	The volume of air that is in the lungs following maximal inspiration	6000ml	Slight decrease
Minute ventilation (VE) TV x f	The volume of air inspired or expired per minute	7500ml	Dramatic increase

To help you understand the different lung volumes, have a go at the following activity.

1. Breathe in as you would normally during normal resting conditions. The volume of air you have just inspired is known as the **tidal volume** and equates to approximately 500ml.

2. Now breathe out as you would normally (you have just expelled 500cm^3/ml or your tidal volume), but before you breathe in again, try to force all the remaining air out of your lungs. This extra volume of air that you have just expired is known as the **expiratory reserve volume** and can measure as much as 1200ml.

3. Now breathe in once more as you did in part 1, but before you breathe out again, continue to breathe in until you have completely filled your lungs. This extra volume of inspired air over and above your tidal volume is known as your **inspiratory reserve volume** and can reach values of 3100ml.

One other volume that you need to be aware of is the **residual volume**. This is about 1200ml of air that remains in the lungs following maximal expiration to prevent the lungs from collapsing. Unlike the other lung volumes, this does not change during exercise.

Lung capacities

Lung capacities result from adding two or more lung volumes together. For example, the **inspiratory capacity** is the sum of tidal volume and inspiratory reserve volume (IC = TV + IRV) and is equal to approximately 3600ml. **Vital capacity** is the sum of the inspiratory reserve volume, tidal volume and the expiratory reserve volume (VC = IRV + TV + ERV) and is typically about 5000ml of air. Essentially, your vital capacity is the maximum amount of air that you can breathe in and out during one inspiration and expiration. One final capacity is the **total lung capacity**, which is basically the sum of all the lung volumes: inspiratory reserve volume, tidal volume, expiratory reserve volume, and residual volume (TLC = IRV + TV + ERV + RV). Total lung capacity averages between 5000ml to 6000ml but generally varies between individuals depending upon their size, height, health and sex.

TASK 3

Do the following lung volumes increase, decrease or remain the same during exercise?
a) Tidal volume
b) Inspiratory reserve volume
c) Expiratory reserve volume

Lung volumes and capacities of individuals are easily measured using an instrument called a **spirometer**. A spirometer produces a chart known as a spirometer trace that clearly identifies the performer's lung function. An example of a trace is shown in Figure 3.05.

HOT TIPS

You will need to be able to identify each lung volume and capacity labelled on the spirometer trace for your examination.

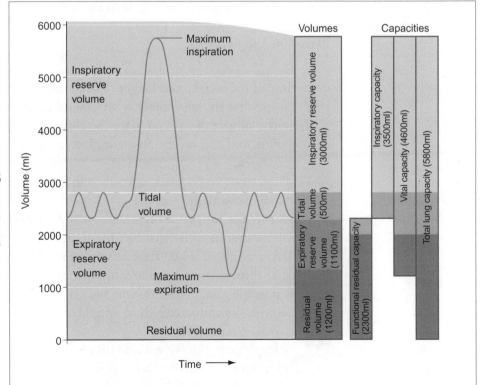

Fig. 3.05 A spirometer trace showing respiratory volumes and capacities

TASK 4

In the spirometer shown in Figure 3.06, a person breathes through a tube connected to an oxygen-containing chamber that floats on a tank of water. The chamber falls during inhalation and rises during exhalation. A container of soda lime is used to absorb all the carbon dioxide in the exhaled air.

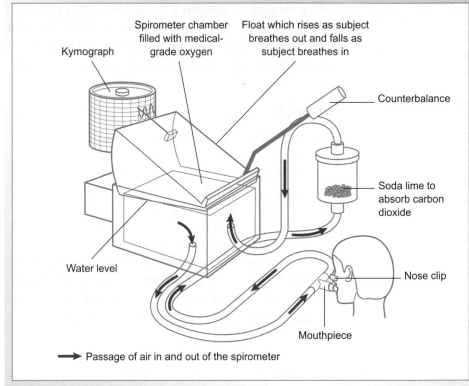

Fig. 3.06 A spirometer

1   Record the weight and height of your subject.
2   Ensure that the spirometer is set up and calibrated correctly.
3   Sit the subject down and place the clean mouthpiece in the subject's mouth, and clip on the nose clip. Leave the two-way tap closed for the time being.
4   When ready to proceed, open the tap just as the subject is finishing exhaling normally.
5   Instruct the subject to breathe normally for about a minute or so.
6   After a minute of normal breathing, instruct the subject to breathe in as deeply as possible and then resume normal breathing.
7   After three or four more breaths, ask the subject to breathe out as much as possible and then to resume normal breathing for a minute or so.
8   Remove the spirometer trace and label the following:
    a) tidal volume (TV)
    b) inspiratory reserve volume (IRV)
    c) expiratory reserve volume (ERV)
    d) vital capacity (VC).

9 From the spirometer trace, calculate the following volumes:
   a) tidal volume (TV)
   b) inspiratory reserve volume (IRV)
   c) expiratory reserve volume (ERV).
10 What is the subject's vital capacity?
11 Estimate the total lung capacity of the subject. Hint: a reasonably
    accurate method of estimating the total lung capacity is to multiply the
    expiratory reserve volume by six.
12 Now calculate the subject's residual volume (TLC – VC).

TASK 5

Figure 3.07 shows a spirometer trace. Copy out the trace.

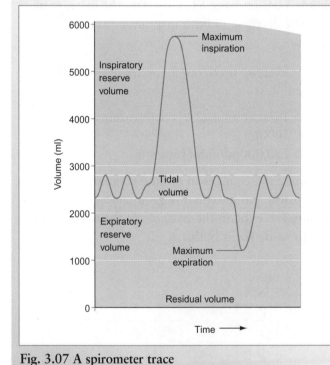

Fig. 3.07 A spirometer trace

1 On your spirometer trace, draw a
   line to show what would happen to
   tidal volume if the subject
   commenced exercise.
2 Write down what happens to:
   a) tidal volume
   b) inspiratory reserve volume
   c) expiratory reserve volume.

Minute ventilation

Minute ventilation (VE) or minute volume is the volume of air breathed in **or**
out per minute. It is calculated by multiplying a person's tidal volume (TV)
by the number of times they breathe per minute or breathing rate (f). At rest,
based on average figures for tidal volume and breathing rate, this will be:

Minute ventilation (VE) = Tidal volume (TV)   × Breathing rate (f)
                        = 500ml   × 15
                        = 7500ml/min (7.5l/min)

However, minute ventilation will increase significantly during exercise.

Ventilation during exercise

 KEY WORDS

Tissue respiration

The process of energy creation through the oxidation of food fuels. It produces energy, carbon dioxide and water.

During exercise, both the rate (frequency) and depth (tidal volume) of breathing increases in direct proportion to the intensity of the activity. This is in order to satisfy the demand by the working muscles for oxygen and to remove the carbon dioxide and lactic acid that has been produced as a consequence of **tissue respiration**. Tidal volume increases by utilizing both the inspiratory and expiratory reserve volumes – consequently, both these volumes decrease during exercise. The tidal volume, however, increases its usage of the overall vital capacity six-fold from about 10 per cent at rest to 60 per cent during exercise. It is not energy-efficient for tidal volume to utilize 100 per cent of the vital capacity during exercise as this will substantially increase oxygen demand of the respiratory muscles.

The spirometer trace in Figure 3.05, on page 51, illustrates the increase in tidal volume and the subsequent decrease in both inspiratory and expiratory reserve volumes during exercise.

Minute ventilation (VE) during exercise therefore increases dramatically – up to 20 or 30 times resting values:

$$\text{Minute ventilation (VE)} = \text{Tidal volume (TV)} \times \text{Breathing rate (f)}$$
$$= 3000\text{ml} \times 50$$
$$= 150,000\text{ml/min (150l/min)}$$

Figures 3.08a and 3.08b compare the changes in minute ventilation (VE) during sub-maximal (low intensity) and maximal (high intensity) exercise. In your exam, you may be required to explain the patterns of the two graphs, so take a few moments now to study them both.

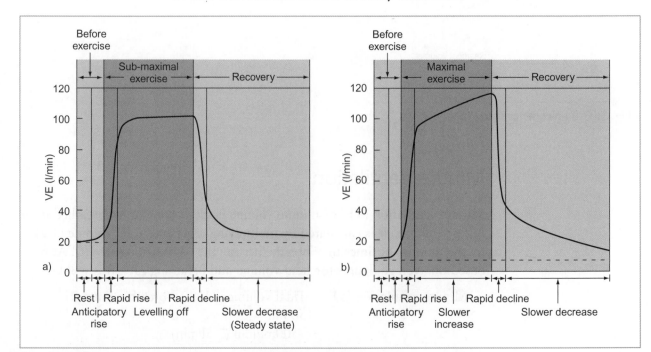

Fig. 3.08 Minute ventilation response to a) sub-maximal exercise and b) maximal exercise

TASK 6

1 Write down the equation used to calculate minute ventilation.
2 Calculate the minute ventilation of an athlete at rest assuming she has a tidal volume of 500ml and a respiration rate of fourteen breaths per minute.
3 Now calculate the tidal volume of the same athlete during maximal exercise where her minute ventilation is 125,000ml/min and her respiration rate is 50 breaths per minute.

TASK 7

Table 3.03

Time (mins)	Minute ventilation (VE) l/min	
	Graph A	Graph B
-2 (prior to exercise)	7	7
0 (exercise commences)	15	20
2	80	80
4	100	100
6	100	110
8	100	120
10	100	125
12 (exercise finishes)	100	125
14	40	50
16	20	40
18	18	30
20	15	25

1 Using the data in Table 3.03, plot the two line graphs on graph paper, illustrating the changes in minute ventilation during exercise. Make sure that you use a large scale and label the axes correctly with appropriate units.
2 Now fully label the different sections of the graphs, explaining the changes that have occurred in minute ventilation in each.

The exchange of respiratory gases

You should now understand how inspiration and expiration move air into and out of the body, but more importantly, you need to discover how oxygen and carbon dioxide are actually exchanged.

There are two sites for gaseous exchange in the body:
1 between the air in the alveoli of the lungs and the blood in the surrounding alveolar capillaries
2 between the tissues/muscles of the body and the surrounding blood capillaries.

To fully understand the process of gaseous exchange, you need to know a little about pressures of gases or **partial pressures**.

Partial pressures

Each gas that exists within a mixture of gases has its own pressure that it exerts, and it behaves as if no other gas is present. The **partial** (part) **pressure** (PP) of a gas is therefore the pressure that is exerted by the individual gas when it exists within a mixture of gases. The gas will exert a pressure that is proportional to its concentration within the whole gas. For example:

Atmospheric pressure is composed of three main gases: nitrogen (approximately 79 per cent), oxygen (approximately 21 per cent) and carbon dioxide (approximately 0.03 per cent). Together they exert a pressure of 760mmHg:

$$\text{Atmospheric pressure (760mmHg)} = PN_2 + PO_2 + PCO_2$$

If we want to find out the pressure exerted by an individual gas and we know its fractional concentration, then we only need to perform a simple calculation. Using the above example, if we want to calculate the partial pressure of oxygen within the atmosphere, then we would perform the following calculation:

Partial pressure of gas (P) = Barometric pressure × Fractional concentration
PO_2 = 760mmHg × 0.21
PO_2 = 159.6mmHg

So why is a knowledge of partial pressure so important? You will recall that gases move from areas of high pressure to areas of low pressure. Knowledge of the partial pressures of oxygen and carbon dioxide at various sites of the body will explain the movement or **diffusion** of these two gases either into and out of the blood at the alveoli or into and out of the muscle tissue.

Table 3.04 Partial pressures of oxygen and carbon dioxide in atmospheric air, alveolar air, blood and muscle cells

	Atmospheric air (sea level)	Alveolar air	Deoxygenated blood	Oxygenated blood	Muscle cells
PO_2	160mmHg	105mmHg	40mmHg	105mmHg	40mmHg
PCO_2	0.3mmHg	40mmHg	45mmHg	40mmHg	45mmHg

Gaseous exchange at the alveoli (external respiration)

Gaseous exchange at the alveoli involves the movement of oxygen and carbon dioxide between the alveoli of the lungs and the surrounding alveolar capillaries. The object of this exchange is quite simply to convert deoxygenated blood returning from the body into oxygenated blood. As

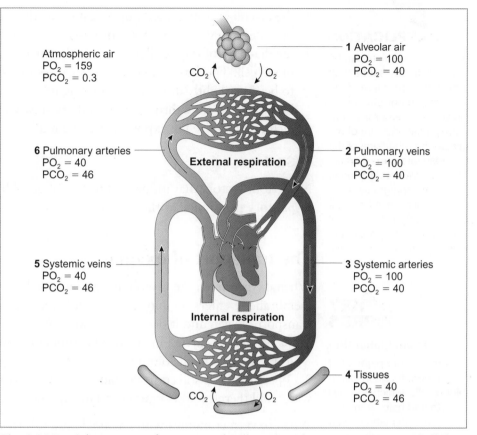

Atmospheric air
$PO_2 = 159$
$PCO_2 = 0.3$

1 Alveolar air
$PO_2 = 100$
$PCO_2 = 40$

6 Pulmonary arteries
$PO_2 = 40$
$PCO_2 = 46$

External respiration

2 Pulmonary veins
$PO_2 = 100$
$PCO_2 = 40$

5 Systemic veins
$PO_2 = 40$
$PCO_2 = 46$

3 Systemic arteries
$PO_2 = 100$
$PCO_2 = 40$

Internal respiration

4 Tissues
$PO_2 = 40$
$PCO_2 = 46$

Fig. 3.09 Partial pressures of oxygen and carbon dioxide at various sites around the body

blood circulates through the alveolar capillaries, oxygen is picked up from the alveoli and carbon dioxide is lost to them so that it can be expired.

Blood entering the alveolar capillaries has a low partial pressure of oxygen (40mmHg) when compared to that of alveoli (105mmHg) (Figure 3.09). Consequently, a diffusion gradient of 65mmHg is created, causing oxygen to diffuse from the alveoli into the capillary blood. This process continues until the pressure on both sides of the respiratory membrane is equal. In the meantime, the partial pressure of carbon dioxide within the blood entering alveolar capillaries is relatively high (45mmHg) when compared to that in the alveoli (40mmHg). Once again, a diffusion gradient of 5mmHg is created, enabling carbon dioxide to diffuse from the capillary blood into the alveoli until the pressure on both sides of the respiratory membrane once again becomes equal.

Diffusion of gases at the alveoli is facilitated by several structural features of the respiratory system:

- the respiratory (alveolar capillary) membrane is very thin, which means that the diffusion distance between the air in the alveoli and the blood is very short
- the numerous alveoli create a very large surface area over which diffusion can take place

APPLICATION

A diffusion gradient can be calculated by subtracting the partial pressure of the gas on one side of the respiratory membrane from the partial pressure of the gas on the other side of the respiratory membrane. Movement along the diffusion gradient will always take place from the area of the highest partial pressure to the area of the lowest partial pressure until equilibrium is reached.

KEY WORDS

Haemoglobin (Hb)

A respiratory pigment of the blood, found in all red blood cells, which attaches to and helps transport oxygen (and carbon dioxide) around the body.

Oxy-haemoglobin (HbO$_2$)

Haemoglobin combined with oxygen.

- the alveoli are surrounded by a vast network of capillaries, which further provides a huge surface area for gaseous exchange
- the diameter of the capillaries is slightly narrower than the area of a red blood cell. This has two effects: a) it causes the shape of the red blood cell to become slightly distorted, increasing its surface area, and b) it forces the blood cells to flow through the capillary slowly in single file. Both these factors maximize the exposure that the red blood cell has to oxygen.

TASK 8

Name four factors that influence the rate of gas diffusion across the respiratory membrane at the alveoli.

The transport of oxygen

When oxygen from the alveoli diffuses across the alveolar capillary membrane, it enters the bloodstream. It is the function of the blood to transport oxygen and it does this in two ways:
1 97 per cent is carried in chemical combination with **haemoglobin** (a red iron-based pigment found in red blood cells) (Figure 3.10)
2 3 per cent is dissolved in the blood plasma (oxygen is not very soluble in water and therefore this figure is relatively low).

When oxygen combines with haemoglobin, it forms **oxy-haemoglobin**:

Hb (haemoglobin) + O$_2$ (oxygen) = HbO$_2$ (oxy-haemoglobin).

Haemoglobin has a very high affinity for oxygen, each molecule combining with four molecules of oxygen so that:

Hb + 4O$_2$ = HbO$_8$

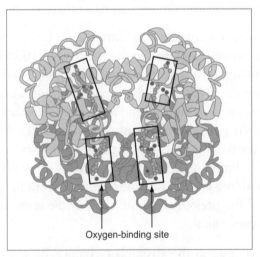

Oxygen-binding site

Fig. 3.10 Transportation of oxygen in the blood. Note that each haemoglobin molecule can transport four molecules of oxygen

The most important factor that determines how much oxygen combines with haemoglobin is the partial pressure of oxygen (PO$_2$). When the PO$_2$ of blood is high, such as in the alveolar capillaries of the lungs, haemoglobin readily combines with large amounts of oxygen until it becomes almost fully saturated (96 per cent). When the PO$_2$ of blood is low, such as in the capillaries of the contracting muscles, oxygen is released by the haemoglobin. This oxygen can now be used by the respiring tissues and muscles. This dissociation of oxygen from haemoglobin occurs since the reaction stated above is easily reversible and is represented by the oxy-haemoglobin dissociation curve.

The oxy-haemoglobin dissociation curve

An oxy-haemoglobin dissociation curve (Figure 3.11) represents the amount of haemoglobin saturated with oxygen as it passes through areas of the body that have very different partial pressures of oxygen (PO_2).

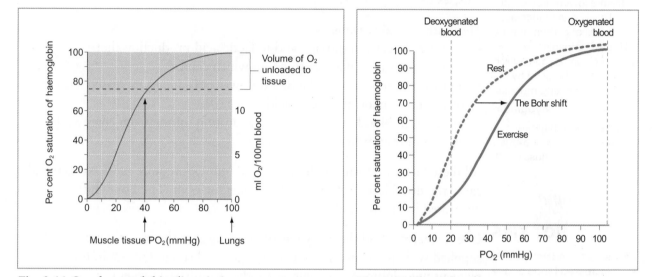

Fig. 3.11 Oxy-haemoglobin dissociation curve at rest

Fig. 3.12 The Bohr effect

You will note that the oxy-haemoglobin dissociation curve is 'S'-shaped. This 'S'-shaped curve means that relatively small changes in the PO_2 can result in a large uptake or association of oxygen at the lungs and a large dissociation at the muscles/tissues.

Now look at Figure 3.12. Note that at very low partial pressures of oxygen, which we would expect at the respiring muscles, the percentage saturation of haemoglobin is very low – approximately 20 per cent, the remaining 76 per cent has been released to the muscles for energy production. At very high partial pressures of oxygen, as we find in the lungs, the haemoglobin is 96–8 per cent saturated.

TASK 10

From Figure 3.12, state the partial pressure of oxygen at 25 per cent, 50 per cent and 96 per cent saturation during resting conditions.

Exercise and the Bohr effect

During exercise, when the muscles require more oxygen, the dissociation of oxygen from haemoglobin occurs more readily, causing a shift of the oxy-haemoglobin dissociation curve to the right. This is known as the **Bohr effect** and frees up more oxygen, which can then be utilized by the working muscles for energy production.

There are several reasons for this:
- increases in carbon dioxide and in lactic acid production that accompanies muscular contraction, which causes
- an increase in acidity of the blood (lower pH) due to increased amounts of carbon dioxide and lactic acid
- increases in blood and muscle temperature resulting from energy released as heat during muscular contraction.

All these factors inform the body that the muscles require more oxygen and cause the dissociation of oxygen from haemoglobin. The Bohr shift is illustrated in Figure 3.12.

One further method the body has of ensuring that the muscles are constantly supplied with adequate amounts of oxygen is through the respiratory pigment **myoglobin**. Myoglobin is another iron-based protein similar to haemoglobin, but it is only found in skeletal muscles. It has a much higher affinity for oxygen than haemoglobin and acts as an oxygen store, saturating itself with oxygen that has dissociated from haemoglobin. You will notice from Figure 3.13 that the myoglobin curve lies well to the left of our regular oxy-haemoglobin dissociation curve. This means that even at very low partial pressures of oxygen, it remains relatively saturated. So, even if the percentage saturation of haemoglobin is low, myoglobin still has oxygen available to supply the working muscles, which can be quickly exploited.

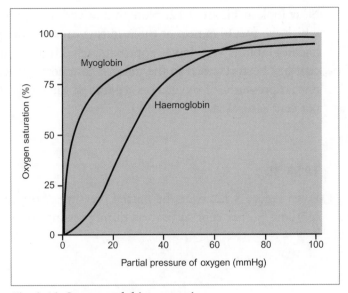

Fig. 3.13 Oxy-myoglobin saturation

Gaseous exchange at the tissues (internal respiration)

You should recall that gaseous exchange at the lungs was determined by the relative partial pressures of oxygen and carbon dioxide. Similarly, gaseous exchange at the tissues is governed by the partial pressure gradients of these two respiratory gases. At the tissue–capillary membranes surrounding the muscles, the PO_2 in the capillary (105mmHg) is greater than that in the tissues (40mmHg), therefore oxygen diffuses from the blood into the muscle tissue until equilibrium is reached. Conversely, the PCO_2 in the tissues (45mmHg) is higher than that in the capillary blood (40mmHg), causing movement of carbon dioxide from the muscle into the bloodstream.

The arterial venous oxygen difference (a-vo$_2$ diff)

The arterial venous oxygen difference represents how much oxygen is actually extracted and utilized by the muscles. It is measured by analysing the difference in oxygen content of the blood in the arteries leaving the lungs and that in the mixed venous blood returning to the lungs. We have already established that after flowing through the alveolar capillaries, blood is 96 per cent saturated with oxygen. During resting conditions, blood returning to the alveoli via the pulmonary artery is still 70 per cent saturated with oxygen. This suggests that at rest our muscles only use about 25 per cent of the oxygen delivered to them. This difference actually equates to about 4–5ml of oxygen per 100ml of blood.

During intense exercise, however, this difference can increase three-fold to about 15ml of oxygen per 100ml of blood and reflects an increased uptake of oxygen by the working muscles.

HOT TIPS

During exercise, the arterial venous oxygen difference actually increases, which indicates greater oxygen extraction and use by the working muscles.

TASK 10

1 What effect does an increase in the carbon dioxide partial pressure have on the oxygen-carrying capacity of haemoglobin?
2 State where in the human body the partial pressure of oxygen and carbon dioxide is likely to be a) high and b) low.

Table 3.05

Partial pressure	Oxygen	Carbon dioxide
High		
Low		

The transport of carbon dioxide

Bicarbonate ions (HCO₃⁻)

An ion formed as a result of the dissociation of carbonic acid. This is how much of the carbon dioxide produced in the body is transported in the blood to the lungs where it is expired.

Plasma

The fluid component of the blood.

Like oxygen, carbon dioxide is transported around the body by the blood. It is carried in several forms:

- **70 per cent** is transported in the blood as hydrogen carbonate (bicarbonate) ions. Carbon dioxide produced by the muscles diffuses into the tissue capillaries and enters the red blood stream where it combines with water to form carbonic acid:

$$CO_2 + H_2O = H_2CO_3$$

However, carbonic acid is a weak acid and quickly dissociates into hydrogen ions (H^+) and hydrogen carbonate or **bicarbonate ions (HCO₃⁻)**:

$$H_2CO_3 = H^+ + HCO_3^-$$

The complete reaction is more accurately written as:

$$CO_2 + H_2O = H_2CO_3 = H^+ + HCO_3^-$$

It is in this form that the majority of carbon dioxide is transported back around to the lungs and expired.

- **23 per cent** combines with haemoglobin in the red blood cells to form carbaminohaemoglobin:

$$CO_2 + Hb = HbCO_2$$

This reaction relies on the partial pressure of carbon dioxide (PCO_2) so that at the tissues where PCO_2 is high, haemoglobin and carbon dioxide readily combine, whilst at the alveoli, the relatively low PCO_2 causes haemoglobin and carbon dioxide to dissociate.

- **7 per cent** is dissolved in the **plasma** of the blood. You will discover in the next section just how important the amount of plasma CO_2 is in the control of the whole respiratory process.

The control of respiration

Breathing happens automatically and is under the influence of the respiratory control centre (RCC) located in the medulla oblongata of the brain. This control centre has two areas, both of which are under involuntary nervous control:

- the inspiratory control centre (ICC)
- the expiratory control centre (ECC).

Breathing patterns at rest

APPLICATION

Note that during normal resting conditions, the expiratory control centre is not involved in the process of expiration. Expiration at rest is a passive process that occurs when the inspiratory muscles relax.

During normal resting conditions, it is the **inspiratory control centre** that determines the basic rhythm of breathing. Inspiration is initiated when nerve impulses from the inspiratory control centre are sent via the phrenic and intercostal nerves to the diaphragm and external intercostal muscles respectively. These nerve impulses last for about two seconds and cause the inspiratory muscles to contract, thus enabling inspiration. You will recall that expiration at rest is a passive process. After the two seconds of inspiration, stimulation of the respiratory muscles ceases and the inspiratory muscles relax, causing expiration. Expiration at rest typically lasts three seconds.

Breathing patterns during exercise

During exercise, the rate and depth of breathing both increase. This increased rate of ventilation, however, causes impulses from the inspiratory control centre to activate the expiratory control centre so that the duration of inspiration is reduced and the rate of breathing can be increased further. Impulses from the expiratory control centre stimulate the internal intercostal muscles and the abdominal muscles, which decrease the size of the thoracic cavity and cause forced expiration.

Factors affecting the respiratory control centre (RCC)

Several factors (Figure 3.14) can influence the basic rate and depth of breathing so that oxygen and carbon dioxide content and acidity levels of the blood are maintained at acceptable levels. These factors include:

- **a low blood pH** (increase in blood acidity) resulting from an increase in plasma concentration of carbon dioxide and lactic acid production, which together stimulate the respiratory control centre, causing an increase in the ventilation rate
- **chemoreceptors** located in the aorta and carotid arteries. Together with the chemosensitive area of the medulla, they detect changes in the concentration of carbon dioxide and oxygen levels in the blood. When stimulated (that is, when PCO_2 is high and PO_2 is low), nerve impulses are sent to the brain, causing the rate of inspiration to increase

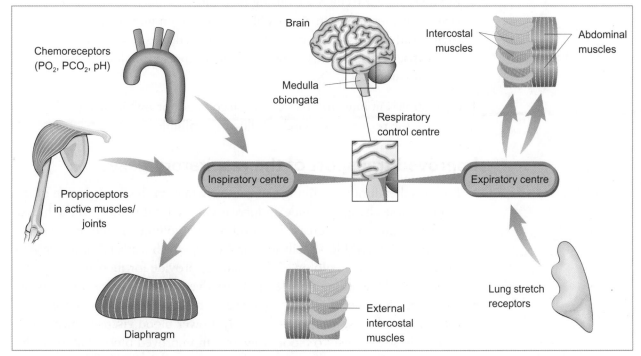

Fig. 3.14 Factors affecting the respiratory control centre

- **mechanoreceptors and proprioceptors** located in the muscles and joints stimulate the respiratory control centre to increase the rate and depth of breathing as soon as exercise commences
- **stretch receptors** in the walls of the bronchi and bronchioles are stimulated when over-inflation of the lungs occurs. These receptors send impulses to the respiratory control centre, causing inspiration to stop and expiration to occur. This safety mechanism, which prevents over-inflation of the lungs, is known as the **Hering-Breur reflex**
- **thermoreceptors** detect increases in body temperature that accompany exercise. This will cause the respiratory rate to increase.

The effects of training upon lung function

A prolonged period of aerobic training signals an improvement in lung function. This is due to several factors including:
- small increases in lung volumes and capacities
- improved transport of respiratory gases, oxygen and carbon dioxide
- more efficient gaseous exchange at the alveoli and tissues
- improved uptake of oxygen by the muscles.

Small increases in lung volumes and capacities

Although total lung capacity remains unchanged following training, there are some small changes to other lung volumes and capacities:
- tidal volume remains unchanged at rest and during sub-maximal exercise but does appear to increase during high-intensity maximal exercise. This ensures as much oxygen as possible is being taken into the lungs with each breath and as much carbon dioxide expelled as possible
- vital capacity also increases slightly, which causes a small decrease in the residual volume.

These increases in lung volumes can be accounted for by the increased strength of the respiratory muscles following training.

Improved transport of the respiratory gases

- Prolonged endurance training can cause changes in the composition of the blood. These changes include an increase in the total volume of the blood (primarily due to an increase in blood plasma volume) and an increase in the number of red blood cells (erythrocytes), which leads to an increase in the content of haemoglobin. These changes provide for increased oxygen delivery to the working muscles and improved removal of carbon dioxide.
- The increase in blood plasma volume also means that the blood becomes less viscous, that is, it flows more freely. Lower blood viscosity means that there is less resistance to blood flow and an improved blood supply to the working muscles.

More efficient gaseous exchange at the alveoli and tissues

- Capillary density (which refers to the number of capillaries that surround the alveoli and skeletal muscle) increases substantially following endurance training, providing for a greater opportunity for gaseous exchange to take place. This enhances the supply of oxygen to and the removal of carbon dioxide from the working muscle.
- Endurance athletes also appear to have enhanced blood flow to the lungs (pulmonary blood flow), which, together with an increase in maximal minute ventilation, causes a significant increase in pulmonary diffusion, that is, gaseous exchange at the alveoli, once again ensuring maximum exchange of oxygen and carbon dioxide.

KEY WORDS

Maximum oxygen uptake (VO₂max)

The maximum volume of oxygen that can be utilized by the working muscles per minute. It is a measure of aerobic capacity.

Improved uptake of oxygen by the muscles

- Endurance training improves the ability of skeletal muscle to extract oxygen from the blood. This is largely the result of increased **mitochondrial** density and **myoglobin content** within the muscle cell, which will cause an improvement in an athlete's **maximum oxygen uptake** or VO_2max by about ten to twenty per cent.
- The enhanced oxygen extraction by skeletal muscle also causes an increase in the arterial venous oxygen difference (a-vo$_2$ diff).

Revise as you go!

1 Outline the path of inspired air from the nasal passages to the alveoli. State the respiratory structures it travels through on its journey.
2 Define the term 'partial pressure'. Explain the importance of partial pressure in gaseous exchange.
3 Define the following lung volumes and capacities:
   a) tidal volume   c) vital capacity
   b) inspiratory reserve volume   d) residual volume.
4 Sketch a graph to illustrate minute ventilation during a) sub-maximal exercise and b) maximal exercise. Explain the shape of both curves. You will need to consider the pattern before, during and following exercise.
5 Explain the ways in which oxygen and carbon dioxide are transported in the body.
6 Explain the importance of plasma carbon dioxide in the control of respiration. What other factors affect the respiratory control centre during exercise?
7 How does aerobic training enhance respiratory functioning?

Chapter 4: Defining and evaluating fitness

Learning outcomes

By the end of this chapter you should be able to:
* provide definitions of 'fitness' and 'health'
* give reasons why the term 'fitness' is difficult to define
* define each of the following components or dimensions of fitness: cardiorespiratory endurance (stamina), muscular endurance, strength, flexibility, speed, power, agility, balance and body composition
* suggest reasons why testing fitness is important to the athlete
* describe a battery of tests that can be used to test each of the following dimensions of fitness: cardiorespiratory endurance (stamina), muscular endurance, strength, flexibility, speed, power, agility, balance and body composition
* explain the terms 'validity' and 'reliability' with reference to fitness testing
* comment upon the validity and reliability of the tests identified for each component of fitness
* comment upon the limitations and ethics of fitness testing
* discuss the relative merits of maximal and sub-maximal tests.

Introduction

In order to improve your athletic performance, it will undoubtedly be necessary to improve some aspects of your fitness. This can obviously be achieved by following a well-structured training programme. However, in order to design this training programme so that it improves the necessary dimensions of your fitness, you will need to gather some information regarding exactly where your fitness strengths and weaknesses lie. This can be achieved by carrying out a battery of fitness tests, which will provide you with some accurate data upon which to base the design of your training programme.

The main body of this chapter seeks to provide a comprehensive guide to fitness testing, but first we must consider definitions of fitness and its various components.

Defining fitness

What is 'fitness'? Exercise physiologists have struggled for many years to come up with an acceptable definition of the term 'fitness'. This is mainly because the term 'fitness' means so many different things to different people. For you or me, being 'fit' might mean being able to cope with the demands of playing a game of squash once or twice a week. However, for somebody like Paula Radcliffe, being 'fit' might be where she is at her peak to compete and break a world record in the marathon! Even elite athletes have a different concept of what it means to be 'fit'. A 100m sprinter, for example, requires completely different dimensions of fitness (speed, power, reaction time) than a marathon runner (cardiorespiratory/aerobic endurance, muscular endurance), so their definitions of fitness will be completely different. One thing that is certain, however, is that elite levels of participation require higher levels of fitness than recreational levels.

When considering our levels of fitness, we must first ask ourselves the question, 'Exactly what are we trying to be fit for?' Only then can we consider exactly how fit we are.

In an attempt to give an all-encompassing definition that meets the requirements of all levels of fitness, whether you are a world-class athlete or a recreational badminton player, we might come up with the following definitions: '**the ability to carry out everyday activities without undue fatigue**', or '**the ability to meet the demands of your environment or lifestyle**'. For a trained athlete, then, being fit means being able to cope with the demands of an activity or competition without becoming so fatigued that you can no longer perform the required skills of the activity.

Defining health

HOT TIPS

Make sure you can distinguish between the definitions of fitness and health for your examination.

The above definitions of fitness, however, should never be confused with the term 'health'. Health has at its core physical, mental and emotional dimensions that allow a person to lead an active and contented lifestyle. A simple definition that is often cited is: '**a state of physical and social and mental well-being, where we are free from disease**'. Considering the terms 'fitness' and 'health' together, it is now possible to see that an athlete may well be physically fit, but if they are suffering from a mental illness such as depression, they can be classed as unhealthy.

The dimensions or components of fitness

A person's overall level of fitness is made up of many sub-components or dimensions. Some are classed as **health-related** components and others **skill-related**. Both types, however, are required in all sports, but depending upon the activity, the relative importance of each may differ. Figure 4.01 categorizes the various dimensions into **health-related** and **skill-related components**. Note that speed and power can be categorized under both headings.

Health-related components of fitness

Those dimensions of fitness that are physiologically based and determine how well a performer can meet the physical demands of an activity.

Skill- (motor) related components of fitness

Those dimensions of fitness that are based on the interaction of the neuromuscular system and determine how successfully a performer can carry out a specific skill.

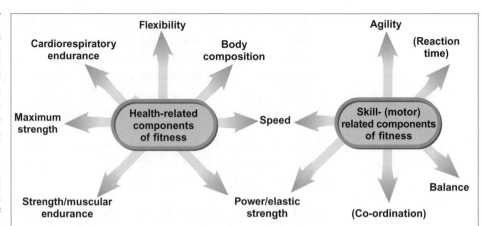

Fig. 4.01 Health-related and skill-related components of fitness (NB: components in brackets are not required for your examination)

TASK 1

Discuss with a partner why you think that the components of speed and power can be categorized under both health-related and skill-related components.

HOT TIPS

For each component of fitness, make sure that you can name a recognized test, give a brief description of the test and suggest a way to evaluate the results of the test.

Figure 4.02 outlines the actual components of fitness that you will be required to know for your examination. For each component, it is necessary that you can provide:

- a definition of the component
- a description of a relevant fitness test to evaluate the component
- a discussion of the reliability and validity of the fitness test(s) that you have described.

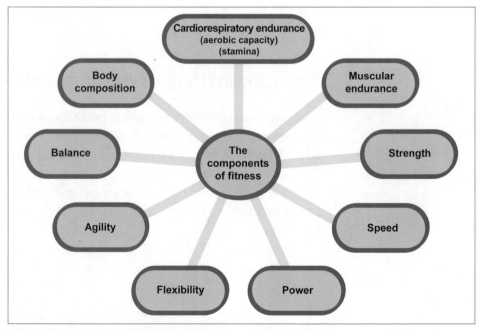

Fig. 4.02 The components of fitness required for your examination

Cardiorespiratory endurance (aerobic capacity)

Cardiorespiratory endurance or aerobic capacity can be defined as:

'the ability of the cardiovascular and respiratory systems to take in and transport oxygen to the working muscles where it can be utilized and aerobic performance maintained'.

Aerobic performance consists of sub-maximal exercise where the activity is of a continuous nature such as long-distance running, swimming and cycling. A triathlete requires high amounts of cardiorespiratory endurance, whereas a weightlifter requires very little. Cardiorespiratory endurance also helps in multiple sprint-type activities and games such as soccer, rugby and hockey since it will help the performer to withstand fatigue, recover during periods of less intense activity and so last the duration of the game.

Several factors influence a person's cardiorespiratory endurance, these include:
- the efficiency of gaseous exchange – both at the lungs and at the muscle cells
- the effectiveness of oxygen transport from the lungs to the muscle cells
- the ability of the muscle cells to utilize oxygen that they receive.

With reference to the above factors, we might expect a performer with high cardiorespiratory endurance or aerobic capacity, such as the triathlete, to possess the following:
- a greater capillarization of the alveoli and muscle
- a greater concentration of red blood cells, and therefore haemoglobin, in the blood, which helps to transport the oxygen to the working muscles
- a greater proportion of **slow oxidative muscle fibres (type 1)**
- a greater concentration of myoglobin within the muscle cell, which helps to store the oxygen and transport it to the **mitochondria**
- a greater number and size of mitochondria, which can utilize the oxygen to provide energy.

Testing cardiorespiratory endurance

Most tests of cardiorespiratory endurance seek to discover a person's VO_2max or maximal oxygen uptake. This is defined as the **maximal volume of oxygen that a person can take in, transport and utilize per minute,** and is usually measured in ml/kg/min (millilitres of oxygen consumed per kilogram of body weight per minute) or more simply l/min.

The most accurate tests of VO_2max are **direct measures** that are determined in the laboratory. **Direct gas analysis,** for example, involves a subject either running on a treadmill or cycling on an ergometer during a test that progresses in intensity until they reach exhaustion. Expired air samples are collected and analysed throughout the test to determine how much oxygen their muscles have extracted and utilized. However, these tests require access

KEY WORDS

Mitochondria

The site of energy production under aerobic conditions (when oxygen is present).

Slow oxidative muscle fibres (type 1)

Muscle fibres that are designed for endurance and are able to produce a large amount of energy over a long period of time assuming that oxygen is present.

KEY WORDS

Direct tests

These are the most accurate types of tests since they give a direct or objective measure of a physiological factor linked to a particular dimension of fitness. For example, a treadmill test actually measures oxygen consumption in ml/kg/min.

Indirect tests

These are not as accurate as direst tests since they will only give a prediction of a physiological factor linked to the particular fitness dimension. For example, the number of shuttles completed in the multi-stage fitness test can only be used to predict oxygen consumption.

to a laboratory that possesses this rather expensive and hi-tech equipment, so some less expensive predictive tests (**indirect tests**) have been developed to estimate the performer's VO_2max.

The multi-stage fitness test

The multi-stage fitness test is a maximal progressive shuttle run test (that is, it gets harder and harder as the test progresses) that gives a prediction of the performer's VO_2max (Table 4.01).

KEY WORDS

Validity of testing

The validity of a test assesses whether the test actually measures what it claims to measure.

Reliability of testing

The reliability of a test considers whether the test will produce the same or similar results when the test is repeated and where there has been no change in fitness levels.

HOT TIPS

For your examination, make sure that you are able to give a critical appraisal of a test for each component of fitness.

HOT TIPS

Make sure you give the units of measurement for all your fitness tests. The unit of measurement for VO_2max is ml/kg/min for weight bearing activities such as running and l/min for partial or non-weight bearing activities such as cycling and swimming.

Table 4.01 The multi-stage fitness test

Facilities and equipment needed	• A marked non-slip 20m track such as a sports hall • Multi-stage fitness test tape and booklet
Testing procedure	Performers run the 20m distance in time to the bleeps emitted from the tape. They should aim to place their foot on or over the line as the bleep sounds. After every minute, the time interval between the bleeps decreases and the performer must increase his/her running speed accordingly. Performers must continue to run in time to the bleeps until they can no longer keep up (exhaustion). This is judged to be when the performer fails to make it to the line as the bleep sounds. At this point, the level and shuttle number attained are recorded
Data collected	The level and shuttle number recorded are compared to the booklet provided, which converts the level and shuttle number to give a prediction of VO_2max in ml/kg/min
Main strengths of the test	• Easy testing procedure • Standardized data that easily converts into a predicted VO_2max score • Large groups can be tested at the same time
Main limitations of the test	• The test is only a prediction of VO_2max, not an absolute measure • The test is maximal and to exhaustion, and is therefore dependent upon the performer's level of motivation • As the test involves a running action, it may favour runners. Test scores for swimmers and cyclists may be distorted
Validity of the test	As a predictor of VO_2max, the test is quite valid. Studies on its validity show correlation coefficients with direct gas analysis of between 0.87 and 0.93 with a standard error of approximately 3.5ml/kg/min
Reliability of the test	Because the test is maximal, it does depend upon the motivation levels of the performer at a given time. With this being equal, the multi-stage fitness test can be a fairly reliable test of VO_2max

Table 4.02 shows some other commonly conducted fitness tests used to evaluate cardiorespiratory endurance. Study the table, taking time in particular to judge the strengths and limitations of each test.

Table 4.02 Other tests of cardiorespiratory endurance (aerobic capacity)

Name of test	Brief description of the test	Strengths of the test	Limitations of the test	Validity of the test	Reliability of the test
Harvard step test	A performer steps up onto and down from a bench in time to a set rhythm for five minutes. Recovery heart rate is recorded and used to predict VO_2max	• Easy to use and organize • Little equipment needed	• Errors in recovery heart rate scores can occur when taking the pulse rate manually • The activity of stepping is not very specific to many sports • The equation used to predict VO_2max has been questioned • Some performers find it difficult to keep up • Some performers find it difficult to maintain the cadence (rate of stepping)	Some validity tests have shown that this test is a poor predictor of VO_2max with correlation coefficients of 0.2–0.5 when compared to laboratory measures	As this is a sub-maximal test, performers' motivation levels should not affect the results. Therefore, all things being equal, this test should be relatively reliable
PWC170 cycle ergometer test	Athletes perform three consecutive workloads on a cycle ergometer. Heart rate is measured each minute for four minutes for each workload. Target heart rates for each workload are stated below: W/load 1 (115–130) W/load 2 (130–145) W/load 3 (145–165). The heart rate for each workload is graphed and a line of best fit drawn. A workload that would elicit a HR of 170bpm can then be extra-polated from the graph	• This is a sub-maximal test that does not require the subject to work to exhaustion • Cycle tests are good as the saddle supports the subject's weight	• As the test is performed on a cycle ergometer, it may favour cyclists • Determining the line of best fit and extrapolating the workload at 170bpm can be open to error • Errors in recording heart rate can occur if performed manually	Some studies have shown a correlation coefficient of 0.9 when compared to laboratory studies and therefore demonstrates high validity	As this is a sub-maximal test, performers' motivation levels should not affect the results. Therefore, all things being equal, this test should be relatively reliable

Name of test	Brief description of the test	Strengths of the test	Limitations of the test	Validity of the test	Reliability of the test
Cooper 12 minute run test	Performers run as far as they can in twelve minutes. The distance covered in twelve minutes is recorded	• Simple to organize • Little equipment needed • Large groups can be tested at the same time	A maximal test that depends upon the performer's level of motivation	Cooper's equation to convert miles covered into a VO_2max score has been questioned. Studies on correlation coefficients range from 0.65–0.9 when compared to laboratory VO_2max scores	Because the test is maximal, it does depend upon the motivation level of the performer at a given time. With this being equal, the distance covered should be similar and the Cooper run is therefore a fairly reliable test

APPLICATION

Validity and reliability correlation coefficients of 0.9 and above mean that the test is very valid and reliable.

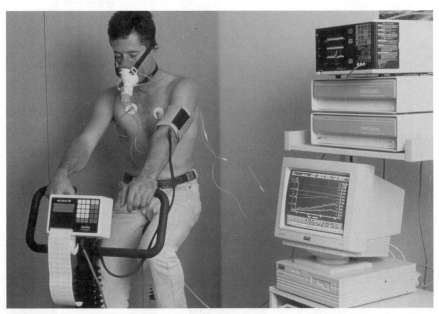

Fig. 4.03 Direct gas analysis

Table 4.03 VO_2 max norms

Rating	VO_2max (ml/kg/min): male	VO_2max (ml/kg/min): female
Excellent	>56	>48
Good	52–6	44–8
Average	44–51	35–43
Poor	39–43	29–34
Very poor	<39	<29

TASK 2

Starting with the greatest, place the following activities in order of expected VO_2max scores:

• rower
• 200m swimmer
• cross-country skier
• weightlifter
• 10,000m runner
• 400m runner.

As a general rule, typical oxygen consumption for female performers is approximately 10ml/kg/min below that of their male counterparts.

Table 4.04 Typical VO$_2$max scores for a range of sporting activities

Activity	Male (ml/kg/min)	Female (ml/kg/min)
Triathlete	80	72
Marathon runner	78	68
Distance swimmer	72	64
Middle distance runner (800m–1500m)	72	63
Games player	66	56
Gymnast	56	47
Weightlifter	52	43

Strength

Strength is the ability of the body to apply a force against a resistance. During sporting activity, this resistance may vary. For example, whilst running, the resistance that you are working against is your own body weight; a swimmer applies force to the water and a shot putter obviously must apply force to the shot, which is acting as the resistance. However, when we are analysing strength during sporting performance, it is how we apply strength that is of most interest. Take the example of the shot putter: when putting the shot, the performer must apply strength rapidly over a very short space of time. Compare this to the swimmer, who might need to apply force to the water over a much longer period of time. Different terms are used to explain more clearly the exact type of strength that we require for our particular sporting activity:

- **maximum strength**
- **elastic strength (also known as power)**
- **strength endurance (also known as muscular endurance).**

Maximum strength

'The maximum force that can be developed in a muscle or group of muscles during a single maximal contraction.'

(This definition also tends to be the universal definition of strength.)

Fast twitch glycolytic (FTG) muscle fibres (type 2b)

A muscle fibre designed for very high intensity, power-based activities such as sprinting, throwing and jumping.

Maximum strength is dependent upon several factors, which include:
- the cross-sectional area of muscle – the greater the cross-sectional area of pure muscle mass, the stronger the performer
- **fast twitch glycolytic (FTG) muscle fibres (type 2b)** are designed more for maximum strength.

A good example of a performer who requires a lot of maximum strength is a weightlifter.

Fig. 4.04 A triple jumper requires high amounts of elastic strength

Elastic strength

'The ability to overcome a resistance rapidly and prepare the muscle quickly for a sequential contraction of equal force.'

A performer with high amounts of elastic strength should also possess a high proportion of fast twitch glycolytic (FTG) muscle fibres (type 2b) since the thick myelin sheath that surrounds these fibres conducts the motor neurone to the muscle more rapidly. This ensures a faster rate of muscle contraction.

Sports performers who require high levels of elastic strength include sprinters, triple jumpers, and gymnasts.

Strength endurance

KEY WORDS

Fast oxidative glycolytic (FOG) muscle fibres (type 2a)

A fast twitch muscle fibre that picks up certain slow twitch characteristics so that they can withstand fatigue for longer. Swimmers and rowers require a good proportion of these fibre types.

'The ability of a muscle or group of muscles to undergo repeated contractions and withstand fatigue.'

For this type of strength, a performer will require a high proportion of **fast oxidative glycolytic (FOG) muscle fibres (type 2a)**, which can withstand fatigue much better than fast twitch glycolytic (FTG) muscle fibres (type 2b). Such sports performers include swimmers, rowers or even Olympic kyakers.

TASK 3

Copy out Table 4.05. For each of the activities listed, state which type of strength is most likely to be required by the performer.

Table 4.05

	Maximum strength	Elastic strength	Strength endurance
400m swim			
Throwing the javelin			
110m hurdles			
Weightlifting			
Track cycling			
Gymnastic floor routine			

Testing strength

Before you decide upon which test of strength to use, you must first decide upon which type of strength you wish to test: for example, maximum strength, elastic strength or strength endurance.

In this section we are only going to deal with tests of maximum strength since we will consider the tests of strength endurance and elastic strength under the headings of 'muscular endurance' and 'power' later in this chapter.

One repetition maximum test (1RM test)

Table 4.06 One repetition maximum test (1RM)

Facilities and equipment needed	A weights room with free weights or multi-gym facility
Testing procedure	Following a thorough warm-up, the maximum weight that a performer can lift just once is determined by trial and error. After each attempt, the weight should be increased or decreased by about 5kg and a recovery period of two to three minutes given between each trial
Data collected	The maximum weight that can be lifted just once (1RM). The weight can be converted to a percentage of the performer's body mass in kg. That is: $\dfrac{\text{Weight lifted (kg)}}{\text{Body mass (kg)}} \times 100$
Main strengths of the test	• Easy testing procedure • Most muscle groups can be tested • Sport-specific actions can be tested
Main limitations of the test	• Requires access to weights or multi-gym facility • Performing maximal lifts increases the likelihood of injury • Only gives a general strength measure
Validity of the test	The data provided does not give precise data concerning the actual force generated within the muscle but can give a general evaluation of muscular strength
Reliability of the test	This test is very reliable since the maximum weight that can be lifted is often repeated

Handgrip dynamometer test

Table 4.07 Handgrip dynamometer test

Facilities and equipment needed	A handgrip dynamometer (Figure 4.05)
Testing procedure	Having adjusted the grip for hand size, the performer holds the dynamometer in one hand at shoulder height. The subject brings the dynamometer down to their side whilst squeezing the handle. Record the highest reading from three attempts for both dominant and non-dominant hand
Data collected	Scores are recorded in kg
Main strengths of the test	• Easy testing procedure • Little equipment needed

Main limitations of the test	• Erroneous adjusting of the handgrip can affect the results • This test only gives an indication of the strength of the handgrip and forearm, and care should be taken if using handgrip scores to comment on general body strength
Validity of the test	As a measure of handgrip and forearm static strength, this test can be considered valid, but it is completely invalid as a measure of dynamic strength of other muscles around the body (for example, leg strength)
Reliability of the test	This test is very reliable since the maximum handgrip score is often repeated assuming appropriate adjustment of the handgrip

NB: dynamometers have also been designed to test the strength of other areas of the body.

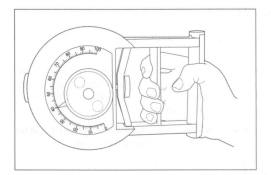

Fig. 4.05 The handgrip dynamometer test

Table 4.08 Handgrip dynamometer norms

Rating: males	Dominant hand (kg)	Non-dominant hand (kg)	Rating: females	Dominant (kg)	Non-dominant hand (kg)
Excellent	>69	>67	Excellent	>40	>36
Good	62–9	56–67	Good	38–40	34–6
Average	48–61	43–55	Average	25–37	22–33
Poor	41–7	39–42	Poor	22–4	18–21
Very poor	<41	<39	Very poor	<22	<18

Muscular endurance or strength endurance

'The ability of a muscle or group of muscles to sustain repeated contractions against a resistance for an extended period of time.'

Muscular endurance is a major component of fitness in those activities where the performer must work at medium to high intensity for periods of up to five or six minutes. A good example is competitive rowing or swimming where muscles of both the upper and lower body are required to work repeatedly for the duration of the event. Performers with high levels of muscular endurance will possess both fast (type 2a) and slow (type 1) twitch muscle fibres and will be able to withstand high levels of lactic acid so that they can avoid fatigue.

The NCF abdominal conditioning test

Table 4.09 The NCF abdominal conditioning test

Facilities and equipment needed	NCF (National Coaching Foundation) abdominal conditioning tape, tape recorder, gymnasium floor, gym mats, stopwatch
Testing procedure	Thoroughly warm up. Follow the instructions on the tape. Subjects are required to perform as many sit-ups as possible whilst keeping in time with the signals emitted from the tape. A partner counts the number of sit-ups completed and times the duration of the work period. The test should be halted when the performer can no longer keep in time with the signals or when their technique deteriorates
Data collected	The number of sit-ups completed
Main strengths of the test	• Easy testing procedure • Little equipment needed • Large groups can be tested at once • The abdominal muscles are easily isolated
Main limitations of the test	• The test is maximal and therefore relies upon the motivation of the performer to work to exhaustion • It is difficult to monitor the correct technique • Full sit-ups should not be completed on a regular basis due to excessive strain being placed on the lumbar region of the spine
Validity of the test	The test does isolate the abdominals assuming the testing protocol is followed correctly. It is therefore a relatively valid test
Reliability of the test	Because the test is maximal, it does depend upon the motivation levels of the performer at a given time. With this being equal, the abdominal conditioning test can be a fairly reliable test of muscular endurance

Table 4.10 Abdominal conditioning norms

Stage	Number of sit-ups	Rating: males	Rating: females
1	20	Poor	Poor
2	42	Poor	Fair
3	64	Fair	Fair
4	89	Fair	Good
5	116	Good	Good
6	146	Good	Very good
7	180	Excellent	Excellent
8	217	Excellent	Excellent

Power (also known as elastic strength)

'The amount of work done per unit of time or the rate at which we apply strength.'

A performer with high amounts of power can exert a great force over a very short period of time. A gymnast performing a vault or a hammer thrower launching the hammer, for example, requires a great deal of power. Powerful athletes should possess a high proportion of fast twitch glycolytic (FTG) muscle fibres (type 2b) since the thick myelin sheath that surrounds these fibres conducts the motor neurone to the muscle more rapidly. This enables the neuromuscular system to recruit the fast twitch fibres as rapidly as possible.

Testing power

Since power is measured in Watts, true tests of power must focus on the amount of work done by the body in a certain time. Perhaps the best test of anaerobic power is the Wingate cycle test.

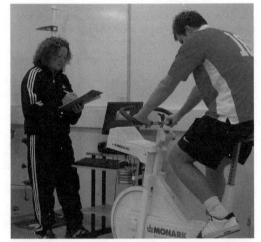

Fig. 4.06 Testing anaerobic power through the Wingate cycle test

Table 4.11 The Wingate cycle test

Facilities and equipment needed	Monarch bicycle ergometer, weight stack (resistance), video recorder, stopwatch
Testing procedure	Thoroughly warm up. With a resistance of 75g per kg of bodyweight, the subject pedals flat out for a period of 30 seconds. Using a video recorder, the number of revolutions is counted for every five seconds of the test. The subject should then perform a cool down
Data collected	Peak power in Watts, power decline, fatigue index, mean anaerobic capacity
Main strengths of the test	• Objective data collected • aspects of power can be evaluated (see data collected)
Main limitations of the test	• The test is maximal and therefore relies upon the motivation of the performer to work to exhaustion • Expensive equipment needed • As it is a cycle test, it may favour cyclists
Validity of the test	When peak power from the Wingate cycle test has been compared to 50m sprint times, the validity correlation coefficient of 0.91 is very high
Reliability of the test	This test is known for its reliability but, as it is a maximal test, it can depend upon the subject's motivation level to perform the test

The standing (Sargent) vertical jump test

A simpler test of leg power is the standing (Sargent) vertical jump test.

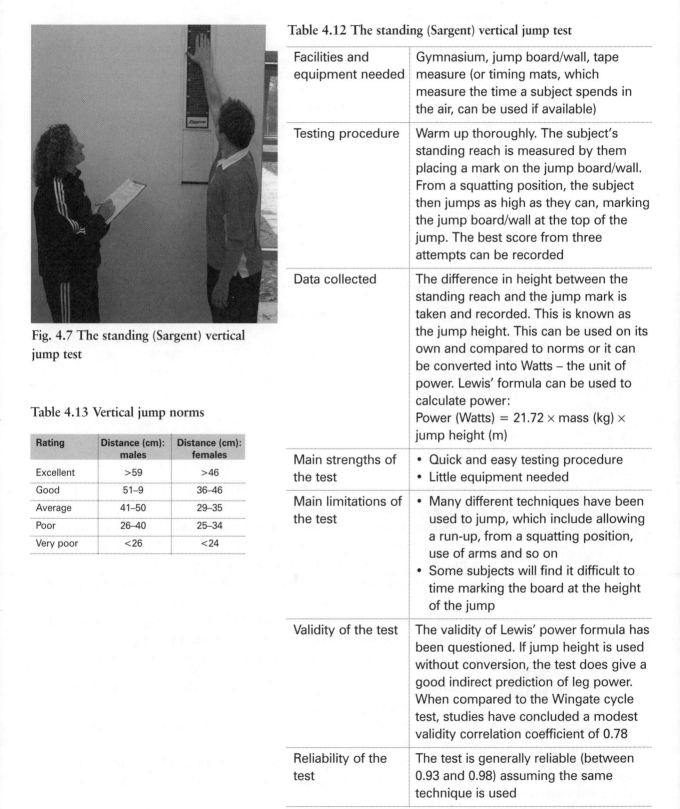

Fig. 4.7 The standing (Sargent) vertical jump test

Table 4.13 Vertical jump norms

Rating	Distance (cm): males	Distance (cm): females
Excellent	>59	>46
Good	51–9	36–46
Average	41–50	29–35
Poor	26–40	25–34
Very poor	<26	<24

Table 4.12 The standing (Sargent) vertical jump test

Facilities and equipment needed	Gymnasium, jump board/wall, tape measure (or timing mats, which measure the time a subject spends in the air, can be used if available)
Testing procedure	Warm up thoroughly. The subject's standing reach is measured by them placing a mark on the jump board/wall. From a squatting position, the subject then jumps as high as they can, marking the jump board/wall at the top of the jump. The best score from three attempts can be recorded
Data collected	The difference in height between the standing reach and the jump mark is taken and recorded. This is known as the jump height. This can be used on its own and compared to norms or it can be converted into Watts – the unit of power. Lewis' formula can be used to calculate power: Power (Watts) = 21.72 × mass (kg) × jump height (m)
Main strengths of the test	• Quick and easy testing procedure • Little equipment needed
Main limitations of the test	• Many different techniques have been used to jump, which include allowing a run-up, from a squatting position, use of arms and so on • Some subjects will find it difficult to time marking the board at the height of the jump
Validity of the test	The validity of Lewis' power formula has been questioned. If jump height is used without conversion, the test does give a good indirect prediction of leg power. When compared to the Wingate cycle test, studies have concluded a modest validity correlation coefficient of 0.78
Reliability of the test	The test is generally reliable (between 0.93 and 0.98) assuming the same technique is used

The standing broad jump test

Table 4.14 The standing broad jump test

Facilities and equipment needed	Gymnasium, mat, tape measure
Testing procedure	Warm up thoroughly. The subject jumps as far as possible (horizontally) with both feet kept together. Take-off must be with both feet and the distance between the start line and the nearest heel is recorded. The best score from three attempts can be used
Data collected	Distance jumped
Main strengths of the test	• Quick and easy testing procedure • Little equipment needed
Main limitations of the test	• This test only predicts leg power through distance jumped • Heavily dependent upon technique • Different techniques have been used including use of the arms, or hands clenched behind the subject's back
Validity of the test	There is no conversion into units of power (Watts) although the distance jumped can give an indirect prediction of leg power
Reliability of the test	The test is generally reliable assuming the same technique is used

Table 4.15 Standing broad jump norms

Rating	Distance (cm): males	Distance (cm): females
Excellent	>240	>190
Good	231–40	181–90
Average	221–30	171–80
Fair	211–20	161–70
Poor	<211	<161

Speed

Speed is a major factor in the successful performance of many sporting activities. From high intensity explosive activities such as sprinting to a rugby player making a break, you simply cannot beat speed. For your study, there are two aspects of speed that you need to be aware of. The first is concerned with moving the whole body from one point to another in the quickest time possible (**the maximum rate that a person can move over a specific distance**), for example when performing a 100m sprint. The other type of speed is concerned with moving perhaps just one body part quickly (**the ability to put body parts into motion quickly**), for example when throwing the javelin where the speed at which the arm moves is of supreme importance.

As with other components of fitness, speed is largely in our genes; however, some determining factors include:

- a high number of fast twitch glycolytic (FTG) muscle fibres (type 2b) within the muscle
- high stores of **phosphocreatine** within the muscle. This is the fuel used to help muscle contraction during very high intensity activities such as sprinting
- highly effective lever systems, which put limbs into motion quickly.

KEY WORDS

Phosphocreatine (creatine phosphate)

A high-energy compound found in the muscle cell, which provides energy very quickly and enables us to perform high intensity activities such as sprinting.

Reaction time

A skill-related component of fitness. It is the time between the onset of a stimulus and the initiation of a muscular response.

Testing speed

Most tests of speed are sprint tests from a flying start. A flying start is preferred over a standing start since this eliminates the effect that **reaction time** might have on the scores. It is possible to conduct sprint tests over almost any distance from 10m to 50m, which helps make the test more specific to a particular performer. Table 4.16 gives an example of the 30m sprint test.

Table 4.16 The 30m sprint test

Facilities and equipment needed	A non-slip 30m track, tape measure, stopwatch (preferably sprint timing gates)
Testing procedure	Thoroughly warm up. From a 1m flying start, the time taken for the performer to cover the 30m distance is recorded
Data collected	Time taken in seconds to cover the 30m distance
Main strengths of the test	• Easy testing procedure • Little equipment needed
Main limitations of the test	• Manual timing can be affected by human error (timing gates should ideally be used over short distances) • Running surface and weather can affect the results • The test is not sport-specific. Most sporting activities are multi-directional and few require us to run in a straight line for 30m
Validity of the test	The sprint test is widely accepted as being a valid test of speed, especially when a flying start is used, which eliminates the effect of reaction time. When compared to other anaerobic tests, such as the Wingate cycle test, correlation coefficients of 0.89 have been shown
Reliability of the test	The use of timing gates greatly improves the reliability of this test to as much as 0.97

Table 4.17 30m sprint norms

Rating	Time (secs): males	Time (secs): females
Excellent	<4.0	<4.5
Good	4.2–4.0	4.6–4.5
Average	4.4–4.3	4.8–4.7
Fair	4.6–4.5	5.0–4.9
Poor	>4.6	>5.0

Static flexibility

The range of movement about a joint when the muscles surrounding the joint are slowly lengthened.

Dynamic flexibility

This considers the speed at which body parts are moved about the joint. For example, a trampolinist performing a straddle jump would demonstrate dynamic flexibility.

Flexibility

'The range of movement possible at a joint.'

Flexibility is an important component of fitness for all sporting activities, from gymnastics and trampolining through to football and hockey. This is because flexibility not only helps in the prevention of injuries, but it also helps us perform some skills more successfully and helps in the generation of faster and more forceful muscular contractions. It is therefore essential that the training programme of any athlete include sessions on improving their flexibility and mobility.

Two types of flexibility have been identified:
• **static flexibility**
• **dynamic flexibility**.

There are many factors that help determine flexibility. These include:

- the elasticity of the ligaments and tendons surrounding the joint – the more elastic these soft tissues, the more movement they will allow at the joint
- the strength of the muscles surrounding the joint, in particular the antagonist muscle – stronger muscles can restrict movement and lead to a more stable joint, therefore limiting flexibility
- the type of joint. For example, the ball and socket joint of the shoulder has a greater range of movement (ROM) than the hinge joint of the knee since the shoulder is designed for mobility whilst the knee is designed for stability
- the temperature of the muscles and connective tissues – the warmer the better
- the age of the performer – we generally lose flexibility and mobility as we get older due to our soft tissues becoming less elastic
- the sex of the performer – females tend to have greater flexibility than their male counterparts.

Testing flexibility

KEY WORDS

Goniometer

An instrument used to measure angular displacement and flexibility.

Although it is difficult to measure the length of a muscle, most coaches accept that angular displacement at a joint is a good predictor of muscle length. Angular displacement at a joint can be measured using a modified protractor known as a **goniometer**. The centre of the goniometer is placed in the middle of the joint whilst the arms are aligned with each of the two body parts as they move. Angular displacement can then be assessed by measuring the degree of movement between the two body parts. The most widely used field test to assess flexibility, however, is the sit and reach test, which is outlined below.

Table 4.18 The sit and reach test

Facilities and equipment needed	Sit and reach box (if this is not available, a bench and a metre rule can be used)
Testing procedure	Thoroughly warm up. In a sitting position with legs outstretched, knees locked and feet flat against the box (with shoes off), slowly reach forward and push the cursor along the calibrated part of the box and hold for a two second count. No bouncing or jerking is permitted and the fingertips of both hands must be level. Record the highest score from three attempts
Data collected	Distance (positive or negative) recorded from the calibrated part of the box or metre rule
Main strengths of the test	• Easy testing procedure • Little equipment needed
Main limitations of the test	• The test only measures flexibility of the lower back and hamstrings – it is difficult to isolate the hamstrings • The extent to which the performer has warmed up can affect the score when comparing against standard norms • Variations in limb length can make comparisons between performers difficult
Validity of the test	The validity of the test is questionable as it is difficult to isolate the hamstrings
Reliability of the test	The extent to which the performer has warmed up can affect the reliability of this test

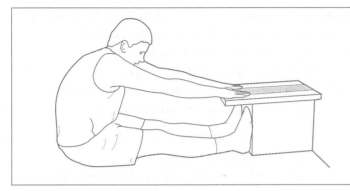

Fig. 4.08 The sit and reach test

Table 4.19 Sit and reach test norms

Rating	Distance (cm): males	Distance (cm): females
Excellent	>34	>38
Good	31–4	33–8
Fair	27–30	29–32
Poor	<27	<29

TASK 4

Copy out Table 4.20. For each of the activities listed, rate on the scale of 1–10 the flexibility requirements of the stated activity (1 = low flexibility requirement, 10 = high flexibility requirement). Write a sentence on each activity justifying your answer.

Table 4.20

Sporting activity	Scale									
Volleyball player	1	2	3	4	5	6	7	8	9	10
Judo player	1	2	3	4	5	6	7	8	9	10
Gymnast	1	2	3	4	5	6	7	8	9	10
Javelin thrower	1	2	3	4	5	6	7	8	9	10
Hockey player	1	2	3	4	5	6	7	8	9	10
Trampolinist	1	2	3	4	5	6	7	8	9	10

Body composition

'The relative components of total body mass in terms of fat mass and lean body mass or fat-free mass.'

Body composition is concerned with ensuring that the performer has an appropriate percentage of lean body mass for their particular activity. Although each sport may have a slightly different requirement in terms of body composition, in general it is safe to say the less body fat, the better. Excess body fat is really dead weight that must be carried around, which is energy inefficient. Lean body mass is much more desirable for those activities that require both cardiovascular and muscular endurance, such as distance running and rowing, since more oxygen can be directed to the working muscles. Ideal body fat percentages for males and females are 14–17 per cent and 24–9 per cent respectively.

APPLICATION

Extreme somatotypes rarely exist. In reality, we are all a combination of the three somatotypes.

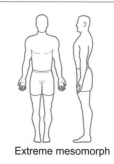

Extreme mesomorph

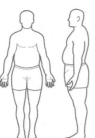

Extreme endomorph

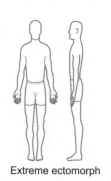

Extreme ectomorph

Fig. 4.09 The three extreme somatotypes

The relative shape of the body or **somatotype** is also linked to body composition. Somatotyping, however, is more concerned with whether our body shape is suited to the activity that we are performing. For example, an ideal body shape for a high jumper is to be very tall and lean, whilst a male gymnast needs to be very muscular with broad shoulders and a narrow waist. A performer's body shape can be categorized according to three extreme somatotypes:

- **endomorph**: pear-shaped body, wide hips with narrow shoulders, fat distributed around the stomach, thighs and upper arms
- **mesomorph**: wedge-shaped body, broad shoulders and narrow hips, very muscular with little body fat
- **ectomorph**: narrow shoulders and hips, little muscle or fat.

In reality, everybody is part endomorph, part mesomorph and part ectomorph, but the relative contribution each makes to our body shape is very individual and differs from performer to performer.

Testing body composition

There are several tests of body composition. The simplest of all tests is perhaps skinfold measurement, which is outlined below.

Table 4.21 Skinfold measurement

Facilities and equipment needed	Calibrated skinfold callipers
Testing procedure	All measurements should be taken from the right-hand side of the body. The thickness of four skinfolds around the body are taken: • triceps • biceps • subscapular • suprailiac spine. The tester pinches the skin and subcutaneous adipose tissue (being careful to avoid pinching any muscle) and applies the callipers 1cm below and at right angles to the pinch
Data collected	The sum of the four skinfold measures in mm
Main strengths of the test	• Easy testing procedure • Little equipment needed • Scores can be used to identify changes in body fat over time
Main limitations of the test	• Does not convert into a percentage of body fat • Inaccuracies in determining the exact site at which to perform the skinfold measure can occur • Pinching muscle tissue can distort the scores • It only considers subcutaneous fat
Validity of the test	Skinfold measurement can only predict the percentage of body fat and is therefore not particularly valid. However, some studies have shown a standard error of approximately +/- 3.5 per cent when compared to other methods of determining body fat percentage
Reliability of the test	Measurements can vary from tester to tester. Assuming the same person is carrying out the test each time, it can be reliable

Table 4.23 Other tests of body composition

Name of test	Brief description of the test	Strengths of the test	Limitations of the test	Validity of the test	Reliability of the test
Biolectric impedance	A small electrical current is passed through the body. Since fat offers greater resistance to the flow of the electrical current, it can be predicted that the greater the current needed, the greater the percentage of body fat	This test gives accurate predictions of body fat percentage	Equipment can be expensive (although it is getting cheaper)	Validity correlations are quite high when compared to hydrostatic weighing	Reliability is high if laboratory equipment is used. However, cheaper handheld 'home' devices can give distorted readings
Hydrostatic weighing (densiometry)	The body is submerged in water. By dividing the body mass of the subject by the volume of water displaced when immersed, body density can be calculated: $\text{Body density} = \dfrac{\text{Mass}}{\text{Volume}}$ Body density can be used to predict the body fat percentage. (NB: air trapped in the airways and intestines must be accounted for.) This works on the principle that because fat floats, a large amount of fat mass will make the body lighter in water, suggesting a higher percentage of body fat	This test gives accurate predictions of body fat percentage	• Can normally only be performed in a laboratory so it is not very practical • Some performers may suffer anxiety from being immersed in water	This is considered to be one of the most accurate measures of the percentage of body fat of the performer	Reliability is high due to the objective nature of this assessment
Body mass index (BMI)	A simple calculation is performed: $\text{BMI} = \dfrac{\text{Weight in kg}}{(\text{Height in m})^2}$	A simple calculation to perform	Does not consider lean body mass – just total body mass	Very poor validity as it only considers total body mass. No distinction is made between fat mass and lean body mass	High reliability. The calculation should come up with the same result all the time assuming no change in height or body mass

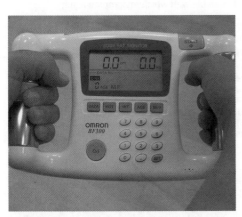

Fig 4.10 Testing body composition through bioelectric impedance

TASK 5

True somatotypes are rare. In reality, we are a mixture of all three. Copy out the delta graph and place the listed sporting activities on the graph:

- high jumper
- male gymnast
- weightlifter
- basketball player
- distance runner
- sumo wrestler.

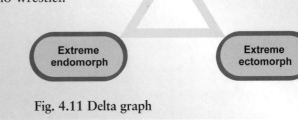

Fig. 4.11 Delta graph

Agility

'The ability to move and change direction and position of the body quickly while maintaining good body control and without loss of speed.'

Most sporting activity is not performed in a straight line, and multi-directional movement and rapid changes of direction are often needed. Take the position of centre in netball, for example: successful performance relies on the performer being able to move into space and lose defenders, which they can only accomplish through dodging and changing direction at speed. Performers in most games will become better if they develop their agility, whether it be a basketball player cutting in to the basket or a squash player moving into position quickly to play a shot. Agility is closely linked to balance since the key to improving agility is to minimize the loss of speed whilst shifting the body's centre of mass.

Testing agility

There are several tests of agility. The most commonly used test is the Illinois agility run test. Other tests of agility include the 'T' drill test and the hexagon obstacle test.

Table 4.24 Illinois agility run test

Facilities and equipment needed	A non-slip 10m × 5m area, tape measure, stopwatch (timing gates would be better), cones
Testing procedure	Thoroughly warm up. Mark out the 10m x 5m area as shown in the diagram (Figure 4.12). The subject lies face down at the starting position. At the signal, the performer moves onto his/her feet and completes the course, weaving in and out of the cones as quickly as possible
Data collected	Time taken in seconds to cover the course
Main strengths of the test	• Easy testing procedure • Little equipment needed • There is a lot of data available with which to compare results
Main limitations of the test	• Manual timing can be affected by human error • Running surface and weather can affect the results • The test is not sport-specific – the agility demands of many sports differ. A hockey player, for example, needs to control a ball with a stick whilst changing direction quickly
Validity of the test	Since agility is influenced by many factors including speed, balance and co-ordination, the validity of the test can be questioned
Reliability of the test	The use of timing gates greatly improves the reliability of this test

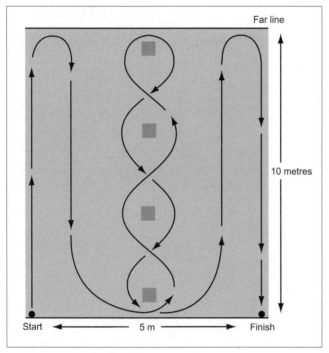

Fig. 4.12 The Illinois agility run test

TASK 6

All fitness tests should, where possible, be sport-specific. For a named activity of your choice, design a test of agility that is sport-specific. Once you have decided upon your test protocol, conduct your test with a group of students within your class. Complete a table, using the headings given below, and discuss your results with others within your class. Include a diagram of the layout of your test of agility.

- Facilities and equipment needed
- Testing procedure
- Data collected
- Main strengths of the test
- Main limitations of the test
- Validity of the test
- Reliability of the test

Table 4.25 Illinois agility run test norms

Rating	Time (secs): males	Time (secs): females
Excellent	<15.2	<17
Good	16.1–15.2	17.9–17
Average	18.1–16.2	21.7–18
Fair	18.3–18.2	23–21.8
Poor	>18.3	>23

Balance

'The maintenance of the body's centre of mass over the base of support.'

Few sporting activities require us to stand still, yet balance is an essential component in the effective performance of most sports. This is because balance can be either static or dynamic. **Static balance** can be seen when a gymnast is stationary, maintaining their **centre of mass (COM)** over their base of support when performing a handstand or an arabesque, for example. **Dynamic balance**, on the other hand, involves the maintenance of a balanced position whilst moving. For example, a gymnast performing a cartwheel – for successful performance, the hips of the gymnast (COM) must remain over their hands (base of support) throughout the movement. Dynamic balance can also be seen in the rugby player who must maintain balance whilst sidestepping or staying on their feet when being tackled. Balance depends upon the co-ordinated actions of the sensory functions of our ears, eyes and proprioceptors.

KEY WORDS

Centre of mass (COM)

The point at which the body is balanced in all directions. In humans, the position of the centre of mass is not fixed but moves according to the positioning of the body's limbs.

Testing balance

Since dynamic balance is difficult to measure, most tests of balance evaluate static balance. One of the most common tests of balance is the standing stork test. Other tests of balance include the use of balance or 'wobble' boards.

Table 4.26 The standing stork test

Facilities and equipment needed	A small non-slip area, stopwatch
Testing procedure	Stand comfortably on both feet with your hands on your hips. Lift one leg and place the toes of this foot against the knee of the other leg. On the signal, raise the heel of the straight leg and stand on your toes. Balance for as long as possible without letting the heel of the foot touch the floor or move the foot away from the knee of the balancing leg
Data collected	Time in balance in seconds
Main strengths of the test	• Easy testing procedure • Little equipment needed
Main limitations of the test	The test is not sport-specific. Most sporting activities require dynamic balance, not static balance
Validity of the test	For gymnasts and other activities where static balance is required, the correlation coefficient is high. However, most activities require dynamic balance and for this reason the validity of this test can be questioned
Reliability of the test	As results may vary, this test is not particularly reliable

Table 4.27 Standing stork test norms

Rating	Time (secs)
Excellent	>49
Good	40–49
Average	26–39
Fair	11–25
Poor	<11

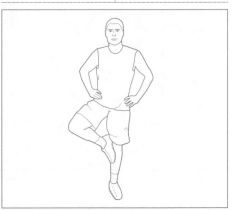

Fig. 4.13 The standing stork test

A quick guide to fitness testing

Here are a few key points to consider before you embark on your chosen fitness tests.

Why conduct fitness tests?

Fitness testing should be an integral part of any athlete's training regime. In fact, testing should be the basis on which their training programme is designed! Fitness testing attempts to measure a performer's individual aspects of performance with the overall aim of improving ability within each component. Think about what the likely benefits of fitness testing might be to the coach and performer. Hopefully you will have come up with some of these:

• identify strengths and weaknesses of the athlete
• monitor progress by comparing against previous test results or even the results of other performers
• enhance motivation – there is nothing more satisfying than seeing yourself improve
• provide information for the design and modification of training programmes – it can be used to measure the success of your current training programme
• talent identification and prediction of physiological potential – it can be used to steer the performer into the most appropriate sport or activity
• help performers set appropriate goals for fitness development.

Fitness tests, though, are not a magic potion; they will not in themselves create a better performer, they should merely be used as a tool, which, when used correctly, can provide the coach and athlete with valuable information to help them improve.

Limitations of fitness tests

For each of the fitness tests outlined in this chapter, some specific limitations have been highlighted. Below is a general summary of the key limitations to fitness testing.

- Many tests are not sport-specific. They do not replicate the specific movements or actions that are required by different activities.
- Many tests are predictive. They do not use direct measures and can therefore be inaccurate.
- Many tests do not consider the sporting environment or the competitive conditions of the activity.

Validity and reliability of testing

To be valid, a fitness test must measure what it claims to. For example, the sit and reach test may be a valid test of the flexibility at the hip, but not at the shoulder joint. The validity of a test is also improved if the test is sport-specific. If the test reflects or mimics one or two of the fitness requirements of that activity, then the validity of the test will be enhanced. A distance runner, for example, should perform a VO_2max test that requires running rather than cycling; a squash player should perform a test of agility that requires sideways movement as well as sprinting forwards. Specificity and therefore validity of the test can also be improved by:

- testing the appropriate muscle groups
- testing the appropriate muscle fibre type
- testing the appropriate energy systems
- replicating the sporting environment (for example, a rugby player should perform a sprint test on grass wearing rugby kit and boots).

Reliability of a fitness test is more concerned with the consistency and repeatability of the test results. If the test is reliable, then the same or very similar test results should be achieved when the test is repeated (assuming no change in fitness levels). There are several factors that can influence the reliability of fitness tests:

- sub-maximal tests are more reliable tests since the performer's motivation to work to exhaustion is not an issue
- the testing environment must be the same each time the test is conducted (for example, consider the weather if the test is to be conducted outside)
- the testing personnel and protocol must be standardized (for example, use timing gates rather than stopwatches in order to minimize human error).

A word on maximal and sub-maximal testing

Maximal tests such as the multi-stage fitness test and the Wingate cycle test require the athlete to work at maximum effort and are invariably tested to exhaustion. Whilst this does give some truly objective data, it does pose some serious problems. Firstly, it is difficult to ensure that the performer is working at their maximum. This may often depend upon how the performer is feeling on the day and their motivation level to push themselves to exhaustion. This can result in some distorted evaluations of fitness. Secondly, there are some ethical considerations and dangers involved in forcing performers to work to their maximum since this can lead to over-exertion and injury.

Sub-maximal tests, such as the PWC170 test, are often favoured since they do not require the subject to work at maximal levels and the motivation of the performer is not an issue. Most sub-maximal tests rely on estimating or predicting maximum work capacity through extrapolation, using data achieved at sub-maximal levels. This, however, also poses some problems in terms of the validity and reliability of the tests used. The results extrapolated to determine work capacity at maximal levels are only estimates or predictions, so they are not totally objective. Also, measurement inaccuracies at sub-maximal levels can also produce large discrepancies in the results when extrapolated.

When selecting the battery of tests, it is necessary to choose tests that are wholly appropriate for the individual performer.

Other ethical considerations

- All performers should be screened before any kind of fitness testing can take place. This can be done through asking subjects to complete a 'Physical Activity Readiness Questionnaire' (PAR-Q).
- Tests should be selected that are appropriate for the subject's age, sex and current fitness level.

TASK 7

Where possible, complete the battery of fitness tests outlined in Table 4.28. Copy out and complete the accompanying table.

Table 4.28

Component of fitness	Recognized test	My score	My rating
Cardiorespiratory endurance (aerobic capacity)	Multi-stage fitness test		
Maximal strength	1 One repetition maximum test 2 Handgrip dynamometer		
Strength endurance (muscular endurance)	NCF abdominal conditioning test		
Elastic strength (power)	1 Wingate cycle test 2 The standing (Sargent) vertical jump test		
Speed	30m sprint test		
Flexibility	Sit and reach test		
Body composition	1 Skinfold measure 2 Bioelectric impedance		
Agility	Illinois agility run test		
Balance	The standing stork test		

Revise as you go!

1 Define each of the following: a) fitness
                               b) health.

2 Validity and reliability are important in any test. How would you ensure that an investigation was both valid and reliable?

3 Explain why fitness testing is necessary for both the coach and the athlete.

Chapter 5: Defining the nature of skill and abilities

Learning outcomes

By the end of this chapter you should be able to:
- identify the characteristics of a skilled performance
- explain the nature of different types of skills and understand how each can influence performance
- classify skills by placing them on various continua and justify your reasons for doing so
- identify the characteristics of gross motor abilities and psychomotor abilities
- understand the relationship between skill and ability.

Introduction

The terms 'skill' and 'ability' are frequently used to describe sporting performance, but are their full meanings actually understood and used in the correct contexts? Hopefully, as students studying the AS Sport and Physical Education course, you will have already developed a wide variety of skills and are applying them effectively both in practice and competitive situations. There are many skills we use daily without even thinking about them because as we develop and refine such skills they become like second nature to us or *autonomous*, for example, writing your name, using mobile phones to text a message and using money to pay for goods. All of these are skills and have developed through practice over time.

During this chapter you will develop an understanding of the relationship between the different terms and how this subsequently affects the development of skill in different performers. As a result, you should be able to answer the question, 'What makes one performer more skilful than another?'

Although some definitions are given, you will not be expected to learn and quote specific examples, merely to interpret and explain them, using appropriate examples to support your answers.

The nature of a skilled performance

We all possess and can execute a variety of skills, even though some people may appear to be more skilled than others. We can all run, throw, catch, aim, dodge and jump. But what makes one performance more highly skilled than another? How can we recognize these skilled performances and justify our reasons?

TASK 1

1 List five skills you use daily (they do not have to be of a sporting nature).
2 List five skills you can apply to a variety of sports (generic skills).
3 List five skills you use that are sport-specific.
4 Compare and contrast your lists with other students. Have you all listed similar skills?

Look at the skills you listed in Task 1. They probably fall into one of three categories:

* some may be a single act, for example a cricket stroke or netball shot
* others may be a series of actions linking with other players and requiring an assessment of the situation, for example a passage of play involving dribbling and passing to create a scoring opportunity
* others may be linked to the quality of the performance and application of techniques within the sporting environment, for example assessing the effectiveness and/or outcome of the actions when compared to previous performances either personally or when compared to others (for example, a gymnastic sequence).

Characteristics of skill

All skilled performances have similar characteristics, even though they may appear totally different in nature. For example, how can the performances of a trampolinist, a volleyball setter, a hurdler and a rugby union prop forward be compared and regarded as skilful? Whilst each may be different in terms of technique and outcome, the characteristics associated with a skilful performance are common to all.

There are many popular definitions of the term 'skill', several of which are outlined below. When you are reading each one, try to highlight similar characteristics to those identified in Task 2.

Knapp:
'Skill is the learned ability to bring about predetermined results with maximum certainty, often with the minimum outlay of time or energy or both.'

Welford:
'Skill is an organized, co-ordinated activity in relation to an object or situation which involves a whole chain of sensory, central and motor mechanisms.'

Robb:
'While the task can be physical or mental, one generally thinks of skill as some type of manipulative efficiency. A skilled movement is one in which a predetermined objective is accomplished with maximum efficiency with a minimum outlay of energy. A skilful movement does not just happen. There must be a conscious effort on the part of the performer in order to execute a skill.'

Fig. 5.01 Jonny Wilkinson place kicking

Fig. 5.02 Tiger Woods playing a shot

TASK 2

Using the photographs of the two performers below or observing a short video clip of a high-quality sporting event, list at least five words to best describe their performance. Compare and contrast your lists with other students.

Hopefully, by comparing the list of characteristics linked to the photographs and reading the definitions, similarities can be seen. Therefore we can conclusively say that a skilled action is:

- *learned* – it requires practice and develops through experience. Being skilled involves a permanent change in behaviour that will stand the test of time
- *goal-directed/has an end result* – each skill has a predetermined objective at the beginning of the movement
- *consistent* – the phrase 'maximum certainty' is a key element, reflecting the ability of the performer to repeat the skill despite differing environmental conditions
- *efficient* – the actions are performed with co-ordination and precision using the required amount of energy necessary
- *fluent* – the actions appear to flow naturally rather than be forced, with good balance and timing
- *recognizable/linked to a technical model* – the skill is instantly recognizable and its execution can be compared to other performers, allowing an analysis of performance to occur
- *aesthetic* – the execution of the skill is pleasing to observe, appearing controlled and effective within the context of the situation.

HOT TIPS

You do not need to remember definitions, but you will need to explain the characteristics of a skill with relevant examples.

KEY WORDS

Subroutine

Phase of a movement pattern that must be executed at the appropriate time in the sequence if the skill is to be successful.

You may be asked to discuss the nature of a skill in terms of its complexity and organization. The complexity of a skill depends on the number of **subroutines** involved, the perceptual and decision-making demands, the time available to process the information and the amount of feedback required (see Table 5.01). The organization of a skill depends on the relationship between the subroutines of the skill (see Table 5.02).

Table 5.01 Complexity of a skill

A simple skill involves:	A complex skill involves:
• few subroutines	• numerous subroutines that need to be performed with the correct timing
• little information to process	• large amount of information to process
• time to evaluate the situation	• limited time to evaluate the situation
Feedback would not be crucial during performance	Feedback would be helpful during and after the performance
Examples: swimming and sprinting	*Examples: trampoline routine and triple jump*

Table 5.02 Organisation of a skill

A low organization skill involves:	A high organization skill involves:
• subroutines that are easily identified and separated from the movement	• subroutines that are difficult to separate and practise in isolation
• subroutines that can be practised in isolation and then developed as part of the whole movement	• development of subroutines that has to usually occur as part of the whole movement
Examples: swimming stroke trampoline routine	*Examples: sprint start and and golf swing*

TASK 3

1 Analyse each of the skills listed below in terms of their complexity *and* organization.
   - Swimming stroke
   - Basketball free throw
   - Triple jump
   - Golf swing
   - Sprint start
   - Hockey penalty flick
   - Netball set play
   - Cycling race
   - Tennis serve
   - Rugby line-out
2 Repeat the task for your chosen activity from the specification for each of the named five core skills.

Types of skills

In order to become an effective performer, there are a variety of different types of skills that need to be mastered and applied to sporting situations. You will already use the types of skills outlined below, but their application may be one reason to explain how performers reach different levels of competence.

 KEY WORDS

Cognitive skill

Involves thought processes and intellectual ability.

Motor skill

Involves physical movement and muscular control.

Perceptual skill

Involves the detection and interpretation of stimuli from the environment.

Psychomotor/perceptual motor skill

A combination of the latter two skills.

The types of skills are:
- **cognitive** – skills that involve thought processes and intellectual ability. Examples include devising appropriate strategies and tactics to outwit an opponent, calculating scores, split times or interpreting data.
- **motor** – skills that involve physical movement and muscular control linked to a specific objective. Examples include a high jump, kicking a ball or badminton serves.
- **perceptual** – skills that involve the detection and interpretation of stimuli from the environment. This may differ between performers, referees and coaches, who may all observe the same situation but focus on different cues and consequently arrive at a different conclusion. For example, during a netball match, players have to quickly analyse the location of teammates, the opposition and their own location on court before deciding on the most effective skill to execute. Those who can do this quickly will develop into the better performers.

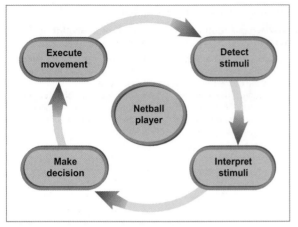

Fig. 5.04 A netball player uses all four types of skills

- **psychomotor** – also known as perceptual motor skills. These skills are a combination of the perceptual and motor skills outlined above and are the type most frequently used during sporting performance. They involve the interpretation of environmental stimuli and the execution of movement. For example, during a rugby match, a player who receives the ball will have to analyse the situation, decide if the best option is to pass, run with the ball or kick and then execute the movement, whilst constantly updating new stimuli and modifying their actions as needed.

Often these skills can be viewed as a never-ending cycle during the course of the performance, as illustrated in Figure 5.04.

TASK 4

For your chosen activity, identify when each type of skill would be used during a personal performance.

Classification of skills

KEY WORDS

Continuum

A sequence of gradations between two extremes.

When analysing skills, it is useful to be able to group together those that may have similar characteristics. This allows the teacher or coach to study the general requirements of a skill and select the appropriate method of practice and learning environment. The process for classifying skills is commonly based on the use of a **continuum** or sliding scale. This allows a general interpretation of the characteristics of the skills to take place and for several skills to be compared at the same time.

Many of the skills you will analyse may have components that could fall into both extremes of the continuum, but for the purpose of this course, it is advisable to analyse the overall movement action rather than subroutines. For example, a bowling action of a cricketer should be viewed as a whole, not merely the wrist action during release of the ball.

HOT TIPS

When asked to classify a skill, always justify your answer. Do not just state its place on a continuum.

Numerous classifications have been proposed, but your studies have to limit the number to four. You are expected to have knowledge of the characteristics of each, give suitable examples to illustrate your understanding and justify your reasons. The classification continua are:
- open/closed continuum
- gross/fine continuum
- self-paced/externally-paced continuum
- discrete/serial/continuous continuum.

Open/closed continuum

This continuum is based on the influence the environment has on the production of the skilled movement. Any number of factors may influence the performance, for example position of players, own position, proximity of the crowd, playing conditions, surface/facilities and so on (see Table 5.03).

Table 5.03 Open and closed skills

Open skills are directly affected by the environment because:	Closed skills are not directly affected by the environment because:
• the environment is unstable and changing • the environment is not predictable • the skills require constant adjustment to suit the situation • the skills are perceptual and involve decision-making • they are usually externally-paced • decisions need to be made quickly	• the environment is stable and constant • the environment is predictable • the skills can be repeated consistently when learnt or habitual • the skills are pre-learned in a set routine and require minimal adjustment • they are usually self-paced • decisions are pre-planned
For example, a tennis player when receiving the ball must evaluate the speed and direction of the ball, their own location on court and that of their opponent, the nature of the surface and the strengths of their opponent before deciding which shot to play.	For example, a springboard diver will experience the same conditions each time he or she competes. The particular dive is selected based on the tariff required, and the dive is performed without the influence of any other competitor.

Fig. 5.05 A tennis rally is an example of an open skill

Fig. 5.06 A dive is an example of a closed skill

There are examples of closed skills being executed within a mainly open environment. A tennis player completing the serve (closed skill) has to consider the position of their opponent, even though they are not directly influencing the skill action itself. Similarly, a player taking a penalty or free throw is executing a closed skill during a break from the usual unpredictable environment.

Gross/fine continuum

This continuum is based on the amount of muscular movement and the precision required during the execution of the skill (see Table 5.04). Many skills combine the two elements during different phases of the action. For example, a cricket bowler's run-up would be classed as a gross skill, while the delivery action of the wrist and hand would be classed as a fine skill.

Table 5.04 Gross and fine skills

Gross skills involve:	Fine skills involve:
• large muscle movements • large muscle groups	• small muscle movements • small muscle groups
Accuracy and precision are not necessarily a high priority	Accuracy and precision are vital factors
For example, running, throwing, jumping or kicking a ball.	For example, snooker shot, throwing a dart or the wrist and finger action of a cricketer when bowling.

Fig. 5.07 A rugby tackle is an example of a gross skill

Fig. 5.08 The wrist and finger action of a spin bowler is an example of a fine skill

Self-paced/externally-paced continuum

This continuum is based on the amount of control the performer has over the execution and timing of the movement (see Table 5.05). This is based on two factors: the timing and initiation of the movement as well as the actual speed/rate of the movement.

Fig. 5.09 Example of a self-paced skill

Table 5.05 Self-paced and externally-paced skills

Self-paced skills involve:	Externally-paced skills involve:
• performers controlling the start of the movement	• performers initiating the start of the movement based on other people's actions or changing events in the environment
• performers controlling the speed of the movement	• performers changing the speed of the movement in relation to other people's actions or changing events in the environment
• usually *closed* skills	• usually *open* skills
For example, gymnastic routine, golf swing or long jump.	For example, sailing, receiving a pass or a sprint start.

Discrete/serial/continuous continuum

This continuum is based on the relationship between the subroutines and identification of the beginning and end of the movement (see Table 5.06).

HOT TIPS

If asked for an example to illustrate your answer, be specific – do not just name a sport, give a definite skill or situation.

Table 5.06 Discrete, serial and continuous skills

Discrete skills involve:	Serial skills involve:	Continuous skills involve:
• a clear beginning and end • short time duration for completion • to repeat the skill, it must be started again	• a linked series of discrete skills • set order or sequence for each subroutine	• no clear beginning or end • extended time duration • the end of one movement is the start of the next
For example, cricket shot, kicking a ball, tennis shot, somersault or catching an object.	For example, triple jump, canoe slalom race, gymnastic routine or basketball lay-up.	For example, swimming, cycling or running.

TASK 5

Place the skills listed below in the correct place on each of the four continua described above. Justify your reasons for each decision.

- Basketball set shot
- Receiving a pass in netball
- High jump
- Tennis rally
- Cycling race
- Gymnastic vault
- Hockey dribble
- Snooker shot

Characteristics of abilities

The terms 'skill' and 'ability' are often used in the same context and are interlinked but are in fact different in their meanings. We now know that a 'skill' is a learned action, but our 'abilities' actually allow us to perform the skills effectively. Below are two definitions of the term 'ability'.

Schmidt:
'An inherited, relatively enduring trait that underlies or supports various kinds of motor and cognitive activities or skills. Abilities are thought of as being largely genetically determined.'

Sharp:
'Abilities are enduring characteristics which underlie a person's potential to acquire skill in one sport or another.'

From these definitions, we can identify generally agreed characteristics of abilities.

- They are *genetic/innate* – our abilities are inherited from our parents.
- They are *enduring* – they remain relatively stable over time, but some development can occur due to training and exercise.
- *Ability underpins skill* – various abilities combine, which allow movement to occur.

HOT TIPS

When asked to outline the abilities required for a skill, explain why they are needed.

When asked to 'list', 'state' or 'name' the abilities required for a skill, the examiner will usually only accept the first answers for the specified number requested.

The terms 'skill' and 'ability' must be regarded as different. Without the necessary levels of specific ability, it would not be possible to excel in a given activity. For example, a springboard diver would require high levels of flexibility, power and co-ordination, whilst a marathon runner would require high levels of stamina with limited levels of the diver's necessary abilities. Performers often possess a general level of each type of ability, but to progress to the highest levels of competition, specific abilities are required for each skill. They should be viewed as the building blocks of movement patterns but a limiting factor of performance. In other words, if the performer does not have the innate abilities required for a particular skill, they will never achieve excellence.

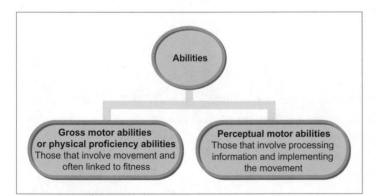

Fig. 5.10 Fleishman's classification of abilities

Types of abilities

There are numerous classifications used to analyse and categorize abilities. One of the most frequently used is that proposed by Fleishman, who subdivided abilities into two categories (Figure 5.10). Each of the categories is outlined in greater detail below (Figure 5.11).

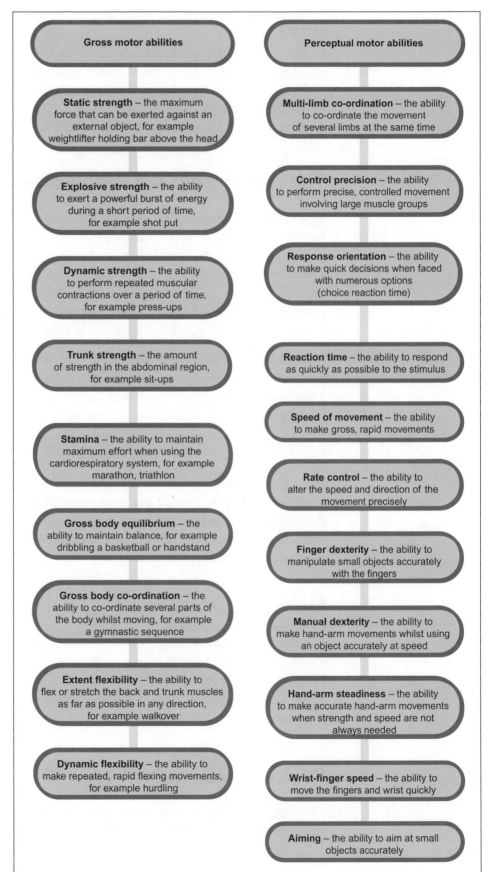

Fig. 5.11 Gross and perceptual motor abilities

TASK 6

1 For the two activities listed below, list the five most important gross motor abilities and perceptual motor abilities required to produce a high level of performance. Justify your reasons for their inclusion.
   a) Trampolining   b) Netball
2 Repeat the task for your own chosen activity.

The relationship between skill and ability

In order to perform any skill, we require specific abilities to execute the movement effectively. Talent identification programmes attempt to measure a person's natural abilities and try to find a corresponding activity that may then allow them to develop into a high-level performer. This alone does not guarantee success, as effective coaching, training and competition programmes are also required to nurture and refine genetic natural abilities. The key factor to remember is that *abilities are skill-specific*.

Another limiting factor of performance may be the range of abilities a performer possesses. Just because they have high levels of one type of ability it does not mean they will necessarily have corresponding levels in all areas. For example, an athlete may have a fast reaction time and good speed but may also have poor response orientation and manual dexterity, which would limit their effectiveness as a games player.

Many skills require similar abilities and often transfer between skills does occur. For example, a decathlete requires speed, explosive strength, flexibility, co-ordination and good reaction time. These qualities are also required for the sport of bobsleigh, and numerous athletes have been successful performers in both sports.

Measuring abilities

Numerous tests have been devised to measure levels of ability, many of which you may use to form the basis of your Personal Exercise Programme (see Chapter 15). Such tests not only allow potential talent spotting to occur, but are a vital aspect in the construction and monitoring of training programmes. A more comprehensive explanation of the tests can be found in Unit 4, Chapter 4.

Revise as you go!

1 State three characteristics of a skilled movement.
2 Name the type of skill that involves large muscle movement during its execution.
3 What is the difference between 'skill' and 'ability'?

Chapter 6: Learning and performance

Learning outcomes

By the end of this chapter you should be able to:
- identify the difference between learning and performance
- outline the stages and characteristics of each phase of learning
- explain and interpret learning/performance curves
- identify possible causes and remedies for a learning plateau
- understand the theories of learning.

Introduction

As performers, we need to be able to understand how we actually learn skills, which will in turn allow us to develop and refine them further. We also need to be able to analyse our own performance and recognize the progress being made, if any! By developing knowledge of how we learn skills, we can adapt and modify practice situations to elicit the most favourable response, which in turn can become a skill and performed effectively within a competitive environment.

During this chapter you will develop an understanding of the difference between 'learning' and 'performance'. How many times have you completed a skill once but never actually been able to repeat it? Why not? We will try to find an explanation. Also, you will discover why, on occasions, there may be no improvement for some time in your skill level: more importantly, you will be able to outline strategies to rectify this problem. Finally, by understanding the theories of learning, you will appreciate the advantages and disadvantages of each in various practical situations, allowing for the optimum use of practice time.

As with the previous chapter, the key to successfully understanding the theoretical aspects is refining the ability to apply them to actual sporting situations. The easiest way to do this is to refer to your own experiences, both positive and negative, and attempt to explain the consequences. Did your skill levels improve or not? If 'no', what could you do in an attempt to develop your performance?

Learning and performance

The terms 'learning' and 'performance' have very different meanings. For example, how often have you revised for a test or exam, passed with flying colours, but when questioned on the same topic several months later cannot remember all the facts? A similar scenario can be applied to sporting performance: how often have you trained hard for a particular event, performed successfully then rested for a period of time and on returning to compete not been as competent? Have you on one memorable day performed like never before and since then been unable to repeat a similar feat?

TASK 1

1 List five general skills you have learnt.
2 List five sporting skills you have learnt.
3 List three memorable sporting performances.
4 Compare and contrast your lists with other students.
5 Attempt to construct a definition for 'learning' and another for 'performance'. Compare and contrast your definitions with other students and those outlined below.

There is clearly a difference between 'learning' and 'performance'. Below are several definitions to highlight those differences.

Learning

Schmidt:
'Motor learning is a set of processes associated with practice or experience, leading to relatively permanent changes in the capability for skilled performance.'

Sharp:
'A person has learned something if their performance shows improvement from one occasion to the next. Such an improvement must be stable and relatively permanent, and not just a transient increase caused, for example, by a change in fitness level or improvement in health.'

Knapp:
'The more or less permanent change in behaviour that is reflected in a change in performance.'

The key characteristics of 'learning' are:
• linked to practice or experience
• relatively permanent
• not a fluke or one-off occurrence.

Performance

Knapp:
'Performance may change because of fatigue or emotion, or alcohol, or the surrounding conditions, but in so far as any change is temporary, it is not learning.'

Singer:
'Performance may be thought of as a temporary occurrence ... fluctuating from time to time because of many potentially operating variables.'

The key characteristics of 'performance' are:

- temporary
- not necessarily repeated.

Stages of learning

In order to develop new skills, we must progress through a series of stages so that when one aspect is refined, another can be added, allowing the skill to become more complex. Fitts and Posner (1967) suggested that when you learn a new skill, there are three stages of learning that must be completed:

- cognitive stage
- associative stage
- autonomous stage.

Some performers may progress through each stage quickly or the skill may be simple, allowing it to be mastered easily, for example the basic action of catching and throwing a ball. However, some may be more difficult and may never be reached due to a variety of factors, for example the skill of juggling.

Cognitive stage

The initial stage of learning involves the performer observing a demonstration or being given verbal instructions (Figure 6.01). The aim is to create a mental picture, which allows for the development of an understanding of the movement requirements. During this time, the performer is attempting to find the answer to all the basic questions concerning the particular skill and its execution. There may be some initial trial and error attempts to complete the movement pattern, often with limited success.

The majority of the feedback is from an external source as the performer has yet to establish a clear understanding of the motor programme and has limited kinaesthetic awareness allowing them to correct any mistakes. However, this stage is usually short in duration.

The role of the coach or teacher is vital during this stage, allowing a clear mental picture to be created. This must be done by maximizing the use of accurate demonstrations, highlighting specific cues, providing time for mental rehearsal, ensuring the learner is paying full attention, avoiding an overload of new information, use of appropriate language and giving reinforcement as required.

- **Practical application**

A novice performer is attempting to learn the Fosbury flop high jump technique. The coach will explain the technique and either demonstrate themselves or show a video highlighting the specific phases and several key points. The performer will try to create a mental image of what they have to do when it is their turn.

Fig. 6.01 The cognitive stage of learning

Associative stage

The second stage of learning is often referred to as the 'practice' stage. It involves the performer developing and refining the movement patterns of the skill via a combination of practice and feedback (Figure 6.02). Initially, gross errors are common, which are gradually eliminated until the recognized and consistent skill emerges.

This stage is often longer than the cognitive stage and may vary in length depending on the ability of the performer, the complexity of the skill, the amount and type of practice completed, and the quality of the feedback.

Initially, the majority of the feedback is still from an external source, which concentrates on gross errors. However, as the performer becomes more accomplished and develops a greater kinaesthetic awareness, they are able to identify errors themselves (internal feedback) and implement external feedback, which focuses on more detailed adjustments.

- Practical application

The performer attempts the Fosbury flop and shows obvious weaknesses in technique. The coach will highlight key points to practise and gradually the weaknesses will be eliminated. As the technique improves, the feedback will become more specific, for example the drive of the take-off knee or the position over the bar. Gradually, the performer will recognize their own mistakes and rectify them as required.

Fig. 6.02 The associative stage of learning

Autonomous stage

The final stage of learning involves the performer becoming highly proficient at executing the skill, to the point where it is completed almost without conscious thought (Figure 6.03). There are numerous advantages created by reaching this stage. It means that the performer is able to focus on other factors happening during the event, such as other players, tactics or stress management techniques, rather than the execution of the skill. The reaction time and decision-making process are improved. It also means that the particular skill can be used as a basis to develop a more advanced skill – it is in effect relegated to a subroutine (see page 149).

The performer is now able to detect and correct the majority of their own errors (internal feedback) and any input from the coach can focus on minor alterations to technique to improve performance.

Once this stage has been reached, it is important for the performer to maintain their level of practice in order to reinforce the movement patterns and ensure the skill can be repeated consistently.

- **Practical application**

The high jumper can now make minor adjustments to their technique during competition, such as altering the run-up, take-off position and timing over the bar. During training, the coach and the performer work together to discuss minor adjustments that may be required to facilitate an improvement.

Fig. 6.03 The autonomous stage of learning

HOT TIPS

For each stage of learning, you need to know the characteristics, the type of feedback primarily used and how to progress to the next level.

TASK 2

Select a skill from a team game, a racket game and an adventurous activity. For each skill, outline what the performer may experience during each phase of learning and comment on how this may affect their performance.

Measuring changes in learning – performance curves

HOT TIPS

Always title the graph and label the axis correctly, including the units.

HOT TIPS

'Plot a graph' means use graph paper, plot the co-ordinates accurately and join with a best fit or smooth line. 'Sketch a graph' means a freehand line is acceptable based on the data provided.

How do we know if we are learning and making progress? Just because time is spent practising a skill, it does not mean there will automatically be an improvement. There may be times when no improvement takes place, which may be demotivating for the performer. It is therefore important to understand how, when and why performance is changing. Each individual progresses at a different rate and the use of a graph is an easy way to interpret such changes. If the results are analysed correctly, training sessions can be modified to achieve a positive outcome and the motivation levels of the performer can be enhanced if they are able to understand the factors influencing their development.

Outlined in Figures 6.04 to 6.08 are several curves that indicate how an athlete's performance varied during the course of trials or during the time of a test/event. It is important you are able to explain how the performance altered during these times and suggest reasons why it may have happened.

Linear curve

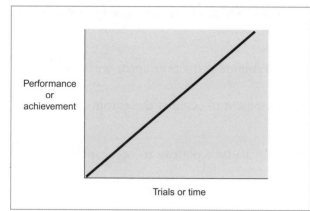

Fig. 6.04 The performance improves in direct proportion to the number of trials or time

Positive acceleration curve

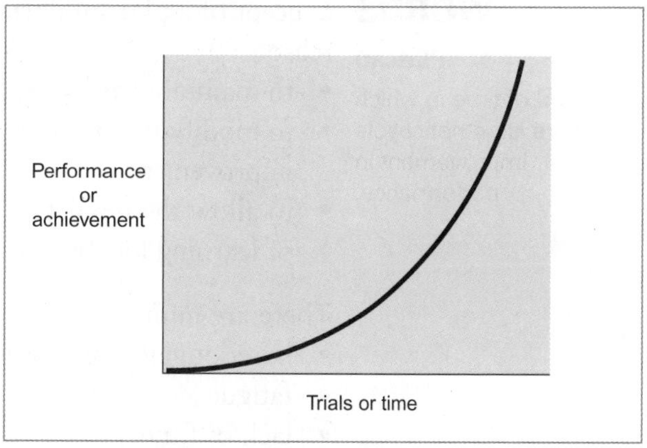

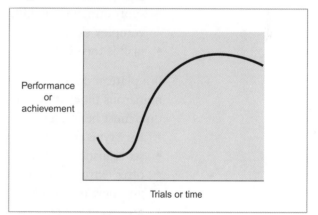

Fig. 6.05 The performance improves slowly during the initial trials but speeds up later

Negative acceleration curve

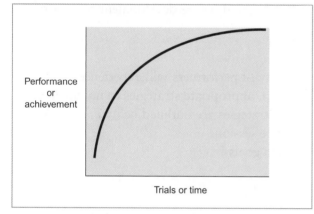

Fig. 6.06 The performance improves quickly during the initial trials but slows down later

Ogive or S-shaped curve

Fig. 6.07 The performance is indicated by a combination of the curves outlined above

Plateau in performance

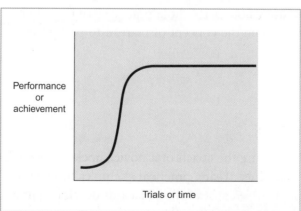

Fig. 6.08 The performance improves but reaches a point at which no further improvement occurs. This may be the final plateau or the first in a series of plateaus

KEY WORDS

Plateau

Period of time in which there is no noticeable improvement in performance.

It is important that both the performer and the coach understand the concept of a **plateau** during the development of performance for a variety of reasons:

- to maintain the motivation levels
- to modify the training regime to minimize the time spent with no improvement
- to allow the next stage of development to occur if the autonomous stage of learning has been reached.

There are numerous factors that may cause a plateau to occur including:

- boredom/lack of motivation
- fatigue
- lack of fitness
- inappropriate practice methods
- poor coaching and guidance
- personal ability
- injury/overtraining
- subroutine mastered/transitional period before development of a more complex skill
- task is too complex.

If a plateau does occur (the majority of performers will experience this numerous times during their career), appropriate strategies to minimize the time must be implemented. Some strategies are outlined below:

- vary type and content of practice sessions
- set realistic short- and long-term goals
- offer extrinsic rewards
- give new responsibility/role
- give recovery periods
- encourage mental rehearsal
- improve physical conditioning/fitness
- improve coaching knowledge
- provide appropriate feedback
- use whole-part-whole practice (see page 121)
- explain the concept of plateau to performer.

HOT TIPS

When asked to interpret a graph, give an explanation of what is happening to the performance and suggest reasons why.

TASK 3

1. You are the coach of a novice hockey team which is failing to make progress. Using practical examples to illustrate your answer, outline three possible causes for this lack of development and suggest three strategies to overcome this plateau.
2. Suggest three alternative factors that may be more relevant to an elite-level performer who may be experiencing a plateau in their performance.

Theories of learning

Now that you know what the term 'learning' means, you need to understand how we actually learn skills. If you can identify the best method to develop a skill, the learning time can be reduced and the result effectively transferred to a competitive situation. There are three theories that need to be understood:
- conditioning theory
- cognitive theory/insight learning
- observational learning.

Conditioning theories of learning

These are also known as 'connectionist' or 'associationist' theories and are based on the 'behaviourist' approach. The basic notion of the theories involves the performer developing a specific link with a certain cue, which is known as the 'stimulus-response bond' or 'S-R bond'. The response is stored in the long-term memory (see page 140) and when the specific stimulus is detected, the appropriate movement is triggered. For example, a cricket batsman will attempt to play a certain type of shot each time the bowler pitches the ball in a particular area, or a netball centre will pass the ball to a specific teammate depending on the agreed call being made.

TASK 4

List five examples of an S-R bond you experience during your major sport.

Operant conditioning

This theory was developed by Skinner, who modified the behaviour of rats in a maze. He altered their environment and depending on their response they received some form of reward or punishment, causing their behaviour to either be repeated or not. He tried to shape their behaviour. If the consequences of their actions were pleasurable, the behaviour was more likely to be repeated. However, if the consequences were unpleasant, they were less likely to be repeated. In other words, the S-R bond will either be strengthened or weakened depending on what happens after the action has taken place. Often the learner will experience 'trial and error' and through a gradual process of elimination will develop the appropriate response with the correct use of reinforcement.

In order for this to occur, the learner may experience either reinforcement or punishment. The former strengthens the S-R bond, while the latter weakens the bond.

Reinforcement may take two forms:
- *positive reinforcement* – this involves the use of a stimulus to create feelings of satisfaction to encourage the repetition of the action, for example praise from a coach, personal satisfaction from completion of

HOT TIPS

Do not confuse negative reinforcement with negative feedback or punishment. For example, the former would be a coach calling out a key point of technique during practice and, when performed correctly, they stop reminding the performer. The latter would involve the coach criticizing the performer.

the movement, visual feedback such as seeing the target being hit or the ball landing in court, applause from the crowd or any other form of reward.

- negative reinforcement – this involves the withdrawal of an unpleasant stimulus when the desired response occurs, for example the coach will stop shouting at the team if their actions are correct.

Punishment may also be used effectively to reduce the likelihood of the actions being repeated. Common forms may include being dropped from the team, penalized for foul play, booked by the referee or fined. However, the continual use of punishment may cause some resentment and have an adverse effect and punishment should be used carefully.

Numerous sports skills are developed using this method, via the use of drills and conditioned practices. Whilst their use does facilitate the learning and refining of skills, a disadvantage may be a lack of understanding as to why the skill is being executed in a particular manner. As a result, when the performer enters a competitive situation, they may not be able to adapt their 'conditioned' skill to a new environment easily and their performance level may drop.

- **Practical application**

A coach is developing the forehand drive of a novice tennis player (Figure 6.09).

1 The coach 'feeds' balls to the player from a specific position in a consistent manner (modifying the environment).

2 The player stands in a certain position and attempts to play the shot repeatedly to a marked area on the opposite side of the court (shaping behaviour).

3 Reinforcement from the coach is provided about the technique in the form of verbal feedback.

4 Reinforcement is obtained by the player via observation of the ball hitting the marked target area.

5 If successful, the player will attempt to re-create the shot and remember the feeling of the movement (kinaesthetic awareness).

6 If unsuccessful, the player will attempt to modify the shot until the correct response is achieved (trial and error).

Fig. 6.09 Example of operant conditioning

TASK 5

Design a series of three progressive practices using operant conditioning for a sport of your choice.

Apply Thorndike's laws to a practical situation you have experienced and evaluate their effectiveness.

Thorndike's laws of learning

In order to make the strengthening of the S-R bond more effective, Thorndike suggested that three 'laws' should be implemented:

1 *law of exercise* – the performer must practise the task regularly in favourable conditions, for example when reinforcement is used

2 *law of effect* – the performer is more likely to repeat the task if their behaviour is followed by experiences of satisfaction, for example positive reinforcement

3 *law of readiness* – the performer is physically and mentally able to complete the task, for example has the appropriate motivation and physiological development.

Drive reduction theory

Hull suggested that learning will occur due to the performer's desire to complete the task and only by achieving their 'drive' will they be satisfied (Figure 6.10). Too much repetition of a skill during the learning phase may actually demotivate the performer and cause 'inhibition'. As a result, Hull proposed that an effective way to strengthen the S-R bond is to ensure the 'drive' or motivation of the performer is always maintained. This will involve the teacher or coach setting new, challenging goals allowing continued development to occur.

• **Practical application**

A coach will initially set a novice tennis player the target of learning to play a basic forehand shot. When this has been mastered, a new goal has to be set to maintain the performer's interest and strengthen the S-R bond, such as the topspin forehand shot. The process continues once this skill has been developed.

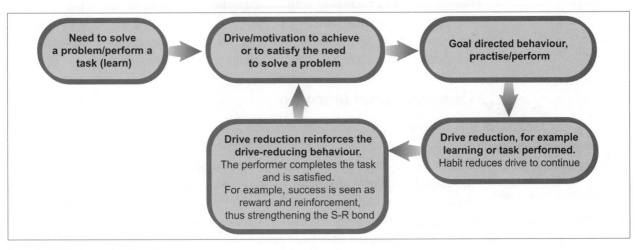

Fig. 6.10 Drive reduction theory

Cognitive theories of learning/insight learning

One of the weaknesses of the conditioning theories is that the performer may not fully understand the relationship between the stimulus and response, as they have been more concerned with the consequences of the action. Therefore their performance may be hindered, as they may be unable to modify their actions accordingly. This occurs because the new situation differs from their established pattern of movement and set environmental conditions.

The cognitive, or Gestalt, theory allows for this deficiency by proposing that the performer learns by thinking about the whole problem. They understand what is required and formulate a response based on previous experiences and the current situation rather than a series of specific responses to various stimuli. They use their perceptual skills to formulate a motor programme suited to the current situation and their own abilities. This form of learning is also known as '*insight*' learning, as there is a clear discovery of the relationship between the stimulus and the response. The 'trial and error' learning is not involved in this process.

The coach would ask the performer to complete the whole movement in order to develop an appreciation of how the timing and subroutines of the movement are inter-related rather than break the skill down into its component parts (as in the conditioning theory). This then allows the performer to adapt their movements more easily to a new situation, for example whether or not to execute a dummy pass/shot during a game depending on the situation at a given moment.

- Practical application

A novice high jumper would be asked to complete the entire sequence rather than be taught in stages, giving them the opportunity to 'work out' the most effective movement for them.

Similarly, a basketball player possesses the required skills to play the game but is not as effective as they could be in the game situation. The coach explains the concepts of offence and defence clearly to the player and they then understand their role within the game and how to deploy their skills for the benefit of the team rather than just themselves. If the player is presented with a variety of situations in training, this knowledge can be used later in the game to overcome any new problems that they may encounter.

Observational learning

KEY WORDS

Significant other

A person that is held in high esteem by the individual, for example a member of their family, peer group, teacher, coach and role model.

Many people learn most effectively by watching others and copying their actions. This is known as a '*vicarious experience*'. It is often more productive than merely giving instructions, as a mental picture is formed allowing the individual to create movement patterns more easily. The use of demonstrations can also be made more effective if reinforcement is used and the model (person demonstrating) is either a **significant other** or a competent performer from their own peer group.

Bandura suggested there should be four key elements in place to allow this process to occur.

1 *Attention* – the amount of notice taken by the learner while observing the model. The coach can aid this process by identifying a small number of specific cues on which to concentrate, ensuring the demonstration is correct and accurate, not too long, the model is attractive to the observer and the skill being observed can be clearly seen.

2 *Retention* – the creation of a mental picture for future reference. The coach should not overload the learner with verbal information but allow them to observe the demonstration several times to create a clear image. They may also be encouraged to picture the movement, a technique known as 'mental rehearsal'. Sometimes a second image may be used to help this image stick in the mind. For example, when learning the techniques of a basketball free throw, to help the learner remember to flick the wrist when releasing the ball, they may be told to 'take a cookie out of the jar'.

3 *Motor reproduction* – the learner must have the physical ability and confidence to copy, attempt and complete the skill either immediately or after a series of progressive practice sessions.

4 *Motivation* – the learner must have the drive and desire to copy the actions of the model. This is often based on the successful completion of the observed skill, its importance, the reinforcement received from others and the perceived status of the model.

• **Practical application**

The coach of a trampolinist wishes to introduce a new, more advanced move into the routine. Rather than attempt the complex move, another member of the training group is asked to demonstrate the move several times. The coach will highlight several key points of technique to remember and possibly relate the feeling/kinaesthetic awareness to a previously learnt skill to make it easier to understand. The coach will also ensure there are no other distractions, allowing the learner to focus entirely on the demonstration, and provide verbal encouragement to boost the performer's motivation level.

Fig. 6.11 Example of observational learning

TASK 6

1 Select a skill, for example dribbling, and devise suitable practices, each based on one of the theories of learning, to introduce it to a group of novice performers.

2 Complete each practice with other students and evaluate its effectiveness.

Each theory has its advantages and disadvantages, and the teacher/coach may find it most effective to evaluate each situation before deciding on the most appropriate to use. Often, within a lesson or training session, a combination may be most suitable depending on the ability and motivation of the participants, the situational factors and the nature of the task.

Revise as you go!

1 Name the three stages of learning.

2 What is the aim of a coach during the first stage of learning? Suggest three methods that may be employed to develop this stage successfully.

3 How does the nature of feedback change as the performer progresses through the various stages?

4 Which stage is usually the quickest?

5 Outline the characteristics of the associative stage of learning.

6 Explain the 'S-R bond'.

7 'Insight' or 'Gestalt' theories are examples of which theories of learning?

8 What can operant conditioning also be referred to as?

9 Explain the term 'associationist learning theory'.

10 Models are often used to aid learning. Give three factors that may enhance their effectiveness.

11 What does the term 'vicarious experience' mean?

12 List the four elements of Bandura's observational learning.

13 Explain why the cognitive approach to learning may be beneficial to the performer during a competitive situation.

14 Explain the three laws of Thorndike.

15 Suggest two ways a teacher/coach may manipulate the environment to develop a specific action or behaviour pattern.

16 What is a 'Plateau'?

17 Which theory suggests that people learn by observing others and then copying their actions?

18 Suggest two factors that may inhibit the performer reaching the autonomous stage.

19 Name two ways to make learning during the cognitive stage easier for the performer.

Chapter 7: Optimizing learning and performance

Learning outcomes

By the end of this chapter you should be able to:
- outline the factors to consider when organizing a training session
- understand the various ways of presenting practices
- explain the different types of practices and when to use each one
- outline various forms of guidance and how to optimize their use
- describe Mosston and Ashworth's teaching styles and outline when to use each effectively
- explain types of motivation and their limitations.

Introduction

Now that you understand what 'learning' actually involves and how it can be achieved, the next stage is to investigate how the process can be made more effective. There are many ways to teach new skills and strategies, some of which are more effective than others. If you can select the most appropriate method for a particular individual or group of performers, not only will the time to learn the skill be reduced, but their motivation levels will remain high and they will retain the information allowing progression to take place.

For each of the areas outlined in the learning outcomes above, you will be expected to explain its characteristics, give practical applications of its use and discuss its various advantages and limitations.

Many of the areas will be familiar, as you will have experienced them yourself during numerous physical education lessons and sports practices. However, you may not have previously considered the theoretical basis behind their use and evaluated their effectiveness. Throughout this chapter, it may be advisable to reflect on your past experiences to help you gain a better understanding of each topic and attempt to implement some of the methods into your current training and evaluate their use.

Factors to consider when planning a training session

If the often limited time available during a training session is to be optimized, numerous factors must be considered. Often a lack of thought and pre-planning can actually limit the amount of learning that occurs.

Key factors to consider include:
- nature of the performer/learner/participants
  - previous experience
  - stage of learning
  - physical and mental abilities
  - age
  - gender
  - motivation
  - size of the group

- nature of the task
  - open or closed skill
  - gross or fine skill
  - discrete, serial or continuous skill
  - self-paced or externally-paced skill
  - simple or complex skill
  - low or high organization skill

- experience of teacher/coach
  - amount of knowledge relating to activity
  - personality
  - relationship with the learner or group

- environmental conditions
  - facilities and equipment
  - time available
  - purpose of the session.

An awareness of all of the factors outlined above will allow the situation to be evaluated, and the most appropriate methods can be utilized.

TASK 1

1 Observe a lesson or practice session. List all the variable factors and methods used to make learning more effective.
2 Discuss with the coach or teacher the factors they considered to be most important and ask them to justify their reasons.
3 Record the information and at the end of the chapter refer back to your notes and analyse their choice of actions. Would you do anything different? If 'yes', why?

Presentation of practices

When introducing a new skill or sequence of movements, the coach has to decide upon the best option that allows the performer to create a clear mental picture and allows for the development of a sound kinaesthetic awareness. This decision often depends on the experience of the performer, the nature of the skill in terms of complexity, ease of breaking it down into subroutines and the ease of transferring subroutines back into the whole sequence. There are two basic methods that the teacher/coach can use:
- whole learning
- part learning.

There are a number of variations of these methods, which will be discussed in detail later.

Whole learning

As the name suggests, whole learning involves the performer attempting the whole movement pattern after observing a demonstration or being given verbal instructions (Table 7.01). Many people feel this is an ideal method.

Table 7.01 Advantages and disadvantages of whole learning

Advantages	Disadvantages
The performer can:	• It is difficult to use with complex skills
• develop an awareness of the entire movement (kinaesthetic awareness)	• It may be difficult for novice performers to execute initially
• understand the relationship between different subroutines immediately	• It is not ideal for dangerous skills
• experience the timing needed to execute the skill successfully	
• develop their own schema (see Chapter 9).	

KEY WORDS

Ballistic

A skill that is performed in a short period of time, usually with maximum power.

The ideal conditions for using this method are when:
- the skill is simple, discrete or **ballistic** (for example, golf swing or throwing a javelin)
- the subroutines lack meaning if performed in isolation
- the performer is motivated and pays attention
- the performer is experienced or approaching the autonomous stage of learning.

Part learning

In comparison to whole learning, part learning involves the performer completing subroutines of the overall movement in isolation before attempting the overall motor programme or skill. This method can have distinct advantages compared to the whole method (Table 7.02).

Table 7.02 The advantages and disadvantages of part learning

Advantages	Disadvantages
• Complex skills can be broken down into different subroutines and learnt in stages	• It hinders the development of continuity and timing of the complete skill
• Specific aspects of the technique can be modified	• It reduces overall kinaesthetic awareness
• It allows the performer to develop confidence when practising the skill	• The transfer from part to whole may not be effective
• It reduces the element of risk in potentially dangerous situations, for example gymnastic vaulting	• The highly organized skills are difficult to break down
• It allows the performer periods of recovery during physically demanding skills	• It is time consuming
• It maintains motivation levels as success can be achieved relatively quickly	

Fig. 7.01 Long jump is ideal for whole learning

Fig. 7.02 Gymnastics routines are best taught by part learning

HOT TIPS

Effective practice should aim to improve performance and maintain motivation.

The ideal conditions for using this method are when:

- the skill is complex, for example hurdling
- the skill involves long sequences, for example gymnastic routines
- there are low levels of organization, for example swimming
- the performer has limited motivation and attention span
- the performer is inexperienced.

Progressive part method

The progressive part method of presentation is a variation on the former method. It involves the performer attempting the skill in stages and linking the phases together after each has been learnt. This method is also referred to as 'chaining'. It is useful when developing gymnastic sequences and set tactical plays such as those used during a rugby match.

Table 7.03 The advantages and disadvantages of the progressive part method

Advantages	Disadvantages
• Complex skills can be broken down and introduced gradually	• It is time consuming
• Novice performers can achieve success	• The performer may become too focused on one particular subroutine
• Performers with limited attention span can remain focused	
• Development of an understanding of the relationships between the subroutines	
• Minimizes the risk involved with potentially dangerous skills	
• Transfer to the whole skill can be made easier	

The ideal conditions for using this method are when:
- the skill is complex
- the skill is serial
- the skill is dangerous
- time is not a constraint
- the performer has limited motivation and attention span
- the performer is inexperienced.

Whole-part-whole method

Whole-part-whole presentation involves a combination of the major two methods previously outlined. The performer attempts the whole movement after observing a demonstration or being given verbal instructions then develops specific subroutines before completing the whole skill again. There are numerous examples that you may have experienced, such as the long jump, in which the take-off is isolated or the flight phase is practised via drills before transferring the new movement into the entire skill. Similarly, a swimming stroke may be developed in this fashion, or the understanding of tactics via a mini-game or restricted practice.

Table 7.04 The advantages and disadvantages of whole-part-whole method

Advantages	Disadvantages
• An overall feel for the movement is developed initially	• Transfer may be difficult from part to the whole skill
• Success is continuous by developing the weaker subroutines	• Some skills are difficult to break down as the overall timing may be affected
• Practice can focus on key areas of weakness	

The ideal conditions for using this method are when:
- the skill can be broken down easily.

TASK 2

Explain how you would present the following skills to a group of novice performers. Justify your answer.
- Triple jump
- Football header
- Basketball lay-up
- Cricket bowling action
- Sprint start
- Gymnastic floor routine
- Golf shot
- Hurdling
- Hockey flick
- Volleyball spike

Fig. 7.03 Set tactical plays are often taught via the progressive part method

Types of practice

After the learner has attempted the skill after the initial instruction (presentation of practice), they now have to spend time developing and refining the movement patterns. The coach must now decide on the most appropriate type of practice to use, ensuring learning actually occurs, motivation is maintained and fatigue does not limit performance. The variable factors are the periods of active work and recovery time.

There are four main types of practice available:
- massed practice
- distributed practice
- variable practice
- mental practice.

Massed practice

Massed practice involves the repeated practice of skills with little or no recovery periods between blocks of trials. This would be used effectively for skills such as shooting at goal/basket or racket strokes.

It would be ideally used when:
- skills are discrete and/or simple
- the performer is well motivated
- the performer is experienced
- the performer has a high level of fitness
- replication of fatigue within a game situation is required.

However, care must be taken to avoid:
- boredom
- fatigue
- overtraining.

Distributed practice

Distributed practice involves the repeated practice of skills with a recovery period before repetition of the skill or the development of a new task. The recovery period may involve some other form of activity other than just rest or it may include the use of mental practice (see below), feedback or simply time to refocus and re-motivate the performer.

It would be ideally used when:
- the skill is new and complex
- there is repetition of gross skills or those that are physically demanding
- the skill is dangerous
- the performer is a novice
- the performer has low levels of motivation
- the performer has low levels of fitness

- the performer has a short attention span
- a recovery period is needed to receive feedback and evaluate performance.

However, care must be taken to avoid excessive periods of recovery as this may lead to:
- demotivation
- loss of concentration
- ill-discipline within groups.

Variable practice

Variable practice involves the coach using a mixture of both massed and distributed practice within one session. It will help to maintain the interest and motivation levels of the performer and limit the effects of fatigue when required.

Fig. 7.04 A weightlifter should ideally use distributed package

Mental practice

Mental practice involves the cognitive rehearsal of a skill without physical movement. This method is particularly useful as it may be utilized before, during and after practice or competition. It is also referred to as 'mental rehearsal' or 'imagery'. The performer will attempt to create a picture in their mind of themselves completing the skill. They can do this in two ways:
- *internal* – involves the performer seeing themselves from within completing the action or in the situation and consequently creating a kinaesthetic feel of the actual movement
- *external* – involves the performer seeing themselves as if they were a spectator or on film. They actually imagine watching themselves performing the skill.

Often, sportspeople can be seen completing such a process immediately prior to competing, for example a high jumper about to jump or a rugby player waiting to attempt a conversion kick. This not only creates a positive mental image, but can also help reduce reaction time, or improve anticipation and control levels of arousal.

It would be ideally used when:
- learning time needs to be reduced, especially for novices
- experienced performers need to prepare for alternative options to situations prior to competition
- the performer needs to concentrate on developing specific aspects or the overall skill
- arousal levels need to be controlled
- confidence needs to be developed
- the performer is injured and some form of practice must be maintained.

Its use may be optimized by:
- finding a quiet location
- focusing on the task and creating a clear picture

- encouraging successful outcomes, not failures
- regular practice
- use during recovery periods.

HOT TIPS

Make sure you understand the difference between presentation of practices and types of practice.

There is evidence to support the theory that by using mental practice the performer can stimulate the neuromuscular systems involved in creating the movement patterns. Whilst the level of nerve stimulation is insufficient to cause actual movement, it does stimulate minor muscular contractions, thus creating a practice situation. The graph in Figure 7.05 compares the effects of different forms of practice on performance.

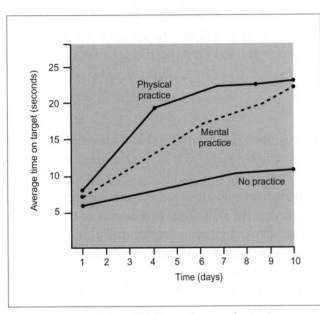

Fig. 7.05 The effects of different forms of practice

TASK 3

1 Subdivide the group into three and record the results of ten attempts. The skill can be anything you choose, for example basketball shot, volleyball serve, badminton serve and so on.
2 After the initial trials, each group experiences a different form of practice:
   - Group A – practise the same skill for five minutes
   - Group B – no practice, actually perform a totally different skill
   - Group C – mentally practise the skill for five minutes.
3 Complete a second set of trials and record the results.
4 Calculate the average scores for each set of trials, sketch a graph and discuss the results.

Forms of guidance

In order to help the learner gain a clear understanding of the skill to be attempted and then actually improve their performance, guidance is used to develop movement patterns and reduce the number of errors made. The form of guidance depends on the situation, the nature of the task and the ability of the performer.

The four main types of guidance are:
- visual
- verbal
- manual
- mechanical.

Visual guidance

Visual guidance involves the performer attempting to create a mental picture of the skill by observing a demonstration, video, pictures, slides or overhead transparencies. The area can also be modified to provide guidance with the use of cones, markings on the floor, hoops or defined target areas.

Table 7.05 The advantages and disadvantages of visual guidance

Advantages	Disadvantages
• Good for performers in the cognitive and associative stages of learning	• Demotivation if the performer is unable to replicate the skill
• Provides a clear idea of the movement pattern to be performed	• Can provide too much information to a novice performer
• Specific cues can be highlighted, which helps to focus the performer's attention	• Poor replication if the skill is inaccurate
	• Static forms of guidance soon lose their impact

To optimize the use of visual guidance, the following factors should be considered:
• demonstrations must be accurate
• all information must be relevant to the age and ability of the performer
• use appropriate verbal guidance to focus on key points
• model/demonstrator must be attractive to the performer
• stimuli must be clear and realistic
• modification of the display to enhance information, for example bright, colourful markers.

Verbal guidance

Verbal guidance involves explaining the motor skill to be performed, either to understand the requirements or to provide feedback. The information may be *general* or *specific* in nature depending on the ability level of the performer. The information may be used to outline the technique of a specific skill or the strategy for a particular game.

Table 7.06 The advantages and disadvantages of verbal guidance

Advantages	Disadvantages
• Good for all stages of learning if combined with other forms of guidance	• Overload of information – key points should be limited to two or three at most
• Very useful for those in the autonomous stage of learning, who may be able to translate the information more easily and correct their faults	• Difficulty in understanding, especially for novice performers
• Feedback can be given immediately, both during and after the performance	• Some movements may be difficult to explain
• Focuses the performer's attention on specific cues when observing a demonstration	• Difficult with large groups and may become boring
	• Over-reliance on feedback during and after performance

Fig. 7.06 A coach uses manual guidance

To optimize the use of verbal guidance, the following factors should be considered:

- information must be clear and accurate with everyone able to hear the instructions
- limiting the amount of information provided
- language and terminology must be relevant to the age group
- use in conjunction with visual guidance to highlight key points
- use immediately after performance (unless combined with video footage).

Manual guidance

Manual guidance involves the performer being physically placed, forced or supported into the correct positions. Examples include a gymnast being supported (Figure 7.06) or a coach holding the batsman's arm and guiding them through a cricket shot.

To optimize the use of manual guidance, these factors should be considered:

- avoid overuse; allow the performer to develop their own kinaesthetic awareness
- combine with verbal guidance to focus on key points
- ensure movement pattern is correct.

Table 7.07 The advantages and disadvantages of manual guidance

Advantages	Disadvantages
• Good for all stages of learning, especially novice performers	• Performer becoming over-reliant on help and support
• Reduces fear and builds confidence	• Lack of intrinsic feedback may not help develop true awareness of the movement pattern
• Helps to reduce the risk in some potentially dangerous situations	• Performer does not learn from their own mistakes and may find it difficult to correct them independently
• Development of the correct kinaesthetic awareness of the movement pattern	• Difficult in large group situations
	• Limited use in ballistic/complex movements

Mechanical guidance

Mechanical guidance is similar in nature to manual guidance but involves the use of some form of device for support. Examples include swimming floats, a trampolining belt harness or any form of apparatus that restricts movement to ensure the correct pattern is followed.

The advantages, disadvantages and methods to optimize its use are similar to those outlined above for manual guidance.

HOT TIPS

You should be able to explain which form of guidance is most appropriate in different situations and justify your reasons.

TASK 4

Outline the forms of guidance you would use to introduce the skills listed below to a group of novice performers. Justify your reasons and give practical examples to illustrate your answer.

- Gymnastic vault
- Swimming – front crawl
- High jump
- Set plays in a basketball game
- Forehand tennis shot

Teaching styles

The teaching style used can have a huge impact on the development of learning. If the appropriate style is used, the learner feels engaged, motivated and secure, which in turn will allow them to develop both the physical capability to perform the skill and understanding of the actions taking place. When considering which style to use, all of the variable factors discussed at the start of this chapter must be considered.

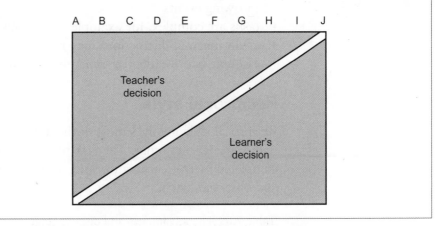

- A – *command* style – all decisions made by the teacher, no performer input
- C/D – *reciprocal style* – decisions made predominantly by the teacher with some input from the performer
- F – *discovery style* – decisions made by the performers with some guidance and input from the teacher
- I/J – *problem-solving* style – all decisions made by the performer, no teacher input

Fig. 7.07 Types of teaching style can be placed on a continuum

Mosston and Ashworth (1986) suggested a continuum of teaching styles could be used based on who makes the decision about the learning environment and the actions that occur within it. Figure 7.07 illustrates the various styles and how the input varies between the teacher and the learner.

Not all the styles have to be remembered. The key styles that need to be learnt are:

- command style (A)
- reciprocal style (C/D)
- discovery style (F)
- problem-solving style (I/J).

Command style

Command style involves the teacher making all the decisions with no input from the learners. The teacher adopts an authoritarian manner and all the performers complete the same actions.

Table 7.08 The advantages and disadvantages of the command style

Advantages	Disadvantages
• Instructions and objectives are clear	• No decision-making or input from the learner
• Control and discipline are maintained	• Possible lack of understanding
• Information can be given quickly if time is limited	• Little social interaction with teacher or other learners
• Large groups can be catered for easily	• Limited individual feedback is given
	• Little allowance for individual creativity and responsibility
	• Demotivation as learner becomes disengaged

The ideal situations for the command style would be when:

- groups are large, for example an aerobics class, or undisciplined groups
- novice performers need to be taught recognized technique
- the situation is dangerous, for example rock climbing and athletics throwing events
- tasks are complex, for example serial skills such as triple jump
- environmental distractions may require issuing of instructions quickly, for example bad weather or 'time-outs' during a game.

Reciprocal style

Reciprocal style involves most of the decisions being made by the teacher with some learner input. The task may be set by the teacher and be completed by the learners working in pairs, alternating the roles of performer and observer/coach.

Table 7.09 The advantages and disadvantages of the reciprocal style

Advantages	Disadvantages
• Instructions and objectives are clear	• May be difficult with beginners
• Social interaction and communication skills are developed	• Learners may lack sufficient communication skills to be effective
• Learners develop some responsibility for their own learning	• Learners may not be able to analyse movement and therefore provide incorrect feedback
• Some individual feedback is received via teacher and partner	• Difficulty in monitoring large groups to ensure they are all on-task
• Learners develop self-confidence and motivation levels may increase	
• Teacher can still maintain overall control	

The ideal situations for the reciprocal style would be when:
- learners are more experienced
- simple skills are involved, for example passing and dribbling
- there is limited danger present
- time is available.

Discovery style

Discovery style involves the teacher guiding the learner to find the correct movement pattern by providing information, giving specific clues or asking questions when appropriate. They act as a facilitator. There may be one or more solutions to the problem and often the performer may have to adapt the response to suit their own abilities.

Table 7.10 The advantages and disadvantages of the reciprocal style

Advantages	Disadvantages
• Encourages creativity and decision-making skills	• Time consuming
• Development of the learner's responsibility for their own learning	• Difficult with beginners or those who lack creativity
• Learners permitted to work at their own pace	• Limited development if learners have poor communication skills
• Development of a greater understanding of the task	• Progress of large groups is difficult to monitor
• Increased motivation and self-confidence	• Learning is not uniform with all learners
• Improves communication skills and promotes group interaction	

The ideal situations for the discovery style would be when:
- creativity is required, for example gymnastic routines or devising tactics
- there is no right or wrong outcome, for example a dance sequence
- performers have good communication and interactive skills or when one of the primary aims is to develop them
- more experienced performers are involved.

Problem-solving style

The problem-solving style involves the teacher setting a problem and the learner devising a suitable solution. It is an open-ended approach, encouraging creativity whilst developing the cognitive and performance elements of the learner.

HOT TIPS

Make sure you learn the characteristics of each style and the situations in which they are most useful.

The advantages and disadvantages are similar to those outlined for the discovery style of teaching. The ideal situations in which to use this teaching style would be when there is no correct outcome, time is not a restriction and the performers are experienced, allowing them to draw on their acquired knowledge.

Generally, as the emphasis on learning moves away from the teacher to the performer, the performer is more likely to be engaged by their learning: motivation and self-confidence will increase and a greater understanding of the task will develop. However, do not presume that the more direct teaching styles do not have a place in learning. Before deciding on the teaching style, all the variable factors have to be considered and the most successful teacher will usually be the one who allows flexibility, utilizing a variety of styles depending on the situation. Often within one session several styles may be used to achieve the desired outcome.

HOT TIPS

You should be able to explain the variables affecting the choice of style: teacher, activity, learner and situation.

TASK 5

Outline the teaching style you would adopt in the following situations and justify your reasons.
- Novice performers throwing the javelin
- Novice performers developing gymnastic sequences
- Experienced basketball players during a team practice developing their free throw technique
- Sixth form students rock climbing for the first time.

Motivation

Motivation is a key factor when developing the knowledge and understanding of a learner. If a performer wishes to improve their skills, tactics, awareness or any other aspect of their performance, they are more likely to remain focused and possess a desire to succeed. Think about the times you have really pushed yourself to master a skill or understand the strategies involved in a game and compare those feelings to a situation where you were not overly concerned about the outcome. What caused those differences?

Motivation can influence your:
- selection and preference for an activity
- persistence
- effort levels
- performance levels relative to your ability level.

There are two broad categories of motivation: intrinsic and extrinsic.

Intrinsic motivation involves gaining self-satisfaction, pride and a feeling of achievement. It often involves overcoming a particular challenge or simply gaining enjoyment from participating. For example, a skydiver will often gain more pleasure from the feelings they experience during the free-fall than from the praise afterwards from well-wishers. The scoring of a goal, winning a competition or achieving a personal best may all create similar feelings and are often sufficient to ensure the performer perseveres with the activity.

Extrinsic motivation, by comparison, involves the performer receiving some form of reward from others, often as a form of reinforcement. These rewards can be subdivided into two categories: tangible and intangible rewards, as illustrated in Table 7.11.

Table 7.11 Tangible and intangible rewards

Tangible rewards	Intangible rewards
• Cups	• Praise
• Medals	• Fame/publicity/social status
• Trophies	• Records
• Money	• Applause
• Certificates	

Whilst the use of motivation is highly desirable, the use of extrinsic motivation must be monitored carefully or it may have an adverse effect. If overused, it may lead to the performer only participating if they will be externally rewarded in some way and the intrinsic motivation will be undermined. If this happens, it may affect their long-term participation in the activity.

The use of National Governing Body award schemes to encourage beginners to participate and strive for improvement is common in many sports. However, they should not be seen as the only factor to encourage participation. Self-esteem, self-fulfilment, success and personal satisfaction are often more powerful to reinforce and direct behaviour in the long term.

To maximize the effectiveness of motivation, the coach should use the appropriate type of reward:
• depending on the nature of the individual, for example one performer may enjoy public praise, whilst another may simply prefer a private feedback session
• as a result of specific behaviour, for example when the correct technique has been achieved
• as soon as possible after the performance, for example give verbal encouragement, highlight that the correct technique has been used, issue

the achieved time, and so on. If this happens, the action is more likely to be repeated

- to motivate the performer. Reward the performer occasionally and then gradually reduce it. The performer should not become over-reliant on extrinsic motivation and not expect it on every occasion.

Ideally, the performer should be motivated by a combination of intrinsic and extrinsic motivational factors, with the former being viewed as the most important.

TASK 6

For each of the examples below, indicate if they are intrinsic or extrinsic. If they are extrinsic, decide if they are tangible or intangible.
- Personal swimming survival badge
- Gold medal
- Monetary bonus for winning a match
- Congratulations from another player
- The coach saying 'well done'
- Being asked for a TV interview after the game
- Election to be team captain

TASK 7

Refer back to your notes from the first task of this chapter. Using the knowledge you have now developed about optimizing learning, analyse the session and make recommendations about aspects you might alter under the following categories: presentation of practices, types of practice, forms of guidance, teaching styles and motivation. Justify your reasons.

Revise as you go!

1 Explain the term 'whole learning'.
2 Which practice method involves the performer attempting to develop specific subroutines of a skill in isolation before putting them into the correct sequence?
3 Suggest three factors a coach should consider when deciding which form of practice would be most suitable.
4 Explain the term 'massed practice'.
5 Which type of practice involves the performer completing a set of tasks and taking a recovery period before progressing to the next set of tasks?

6 Suggest three ways in which the recovery period during distributed practice can be used effectively.

7 Explain three ways of how mental practice can help the performer.

8 What form of guidance is the most effective to help the performer create a mental picture of the action?

9 Give three examples of how a coach may use visual guidance.

10 Suggest two advantages of mechanical and manual guidance.

11 Suggest three factors that need to be considered before deciding on the most appropriate teaching style.

12 Explain what is meant by the 'command style' of teaching.

13 Give two disadvantages of the command style of teaching.

14 Which form of motivation involves gaining self-satisfaction or pride from achievements, challenging yourself, or just taking part for enjoyment?

15 Which form of motivation involves receiving some form of reward for participation from others?

16 Give two examples of a tangible reward.

17 Give two examples of an intangible reward.

18 Explain why the coach should be careful in their use of extrinsic motivation.

19 Explain two advantages of the reciprocal style of teaching.

20 Why might the discovery style of teaching be inadvisable in some situations?

21 Name the most appropriate style of teaching when developing the basketball lay-up skill with a group of Year 11 GCSE students.

22 Suggest two advantages of the problem-solving style of teaching.

23 Why should a variety of teaching styles be used?

Chapter 8: Information processing

Learning outcomes

By the end of this chapter you should be able to:
- outline the basic stages of recognized information processing models
- explain the stages involved in the memory process
- discuss factors that affect decision-making, including reaction time, Hick's Law and the psychological refractory period
- explain the function and value of feedback.

Introduction

One of the key aspects of this chapter is to understand how you gather, interpret and make use of the various pieces of information your senses are constantly gathering. The effectiveness of your information processing system is a vital factor in your ability as an individual and can have a big impact on the level of your performance. Often it is not the performer who is the most skilful that succeeds, but the one that is most able to identify the relevant cues, ignore those that are irrelevant and, based on that information, select the appropriate action in the quickest time.

For each of the areas outlined in the learning outcomes above, you will be expected to explain its characteristics, give practical applications of its use and discuss its various advantages and disadvantages. You will also be expected to explain how each of the processes may be maximized using relevant practical examples.

As with previous chapters, often the best way to gain a fuller understanding of each topic may be to refer back to personal experience and then apply some of the acquired knowledge to your current performances.

Models of information processing

KEY WORDS

Display

The physical environment surrounding the performer, containing various stimuli or cues, from which the performer has to select those that are relevant at the time.

The majority of the models of information processing are based on the assumption that our brain functions in a similar fashion to that of a computer and as such works in stages to arrive at the output phase. The main stages involved are:
- input – information is gathered from the environment/**display**
- decision-making – gathered information is used to formulate a motor programme
- output – motor programme is completed by the performer
- feedback – information is gathered during and after the performance.

KEY WORDS

Selective attention

A process that filters irrelevant information gathered by the sensory system and prioritizes the stimuli that can affect that particular situation.

Motor programme

Organizes a series of subroutines into the correct sequence to perform a movement, adapting it to changes in the environment. They are based on a hierarchical structure, involving movements that are autonomous at the lower level with more complex subroutines at the peak.

The two most commonly used models to illustrate information processing are those of Whiting and Welford. Whilst they differ slightly in their structure and terminology, their basic process is very similar, involving three stages:

- **stimulus identification** – information is collected from the display via the sensory system. This involves the performer using their **perceptual mechanism**. Any information deemed irrelevant is filtered via **selective attention** to increase the speed of the decision-making process. For example, a netball player will gather information regarding the speed and direction of the ball, the location of teammates and opponents, personal location on court and specific strategies being adapted. Shouts from spectators and location of the umpire will be ignored as this will slow down the decision-making process

- **response identification** – the relevant information is assessed and a decision made based on previous experience, which is stored in the memory. For example, the netball player will decide upon a particular type of pass to use to a specific player

- **response programming** – the **motor programme** is completed via the **effector mechanism** and the muscular system. For example, the netball player completes the pass to their teammate.

 KEY WORDS

Perceptual mechanism

The interpretation and analysis of information gathered from the environment by the sensory system.

Translatory mechanism

Uses the information gathered from the environment and makes the appropriate decision.

Effector mechanism

Transfers the decision that has been made to the muscular system via motor nerves.

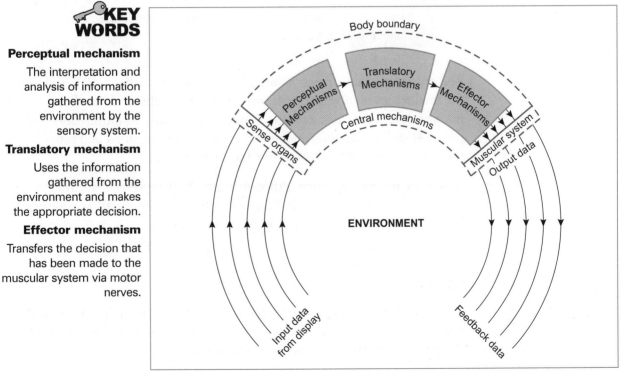

Fig. 8.01 Whiting's model

Whiting's model

The input is gathered via three forms of receptors in the sensory system (Figure 8.01):

- **exteroceptors** – information gathered from outside the body – extrinsic, for example sight, sound, touch, smell and taste (the first three are the most important to sports performers)
- **proprioceptors** – information gathered from inside the body via nerve receptors in the muscles and joints – intrinsic, for example the feeling of the movement or kinaesthetic awareness
- **interoceptors** – information from the internal organs, which is passed to the central nervous system, to control functions such as blood flow, blood pressure and body temperature.

The intensity of the stimulus can affect the ease of 'signal detection' and the resultant motor programme; that is, if the stimulus is easier to detect, usually the motor programme can be initiated sooner. Often the teacher or coach may modify the situation to make the identification of cues easier.

TASK 1

1 Play a game of your choice but inhibit the sensory system to limit the amount of information received. For example, wear earplugs, an eye patch, blinkers, thick gloves, and so on. Do not restrict all your senses at once!
2 Alternate the inhibition. Discuss the effects and implications on performance with a partner.

The central mechanisms on Whiting's model are as outlined previously, and the final stages involve the performer receiving feedback about their performance. This can be received either extrinsically or intrinsically (see page 146), allowing adjustments to be made when required and retention of the information in the memory for future reference.

It must be remembered that although Figure 8.01 represents a static situation, our environment and the components of the model are constantly changing and being updated. It is dynamic in nature.

TASK 2

For each of the major sensory exteroceptors (vision, auditory and touch), suggest ways in which the intensity of the stimulus may be altered to aid the detection of the stimulus and processing of information.

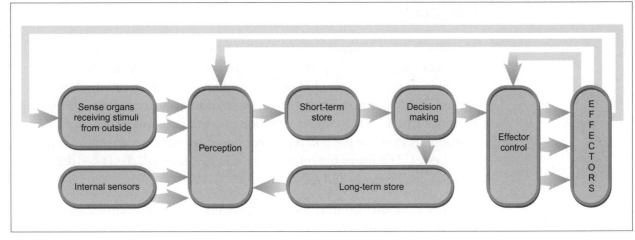

Fig. 8.02 Welford's model

Welford's model

Figure 8.02 represents the major stages as outlined in Whiting's model but is more detailed. You must be able to explain how the information is used and the processes that are involved in producing a motor programme.

- **Input** (sense organs and internal sensors) – the information is gathered via the sensory system from the display, and the perceptual mechanism interprets those stimuli.
- **Perception** involves three stages – the DCR process:
  - ○ detection – the identification of a stimulus
  - ○ comparison – the gathered stimuli are compared to memory stores
  - ○ recognition – the stimuli is matched to one stored in the memory.
- **Memory** (short-term store and long-term store) – involves the gathered information being interpreted and compared to past experiences before a decision is made. The process involves the short-term sensory stores, short-term memory and long-term memory (see page 140).
- **Decision-making** – involves the formulation of a motor programme most appropriate to the current situation. This is also known as the translatory mechanism.
- **Effector control** – the selected motor programme or **schema** (see page 153) is sent via the body's nervous system to the muscular system (effectors) allowing movement to occur.
- **Feedback** – once the action has been initiated, the performer gathers information about the effectiveness of the motor programme, either internally or externally, allowing modifications to be made (see page 146 for a further detailed explanation).

KEY WORDS

Schema

A generalized series of movement patterns that are modified to adapt to the current environment and situation.

HOT TIPS

You may be asked in your exam about specific information processing models or selective components within an expanded model, for example memory, decision-making or output.

TASK 3

Select a sporting situation you have encountered and complete the stages of one of the models to explain your own experience.

Memory

Memory is a key element in information processing. Learning is concerned with acquiring relatively permanent changes in behaviour, therefore this information must be stored in some way allowing us to recall it when needed. When performing in a sporting environment, we are always making decisions based on the current situation and our previous experience, allowing us to make the correct choice based on our own strengths and weaknesses. The faster the information can be retrieved, the faster the decision can be made and executed.

Memory is subdivided into three components and their relationship is illustrated in Figure 8.03.

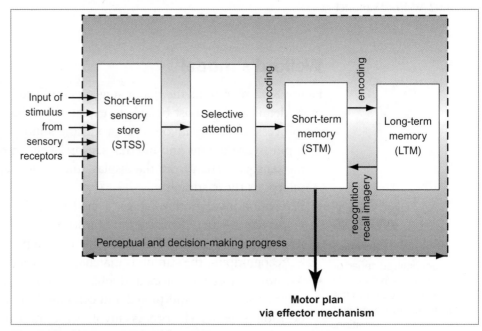

Fig. 8.03 The components of memory

Short-term sensory store (STSS)

The short-term sensory store collects all the information entering the body via the sensory system. It has a huge capacity to receive information but can only retain it for a short period of time – up to one second before it is lost. The information is prioritized and irrelevant stimuli are discarded. This process is known as selective attention.

Selective attention allows the performer to gather only important information and consequently speeds up the decision-making time. Many theories suggest there is only a limited amount of information that can be processed at any one time and by focusing on a smaller number of cues, we react faster to them. For example, a tennis player will attempt to focus on the ball, their position on court and their opponent. They will attempt to ignore the crowd, advertising boards and the consequences of the match.

Often a performer with the ability to focus and block out distractions will be more effective than a potentially more skilful player who cannot concentrate fully. Sometimes athletes have referred this to as 'tunnel vision'.

A performer can improve their selective attention by:
- using appropriate practice and presentation methods
- highlighting specific cues on which to focus their concentration. This can be done by using different guidance methods
- altering the intensity of the stimulus, for example colour and speed of the object, loudness of the sound, and so on
- referring to past experiences
- making the stimuli meaningful or unique, for example make the performer think about the action in a different way. A basketball player snapping their wrist when taking a free throw may be told to think of 'waving the ball goodbye'
- reaching the correct level of arousal and maintaining motivation.

HOT TIPS

Practise drawing the memory model diagram on page 139 including the correct number and direction of the respective arrows.

Short-term memory (STM)/working memory

The short-term memory or working memory receives the filtered information and compares it to stored information from past experiences before the final decision is made. It has a limited capacity of five to nine pieces of information, which can be retained for approximately 30 seconds. If the information is practised and learnt, it is transferred to the long-term memory for future reference or it is released. This has implications for a coach, as outlined previously when discussing guidance. If they overload the performer with information, the performer will not be able to process all of it at once and their learning will be less effective.

A performer can improve their short-term memory by:
- *chunking* – the information is arranged into larger units or 'chunks', allowing more pieces of information to be stored. For example, a set play in a game situation will be remembered by a single call
- chaining – the linking together of pieces of information, as used in the progressive part method of practice (see page 120), for example, when a gymnast is developing a sequence
- using selective attention – limiting the amount of irrelevant information passing into the short-term memory.

TASK 4

1 Compile a list of random numbers, the first comprising four digits, the next five digits, and so on until there are 12 digits in the sequence.
2 Read each number in turn to your partner, who must recall and record the sequence immediately. Check the answers and reverse roles with a new set of numbers.
3 Compare results – who has the best short-term memory?

Long-term memory (LTM)

Long-term memory is the permanent retention of information through repetition or rehearsal. It has the capacity to store vast amounts of information for an unlimited period of time. When the performer is faced with a new situation, the relevant stimuli are passed on from the short-term memory, where a comparison is made with any similar experiences. If any recognition does occur, the similarities are noted and a decision is made quickly. If the situation is new, a motor programme will be formed based on available knowledge, but this may take slightly longer and delay the decision-making process.

A performer can improve their long-term memory by:
- improving the capability of the short-term memory
- practising and repeating movements, causing 'over-learning' of motor programmes
- developing a range of past experiences, for example modified games and realistic practice situations
- using mental rehearsal
- making the information meaningful, relevant and interesting to the performer.

HOT TIPS

Make sure you know the characteristics and relationship between the different components of memory and are able to relate them to practical examples. You should be able to outline methods to improve memory.

Table 8.01 compares the possible memory process of both a novice and an experienced performer when confronted with the same situation. Both are playing in a rugby match, in possession of the ball, with support players on either side. They are confronted with a defender attempting to make a tackle.

Table 8.01 Memory processes in novice and experienced performers

	Novice performer	Experienced performer
STSS	Gathers information about some of their own team, opponents, own position; aware of crowd and coach calling instructions	Gathers information about their own team, opponents, personal position
STM	Some relevant stimuli collected, for example location of defender and position of one support player plus some irrelevant cues, for example shouts from the crowd about what to do	Eliminates some stimuli, for example crowd noise and location of players who would not be an option to involve, but retains information about several possible teammates and defender's position
LTM	Limited reference data available, distracted by the crowd and either makes the pass to the closest support player or runs into the defender	Large amount of previous experience allows the player to select from a range of options, to pass to the support player in the best position or to kick the ball into a suitable space or to another player

Reaction time and decision-making

Another key element in the decision-making process is the amount of time the performer takes to receive, interpret, analyse stimuli and formulate an appropriate response. The faster this can be achieved, the more time the performer is likely to have in order to complete the selected skill successfully.

We often attempt to confuse our opponents by giving them false cues, for example a dummy, feint or change of tactics, to keep them guessing and ultimately slow their reaction time. A performer with a faster reaction time can delay the start of their movement, giving them a greater opportunity to fully assess the situation and eliminating the need to guess what may happen. For example, a hockey defender may wait until an attacker is closer before committing themselves to the tackle and risk either giving away a foul or being beaten by a dummy movement.

There are three key terms that need to be understood when discussing this section:

- *reaction time* – the time between the onset of a stimulus and the initiation of the response. It is the time the information processing system takes to interpret the situation, formulate a motor programme and transmit the information to the muscular system. An example is the time taken when a striker thinks they have the opportunity to score a goal and the start of the shooting action.
- *movement time* – the time between the start of the movement and its completion. It is the time the performer takes to physically complete the movement when the muscular system has received the message from the brain via the effector system, for example, the time it takes the striker to move their limbs to strike the ball.

Fig. 8.04 Components of response time – reaction time/movement time and response time

HOT TIPS

Make sure you know the definitions of each term, their relationship and are able to apply them to practical examples.

- *response time* – the time from the onset of the stimulus to the completion of the movement. It is the combination of the reaction time and the movement time, for example, the overall time the striker takes to complete the shot from first seeing the ball, their position and the goal.

There are numerous factors that affect the speed of a performer's reaction time including:

- age – reaction times improve until the early twenties but then become slower
- gender – males generally have faster reaction times but as we become older, the difference becomes less
- fatigue – tired performers tend to have slower reaction times
- intensity of the stimulus – the more intense, the faster the time, for example brighter and louder stimulus help increase reaction time
- probability of the stimulus occurring – if the stimulus is expected, there is a reduced element of doubt and anticipation, for example an opponent always plays the same shot in a particular situation
- presence of a warning signal – this may be a call or gesture, for example the starter at the beginning of a race issuing commands or coloured lights to begin a grand prix race
- personality – introverts tend to have slower reaction times than extroverts
- sense used to detect the stimulus – sight, sound, touch and kinaesthetic awareness all produce differing reaction times
- previous experience – the greater the experience, the faster the recall from the long-term memory
- arousal level – optimum arousal will cause heightened concentration levels and allow the performer to only focus on key stimuli
- stimulus-response compatibility – the reaction time is faster if the required action is normally linked to the stimulus, for example a batsman facing a bowler will select a shot based on how they think the ball usually bounces, depending on the bowler's action and where it pitches on the wicket. If the ball bounces differently, the batsman's reaction time may be slower as an adjustment is required
- body temperature – reaction time is slower if the body is cold
- limbs used – the further the nerve impulse has to travel, the slower the reaction time, for example hand movements tend to be completed faster than foot movements.

There are two forms of reaction time performers must use, which are dependent on the number of stimuli present and the number of possible responses available. They are:

- *simple reaction time* – involves one stimulus and one possible response. One example is the time a sprinter takes to start moving off the blocks when the gun has been fired
- *choice reaction time* – involves the performer being presented with numerous stimuli, each with a different response. This situation occurs in all open skills, causing the performer to make decisions largely based on past experiences. For example, a water polo player in possession of the

ball has to decide whether to pass, move with the ball or shoot, and their situation will constantly alter requiring another decision to be made.

TASK 5

For this task you will need playing cards and a stopwatch. In pairs, one times and the other performs; then swap roles. The performer has to complete each of the tasks below.

1 Divide the cards into two piles either red or black.
2 Divide the cards into four piles, one of each suit.
3 Divide the cards into eight piles, each suit with picture cards and numbers.

Plot a graph and discuss the results.

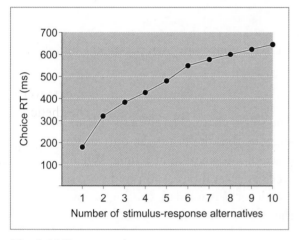

Fig. 8.05 Response time curve

Hick's Law

Hick's Law suggests that reaction time will increase in a linear fashion as the amount of information to be processed increases. Based on your results from Task 5, you should observe that your choice reaction time gets slower as the number of options increases, and your graph will probably look similar to Figure 8.05.

This knowledge, when applied to sporting situations, has great implications for the quality of performance. If a performer can develop a range of skills and employ them effectively when faced with a number of different situations, their opponent will not know what is going to happen and as a result will have to delay their decision-making process until the last moment, which may be too late for them to respond correctly. For example, a squash player who is able to play a variety of shots from differing positions will find it easier to outwit and deceive an opponent.

If, on the other hand, the player is facing a skilled performer, specific cues must be identified in an attempt to limit the number of options and reduce the choice reaction time. For example, the performer may always have a particular mannerism just before executing a shot, or by observing previous performances it may be possible to identify particular shots that are more commonly used in specific areas of the court.

The increase in reaction time can be explained using the psychological refractory period (PRP) (Figure 8.06). The delay is caused by an increase in the

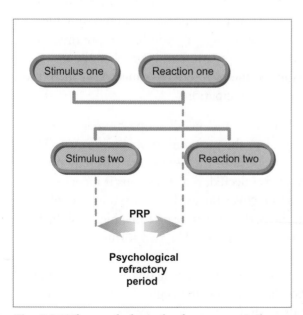

Fig. 8.06 The psychological refractory period

143

information processing time when the initial stimulus is closely followed by a second stimulus. The reaction time is slowed because the first piece of information must be cleared before the second can be processed, as explained by the single channel hypothesis (see below).

The practical implications of this to a performer are considerable. If the performer can fake or dummy a movement successfully, often the opponent will be unable to clear the first stimulus in time, causing a delay in the overall response time, thus creating a clear advantage, allowing the move to be completed with slightly less pressure. For example, a badminton player may look as if they are about to execute a smash shot, but at the last moment actually plays a drop shot. Their opponent will find it difficult to react to the rapid change of shot and direction of the shuttle.

HOT TIPS

Practise drawing the relevant diagrams relating to Hick's Law, single channel hypothesis and PRP.

TASK 6

Complete the diagram of the PRP with your with own practical example you have experienced.

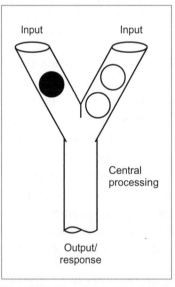

Fig. 8.07 The single channel hypothesis

The single channel hypothesis (Figure 8.07) suggests that the brain can only deal with one piece of information at a time. When it receives several pieces in rapid succession, a 'bottleneck' is formed, causing a slowing of the decision-making process.

Improving response time

If the performer can improve their response time, their performance can improve significantly as they will have more time to assess the situation and complete the task. One of the most effective methods can be the use of anticipation.

Anticipation depends on past experience and involves the recognition of specific cues. The performer attempts to predict the actions of the opponent. This may prove to be effective if the correct choice is selected, but disastrous if incorrect, as there would be insufficient time to recover (as explained by the psychological refractory period). It can mean the performer appears to be highly skilled, executing the skill with plenty of time to spare. The two forms of anticipation are:

HOT TIPS

Make sure you are able to outline the positive and negative effects of anticipation on performance.

- **spatial anticipation** – involves the performer predicting what will happen. For example, the badminton player detects the slight difference in the shot action and is expecting the drop shot

- **temporal anticipation** – involves the performer predicting when the action will happen. For example, a football defender tries to guess when the attacker will actually pass the ball.

Other methods used to improve response time include:
- relevant practice responding to specific cues or stimulus
- mental rehearsal
- concentration on early warning signals
- improvement of selective attention
- control of arousal levels
- improvement of physical fitness
- altering the intensity of the stimulus
- identification of specific actions/cues used by opponents (studying their game).

Feedback

The final stage of information processing is feedback, which is vital to the learning process. It links the output and input phases, effectively 'closing the loop'. We learn from experience either to modify our movements at the time or store the information in our long-term memory for future reference. Feedback has several purposes including:
- detection and correction of errors causing a change in performance
- motivation – incentive to continue and increase effort
- reinforcement of learning – Thorndike's law of effect (see page 113).

There are numerous types of feedback and they must be subdivided. The two major categories are:
- **intrinsic or internal feedback** – this is received from within the performer via proprioceptors and is known as kinaesthetic feedback. As the performer becomes more skilled, they are able to detect and correct their own errors more easily. For example, an experienced trampolinist will be able to make minor adjustments during their routine, whereas a novice will not be able to do so without the help of their coach
- **extrinsic or external feedback** – this is received from outside the performer, usually via sound or vision, via their exteroceptors. It may also be known as augmented feedback. The information is given by a coach, teacher, supporters, teammates, video or photographs. It is particularly useful in the cognitive and associative stages of learning, as the performer has yet to develop their kinaesthetic awareness, which allows them to correct their errors via intrinsic feedback.

In addition to these two broad categories, there are other forms of feedback.
- *Continuous feedback* is received during the performance via the proprioceptors and kinaesthesis, for example the feel of the shot when playing badminton, or via the coach issuing instructions.

- *Terminal feedback* is received after the performance. It may be issued immediately by the coach or given later, for example when observing a video recording of the event.
- *Positive feedback* is used as a form of reinforcement, encouraging the performer to repeat the action. For example, the coach praises a shot or the performer sees that the result is effective.
- *Negative feedback* is used if the technique was incorrect to discourage a repetition of the action. For example, the coach would highlight incorrect points of technique or the performer may correct the error themselves if the shot was out.
- *Knowledge of results (KR)* – feedback that the performer receives concerning the outcome of the action. It may be the number of goals scored, recorded times and distances, or the statistics collected concerning accuracy and completed shots or passes. It is an external form of feedback and particularly useful in the early stages of learning.
- *Knowledge of performance (KP)* – this is information that the performer receives about the quality of their technique or performance. It can be internal or external feedback, depending on the stage of learning. For example, a coach of a swimmer may analyse their techniques with the use of video and adjust the training programme accordingly.

HOT TIPS

Make sure you are able to outline each term. You should be able to discuss the use of feedback and relate the use of feedback to the various stages of learning.

Table 8.02 compares knowledge of results and knowledge of performance for two activities.

Table 8.02 Knowledge of results and of performance

	Knowledge of results	Knowledge of performance
Long jump	7.24 metres	More drive needed from the knee during take-off
Tennis shot	Ball was wide of the tram line	Racket face was too open

Making feedback effective

If feedback is used correctly, it can accelerate the learning process and boost motivation. If used incorrectly, it can confuse and discourage a performer. The coach should consider the ability level of the performer and the nature of the task when deciding on the most appropriate form to use.

Here are some key points to using feedback successfully.
- It must be relevant and modifications made according to the ability range of the performer.
- It should be limited – no more than three points of information or the performer will be overloaded with information.
- It must be accurate and specific – give parameters, for example direction and speed.
- Ideally issue immediately when the action is fresh in the performer's mind.
- Allow time to digest the information and to make modifications, possibly combined with mental rehearsal.

- Keep it brief – do not get bogged down with long, detailed instructions.
- Do not overuse – the performer may become over-reliant on feedback and fail to develop their own understanding.
- Set appropriate goals or targets to improve motivation.

TASK 7

1 In pairs, select any aiming skill to be completed blindfolded, for example, badminton serves into a hoop. The performer completes five attempts under each of the following conditions:
   - no feedback
   - limited feedback – simply 'yes' or 'no'
   - detailed feedback – direction, force, and so on.
2 Record the results and discuss the implications of feedback on performance.

Revise as you go!

1 Explain the term 'perception'.
2 What provides intrinsic information about the movement and balance of the body during movement?
3 Place the following terms in the correct sequence when a decision has to be made involving memory: long-term memory, short-term memory, short-term sensory store, selective attention.
4 State another term often used for the short-term memory.
5 Outline the capacity and duration of long-term memory.
6 Explain the term 'movement time'.
7 What is 'simple reaction time'?
8 Suggest two reasons why feedback is used.
9 What kind of feedback is received via the proprioceptors, developing a performer's kinaesthetic awareness?
10 What is the term given to feedback that is given after the activity?
11 Explain the term 'knowledge of results'.
12 Explain the term 'extrinsic feedback' and give two examples of how a performer may receive this form of feedback.
13 Why is continuous feedback useful to a performer?
14 Suggest two ways in which the coach can use feedback most effectively.

Chapter 9: Motor programmes and movement control

Learning outcomes

By the end of this chapter you should be able to:
- explain the term 'motor programme' and identify specific subroutines
- understand how movement is controlled with reference to the open and closed loop theory
- apply the knowledge of motor control to practical situations
- outline schema theory and the sources of information used to modify movement
- explain the concept of transfer and apply that knowledge to aid the learning process.

Introduction

The final chapter of the psychological section involves the actual movement phase of the skill action. It is the 'output' phase of the information processing model. You will need to understand how movement patterns are constructed and how this information can be utilized when designing the most appropriate form of training session, allowing the learner to achieve more effectively.

There are several theories that attempt to explain how movement actually occurs and is modified. You must be able to outline and evaluate each one as well as discuss the practical implications this may have on learning and performance.

Often, performers appear to have the ability to participate successfully in an activity in which they have little experience. How is this achieved? The performer may have little time to actually learn all the new skills involved, but seems to be able to adapt existing skills to a new situation and refine them as the game progresses. This chapter will attempt to explain why this may occur and outline the implications for a successful training regime.

For each of the areas outlined in the learning outcomes above, you will be expected to explain the characteristics of each one, give practical applications of their use and discuss their various advantages and disadvantages. As with previous chapters, often the best way to gain a fuller understanding of each topic may be to refer back to personal experience and then apply some of the acquired knowledge to your current performances.

Motor programmes

Executive motor programme

A series of subroutines organized into the correct sequence to perform a movement.

When we develop a new skill, during the cognitive and associative phases of learning, it is transferred into the long-term memory. When a specific action is required, the memory process retrieves the stored programme and transmits the motor commands via nerve impulses to the relevant muscles, allowing movement to occur. This is known as the '**executive motor programme**'. This programme is recalled when needed, modified after execution and stored for future reference. If the skill is well learnt or autonomous, the recall process (reaction time) is very short, but during the early stages of learning this may take some time or the movement patterns may not be completed correctly.

Each executive motor programme has an organized series of subroutines, which must be completed in the correct sequence and adapted to the changing environment. For example, Figures 9.01 and 9.02 illustrate the subroutines of a high jump and a cricket shot.

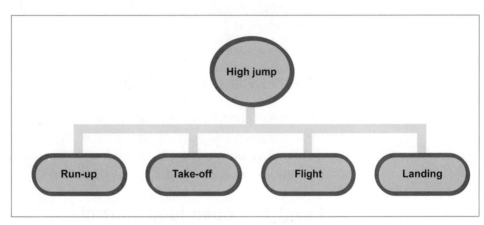

Fig. 9.01 Subroutines of a high jump

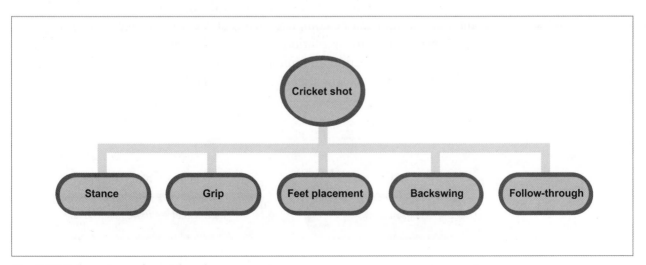

Fig. 9.02 Subroutines of a cricket shot

Motor programmes are based on a hierarchical structure involving movements that are autonomous at the lower levels with more complex subroutines at the peak. As the performer becomes more skilled, the existing executive motor programme is relegated and superseded by a new programme. It becomes autonomous and over-learned. For example, the cricketer, after mastering the subroutines as shown in Figure 9.02 of how to make contact with the ball correctly, will then develop more specific shots depending on the line of the ball, where it pitches and how it moves after bouncing.

HOT TIPS

Make sure you can discuss the limitations of motor programme theory.

Identification of subroutines may help the coach pinpoint specific weaknesses and incorporate a particular type of practice into the training session, for example, whole-part-whole or progressive part practice. Some skills may not be broken down so easily, such as running or dribbling skills, and another form of practice may be more appropriate.

TASK 1

1 Identify the core skills required in your chosen coursework activity.
2 For each core skill, identify the subroutines and highlight two key points of technique for each.

Open and closed loop control theory

Once the executive motor programme has been selected, the movement has to be regulated and adapted. It has been suggested that performers achieve this on three different levels, depending on the extent to which the central nervous system is involved.

Level 1 or open loop control

This level involves the completion of the movement automatically, with no conscious control (Figure 9.03). These movements are well learnt, stored in the long-term memory and retrieved very quickly when required. They are autonomous and can be completed without the need for feedback and adjustment during the execution of the task. It is also known as the 'memory trace', allowing selection and initiation of the movement, but it has no influence over the control after the action has started.

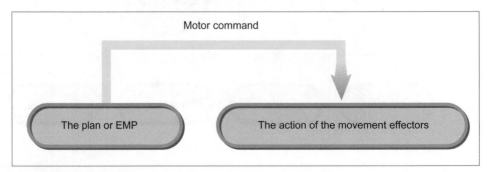

Fig. 9.03 Level 1 or open loop control

Muscle spindles

Receptors that lie between the muscle fibres, detecting the degree of stretch within the muscle, transmitting information to the spinal cord and the brain about the length of the muscle.

Fig. 9.04 An example of open loop control

Fig. 9.06 An example of closed loop control

This process usually occurs during the execution of a closed skill, such as skipping, basketball free throw (Figure 9.04) or a golf swing, but may also occur during open skills such as catching or kicking a ball.

Level 2 or closed loop control

This level involves some feedback, which is received via kinaesthetic awareness and the **muscle spindles**. Errors are detected and adjustments are made at a subconscious level, with little direct attention from the performer, for example maintaining a static balance, such as a handstand, or dynamic balance, such as sidestepping an opponent in a rugby match.

Level 3

This is also closed loop control but involves a conscious decision by the performer based on feedback received (see Figure 9.06). The performer pays attention to specific details and has to concentrate and make a deliberate attempt to alter the movement pattern. Often performers in the associative phase of learning will rely on level 3 control to develop their skill level. For example, a novice basketball player may have to think about changing hands and the force used when dribbling the ball.

Levels 2 and 3 are also known as the 'perceptual trace', allowing comparison and modification of movements when compared to a stored model. This is developed through practice and feedback, either received during or after completion, allowing errors to be detected, corrected and updated for future reference. For example, a gymnast completing a routine will constantly evaluate the movements being performed during the sequence and make adjustments as required to maintain balance, speed and control based on their knowledge of how each component should feel.

Most performers will experience both open and closed loop control during their performance depending on their skill level and the task difficulty.

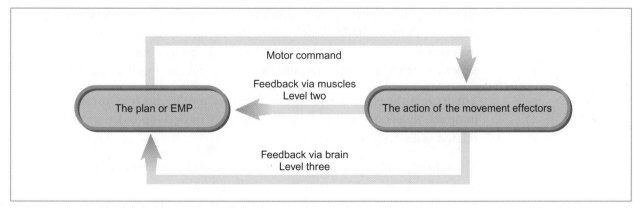

Fig. 9.05 Level 2 or closed loop control

HOT TIPS

You should be able to explain the difference between each form of control and the stages of the open and closed loop theory with reference to a practical example, and also the limitations of the theory.

However, there are some criticisms of the theory.

- It assumes that there is a separate memory trace for each movement pattern, which has to be accommodated and recalled from the long-term memory.
- It also suggests practice should be accurate and variance would hinder learning, which recent research has refuted.
- Performers sometimes produce movements that are spontaneous and unusual, for which a memory trace could not be stored.

TASK 2

Look at the skills outlined below and decide if the movements are under open or closed loop control.

- Continuous chest pass
- Forward roll to balance
- Hockey push pass
- Walk along an upturned bench
- Run 200 metres in 40 seconds, with the aid of a stopwatch to monitor your time
- Dribble a football between a series of cones
- Badminton rally
- Five basketball free throws

Discuss the results with a partner.

Schema theory

One of the major criticisms of the motor programme theory is the suggestion that all movements are pre-planned and stored in the long-term memory. The schema theory, proposed by Schmidt, argues that rather than using memory and perceptual traces to initiate movement, we store in our memory a generalized series of movement patterns that we modify to adapt to the current environment.

When we learn new skills or are playing a game, the performer will recall and alter stored motor programmes to complete the task successfully. For example, during a badminton match, the performer cannot possibly have experienced every type of shot that they have to face, but based on experience they adapt the required stroke to suit the specific situation.

There are a variety of basic schemas that we modify, such as running, jumping, throwing and catching, allowing us to develop more specific sport-related skills.

The schema are initiated, evaluated and updated by two processes:
- *recall schema*, which actually start the movement
- *recognition schema*, which control and evaluate the movement.

Recall schema have two sources of information.

1 *Knowledge of initial conditions* – refers to information about the location of the performer, their environment and limb position. This information is compared to previous experiences. Performers ask themselves, 'where am I?'

2 *Knowledge of response specifications* – refers to information about the task to be completed, the speed, force, options available and the formulation of a suitable movement. Performers ask themselves, 'what have I got to do?'

Recognition schema also have two sources of information.

1 *Sensory consequences* – refers to the feelings experienced during and after the movement, the kinaesthetic feeling, the sound and any other information gathered via the sensory system, allowing suitable adjustments to be made. Performers ask themselves, 'what does the movement feel like?'

2 *Response outcome* – refers to the end result and a comparison being made with the intended outcome. This information is vital for updating the memory store for future reference when confronted with a similar situation in the future. Performers ask themselves, 'what happened as a result of the movement?'

These sources of information are called *parameters* and are taken into account the next time the skill has to be completed. The parameter is stored within the schema and is used to initiate a response with the correct speed, force and direction required. A performer who develops a wide range of parameters will have a better chance of successfully executing the skill, as they will be more familiar with the specific requirements when faced with the situation during a game. For example, a basketball player who shoots from different places on court will develop a slightly different action for each. However, a player who only practises from the free throw line will find it more difficult to adjust during a game when having to shoot from a variety of locations, as they will find it more difficult to select the exact response required.

HOT TIPS

You should be able to explain the different types of schema and sources of information used to control motor programme and link them to specific practical examples. Do not confuse schema theory with 'transfer of learning' (see below).

For example, David Beckham has developed a wide range of schema relating to striking a football. When faced with a free kick, he assesses the situation and selects the type of shot he wishes to execute to avoid the defenders and goalkeeper (recall schema). The wide range of parameters enables him to take free kicks from a variety of locations, producing effective end results. He controls the execution of the shot and assesses its outcome, retaining any information that may be useful in the future if faced with a similar situation (recognition schema).

Implications for training and development of schema

The coach can use this knowledge and develop a range of schema and parameters. This can be achieved in a variety of ways including:

- variation of practice
- avoiding blocked practices (repeated practice of the same skill)

- setting small parameters to facilitate fine adjustments of technique
- ensuring practice is relevant to the competitive situation
- provision of accurate knowledge of results and feedback
- challenging and progressive tasks
- developing as many schema as possible.

Transfer of learning

In order to make the learning of skills more effective, the concept of 'transfer' must be understood. Transfer is the effect that the learning or performance of one skill has on the learning or performance of another skill. If the teacher/coach can apply this knowledge correctly, they can decrease the learning time, maximize the use of the time available, develop relevant conditioned practices associated with the full competitive situation and identify areas that may hinder learning.

The notion of transfer is liked to the schema theory, allowing us to modify movement patterns to suit new situations. For example, a basketball player would be encouraged to use the skills of movement, spatial awareness and ball handling when being introduced to the game of netball. However, some skills that are well learnt may be more difficult to eliminate and hinder the performance, such as dribbling with the ball and shooting with the aid of a backboard.

There are numerous forms of transfer including:
- *positive transfer* – involves previously learnt skills helping the development of new skills. Various movement patterns may be adjusted to suit the new situation, as illustrated in Figure 9.07. The coach is able to identify similarities and make comparisons, illustrating to the learner how the movement should basically feel.

Fig. 9.07 Example of positive transfer

Other examples include a diver using a trampoline and harness to practise complex moves, and team games often use modified practices such as 3 v 2 or 2 v 1 to develop an understanding of spatial awareness and timing.

- *negative transfer* – involves previously learnt skills hindering the development of new skills. Usually this is temporary and can be eliminated with relevant practices and the coach highlighting the potential difficulties immediately. For example, a tennis player, when playing badminton, may not be able to generate the power needed to hit the shuttlecock effectively because they are used to playing with a firm wrist rather than the flexible wrist action required.

- *bilateral transfer* – involves the transfer of learning from one limb to another, rather than from skill to skill. Often the kinaesthetic awareness from the dominant limb when applied to the other limb can improve performance and allow the performer to develop a wider range of skills and be able to apply them in a greater range of situations. Think back to the section on reaction time and the psychological refractory period in Chapter 8 and how such an advantage could slow an opponent's response time significantly. For example, a games player who can use both feet and hands equally well has a distinct advantage over one who is only comfortable using their dominant limb.

- *proactive transfer* occurs when the skill being learnt has an effect on skills developed in the future. A coach may gradually increase the level of difficulty, develop specific subroutines or employ the progressive part method of practice to ensure the skill is fully understood and mastered. For example, a young tennis player will learn the basic forehand and backhand ground strokes before developing topspin and more advanced shots, but the fundamental movement patterns are the same.

- *retroactive transfer* occurs when the skill being developed has an effect on one that has been previously learnt. For example, an experienced tennis player may have to alter their basic technique as more advanced shots are developed. When developing the forehand stroke, they are taught to move into a side-on position, but as their skill levels progress, they often have a more open stance and alter the basic movement pattern.

TASK 3

Select a skill, for example a badminton serve or basketball lay-up, and attempt to execute the skill with your non-dominant hand. Discuss with a partner your experiences and explain how you modified your technique in an attempt to improve.

Implications for training

The coach must use this information to structure the training session to maximize the learning opportunity. This can be achieved by:

- identifying elements of the skill that are transferable, improving and hindering learning

- developing good basic movement patterns initially and then progressing to more complex skills
- making practice situations relevant and realistic to the competitive environment, for example swimmers need to practise for the majority of the time in the water, not land-based activities; team games need to practise against opposition, not simply unopposed
- eliminating the opportunity for bad habits to develop – negative transfer.

TASK 4

Compare the activities listed below and identify examples of positive, negative and bilateral transfer that may occur between each. There may be more than one form present.

- Netball • Rugby • Basketball • Gymnastics • High jump

Revise as you go!

1 Explain the term 'subroutine'.
2 Suggest how the high jump event may be divided into subroutines.
3 Which schemas are responsible for starting the movement?
4 Which schemas are responsible for controlling and evaluating the movement?
5 Explain the term 'sensory consequences' when referring to recognition schema.
6 Explain the term 'response outcomes' when referring to recognition schema.
7 Which form of transfer occurs when a skill currently being learned has an effect on a skill in the future?
8 Explain the term 'bilateral transfer' and give an example to illustrate your answer.

End of Unit 1 Questions

Unit 1: Physiological and psychological factors which improve performance

1   Gymnastic activities rely on repetitive patterns that require high levels of fitness.

a) In schools, gymnastics can be taught as educational gymnastics, which corresponds to a *problem-solving* teaching style. What are the advantages of this approach when teaching gymnastics? **(3 marks)**

b) On occasions, a teacher may need to adopt *command style* teaching. In what situations would this be necessary? **(2 marks)**

c) Explain **four** factors a teacher should consider when selecting an appropriate teaching style. **(4 marks)**

d) What do you understand by the term 'body composition'? Explain why a gymnast's body fat needs to be low. **(2 marks)**

e) Flexibility and strength are important fitness components for a gymnast. Using examples, explain where each is used in gymnastics. **(2 marks)**

f) A coach may require their gymnasts to regularly undergo a series of generalized fitness tests. What purpose does such fitness testing serve and what are the limitations to such testing? **(5 marks)**

(Q2, January 2004)

2   a) During exercise, the flow of blood to different parts of the body will alter, as shown in Figure 2.

Part of the body	Rate of blood flow (cm^3 min^{-1})	
	At rest	**During exercise**
Muscle	1000	16000
Heart muscle	300	1200
Gut and liver	3000	1400
Brain	750	750
All other organs (except lungs)	1550	1550

Fig. 2

   i) Use the figures in Figure 2 to calculate the *cardiac output* at rest. **(2 marks)**

   ii) State **two** reasons for increased cardiac output during a period of exercise. **(2 marks)**

b) Describe how the *sinoatrial node* (SAN) and the *atrioventricular node* (AVN) control the increase in heart rate during exercise. **(6 marks)**

c) When instructing their performers, coaches often try to ensure that practice conditions are as varied as possible, since *variability of practice* is supported by Schmidt's schema theory.

i) What are the main principles of *Schmidt's schema theory*? **(6 marks)**

ii) What implications does *Schmidt's schema theory* have for the way in which sports skills should be taught? **(2 marks)**

(Q2, May 2003)

3 a) Figure 1 shows phases of a tennis stroke.

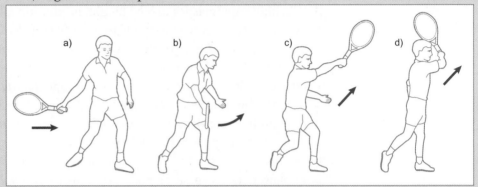

Fig. 1

What joint actions are taking place at:

i) the **right shoulder** during the sequence **b–c**

ii) the **right elbow** during the sequence **c–d**? **(2 marks)**

b) i) In the same sequence **c–d**, name the *agonist* causing the movements at the elbow joint, and name the type of muscle contraction involved. **(2 marks)**

ii) In which **plane** and around what **axis** does this elbow movement take place? **(2 marks)**

iii) **Name** and **sketch** a fully labelled diagram to show the lever system that operates at the elbow during this action. **(3 marks)**

c) Professional tennis players are able to serve the ball at very high speeds. It takes 0.17 seconds for the ball to reach the receiver once it has left the server's racket.

• The time taken by the receiver to decide on an action is approximately 0.15 seconds.

• The time taken for the receiver to play the return having decided on a stroke is 0.2 seconds.

Using the information provided, calculate the receiver's:

i) reaction time

ii) response time

iii) movement time. **(3 marks)**

d) Using your knowledge of information processing and decision-making, explain what strategies the receiver could use to return the ball successfully in situations such as that described in part (c). **(3 marks)**

e) Suggest reasons why novice performers often find it difficult to return a serve successfully, even when it is delivered at a speed that they should be able to respond to. **(3 marks)**

(Q1, January 2003)

Unit 2: Socio-cultural and historical effects on participation in physical activity and their influence on performance

Chapter 10: The changing nature of British society

Learning outcomes

By the end of this chapter you should be able to:
- trace the development of British society from the middle of the nineteenth century (the Victorian era) to the present day
- appreciate the term 'rational recreation' as opposed to 'popular recreation'
- understand the role and influence of the three distinct social classes (upper, middle and lower) on sport and society
- explore the growth in leisure time for the masses
- highlight the developments in transport, communications and technology as they influence sport in society
- understand the changing attitudes and influence of the church in the development of sport
- identify the significant developments in a variety of sports, including technical and administrative details.

KEY WORDS

Industrialization

Process in the eighteenth and nineteenth centuries when Britain moved from a predominantly agricultural base to one where the economy was dominated by manufacturing.

HOT TIPS

Although pre-industrial Britain is not directly examined, you need to have a reasonable understanding of this period in history in order to appreciate the significant developments that occurred in sport and in society.

Introduction

Before we can understand how sports have developed, we first have to appreciate that sport is not a separate entity but an integral part of society. For the purposes of this specification, you will need to understand three basic phases in British society:
- pre-industrial society
- **industrialization**
- post-industrial/advanced technological society.

It will soon become clear that the developments in sport tend to mirror the developments in society, for example as society began to become 'civilized', so, too, did many of the sporting recreations of the time. This was reflected in the development of rules, skills and etiquette for many games.

KEY WORDS

Civilizing of society

The evolution of human manners, in particular the practising of self-restraint in social situations. Codes of behaviour and etiquette became the norm. Sports became less violent in their nature.

Urbanization

The process whereby the mass of the population changes its lifestyle from living in villages and rural areas to living in towns and cities.

Popular recreation

Recreational pursuits that occurred before the Industrial Revolution. These activities were characterized by being played occasionally, by the lower classes, having few rules, reliant on physical force rather than skill and with limited structure.

We will chart some of the major social changes occurring during the Victorian era and into the twentieth century and then, most importantly, demonstrate the effect these changes would have on the development of sport and recreational activities.

Sport and leisure were no exceptions to the forward momentum and the **civilizing of society**. It was no coincidence that the birth of modern sport began in Britain, the first industrialized country in the world. Modern sport developed in an atmosphere where certain social and economic conditions occurred:

- industrialization
- effective communications
- **urbanization**
- affluent society
- a population with sufficient leisure time and surplus disposable income.

Pre-industrial Britain (approximately pre-1750) was characterized by the majority of the population living in rural areas and working on the land. The upper classes were the wealthy landowners who held political power. The working classes had little free time and their lives were harsh, but they had a strong sense of community that would be lost with the onset of industrialization. Due to this lack of free time, their recreations only took place occasionally and mostly on religious holidays and festivals. As they did not participate regularly in recreational activities, many of the activities did not develop structurally but retained their traditional nature over hundreds of years. The term given to this type of recreation was **popular recreation**, for example mob football. The peasants were also uneducated, as schooling was not to become compulsory until 1870, whereas the upper classes had been educated in their elite public schools for centuries.

Characteristics of popular recreation, for example mob football:

- being occasional due to little free time
- having only a few simple unwritten rules
- the activity being participation-based rather than spectator-based
- physical force rather than skill
- many injuries/violent
- lower-class involvement
- local rather than regional or national events
- limited structure, equipment and facilities.

The Victorian era (1839–1901)

The Victorian era (when Queen Victoria was on the throne) was from 1839 to 1901. This era witnessed a major transition in society. The image of Victorian Britain is that of a country with immense contrasts between rich and poor people, but it is also seen as a period when the nation was prosperous and stable. For our purposes, we need to have some understanding of life in Victorian times and into the twentieth century. In particular, we need to discover how these changing social and economic conditions affected leisure and the development of sport.

The Industrial Revolution (c.1750–1850) was in full swing during Victoria's reign and most people's lives had undergone dramatic changes, most notably the move from the countryside to the towns (urbanization) with their cramped living and working conditions.

The resulting change in working patterns from agriculture and cottage industries to working in factories posed problems for employers and employees unused to such regulated activities. In the middle of the nineteenth century, Britain was seen as 'the workshop of the world'.

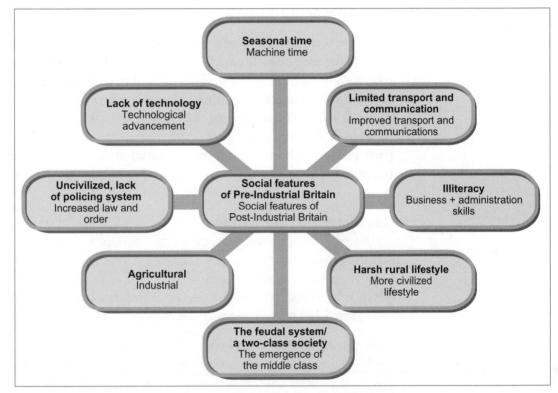

Fig.10.01 Pre- and post-industrial factors that influenced sport
Text used by permission of Sarah van Wely.

Britain was the first European country to undergo an industrial revolution with the growth of factory production replacing craft workshops, and its economy expanded. By the middle of the nineteenth century, Britain was the world's leading industrial power. Britain was the most highly specialized country in manufacturing: in 1901, fewer than ten per cent of its labour force worked in agriculture, and it was also the most urbanized country at this time. By 1851, half the population lived in towns or cities, and this had risen to three-quarters by 1901. The upsurge in the population was a visible sign of economic growth. Over the period of the Industrial Revolution, the population nearly trebled to 37 million by 1901.

Working conditions needed to be addressed as industrialization initially restricted the recreational opportunities of the working classes. The new urban population was a cause of some concern, particularly the hours that women and small children worked in the textile and coal industries. The working week was twelve hours a day, six days a week, and on the seventh day the working class were expected to attend church, so there was little time for rest and leisure. The term 'machine age' was coined and with it came a mixture of anticipation and anxiety. The material prosperity that was accumulating did so at a cost to the environment and people's lives. Issues such as urban squalor, spoiled landscapes and dislocated communities would have to be tackled.

Gradually, improvements were made. Numerous factory reforms were introduced (the Reform and Factory Act 1832, the Ten Hours Act 1847 and the Factory Act 1878) to try and combat this problem.

The drive towards new model trade unions was an attempt to provide some security for members. Gradually, the working classes enjoyed some more free time with the advent of the half-day Saturday, early closing for shop workers on Wednesdays and the granting of bank holidays from 1870 under Lubbock's Act. The concept of the bank holiday was a significant step forward in the provision of nationally recognized leisure time for all and particularly for those without the industrial muscle to insist on it. Wages began to increase, giving the working classes some disposable income.

Legacy for sport and recreation

Many of the traditional pastimes of the working classes, such as mob football, could not be accommodated. The cramped towns were now housing a vast amount of people but with few facilities. The combination of little free time, poor wages and poor health meant the working classes were restricted in their recreational opportunities.

Later, as conditions improved, the working classes were able to participate in more activities, and spectator sports and facilities began to develop. Increasing disposable income meant they had more money to spend on leisure. On the first ever August bank holiday, people set out on excursions to the seaside, by train, steamer and on foot, on an unprecedented scale. The cyclists covered the roads, and the town and city parks were full. Within twenty years, the bank holiday saw 500,000 people leave London for the coast and country.

Scientific and industrial invention thrived during the Victorian era. This was demonstrated in 1851 when Queen Victoria opened the Great Exhibition in the Crystal Palace, which was a testament to modern architectural design in iron and glass. Edison invented the first electric light bulb and improved numerous other inventions such as the telegraph, telephone and motion picture projector.

Legacy for sport and recreation

Scientific inventions were not confined to industry. Sports were being invented, such as rugby football, lawn tennis, basketball and volleyball. Sports equipment was being developed, such as the new lawn tennis kits, and the change in golf clubs and golf balls began to price working-class people out of a sport that had initially belonged to them. New technology like the steam press enabled the working classes to purchase cheap newspapers and interest in sport and leisure boomed. The invention of the bicycle added to the options of transport, particularly cheaper modes of transport, but also became an accepted leisure pursuit for ladies, for whom less restrictive, more practical clothing was designed, as in the article of clothing the 'bloomers'. Commercialization of leisure was well underway by the latter quarter of the nineteenth century.

Transport for people and goods began with rivers and that is the reason why many early towns were built close to waterways. Many aquatic activities, such as rowing and swimming, began as functional activities needed by those societies and later developed into sports, developing rules of competition. Roads came next with the gentry 'horse and carriage' and were later developed to accommodate the boom in cycling. The railway was the significant development in transport for the Victorian era, enabling goods, people and ideas to be transported nationally and internationally.

Legacy for sport and recreation

The railways encouraged the popularity of the excursion, such as day trips to the seaside. Work holidays also added to the establishment of the seaside resorts, with whole communities travelling together, re-creating the community spirit of pre-industrial Britain. Blackpool was developed for the workers in the Yorkshire textile industry and goods such as postcards, ice cream, fish and chips, and so on, all helped to redefine leisure as it evolved in the Victorian era. Outdoor and adventurous activities, such as rambling, fishing, cycling and mountaineering, were all given a boost as the railways allowed access to more isolated parts of the country, with return possible in a day. Football fixtures occurred further afield and spectators were increasingly able to travel with their team, leading to the 'home and away' tradition.

KEY WORDS

Rational recreation
The middle classes changed the recreations of the working classes, giving them rules and codes of conduct.

The old popular recreations were giving way to **rational recreation**. Popular recreations were finding it hard to survive in this 'newly' civilized and increasingly moral environment. The cramped living conditions resulted in a severe lack of space, making it impossible for popular recreations like mob football to survive. The middle and upper classes required disciplined and productive workers, and were also keen to suppress excessive behaviour amongst the working classes. This was exemplified by their popular recreations such as cock fighting and mob games. Crowds of working-class

HOT TIPS

Blood sports were merely a part of a violent and cruel society. The emergence of the middle classes, with their civilizing and moral impact, led to many of these activities being banned. Interestingly, today, the debate about fox hunting is continuing at the highest levels.

KEY WORDS

Philanthropists

People who practise performing charitable or benevolent actions.

people involved in riotous behaviour were considered a threat to the authorities, properties and productivity. It was deemed necessary to control leisure, as society was suffering political unrest in the form of a discontented workforce and appalling problems of public health.

Characteristics of rational recreation:
- regular participation
- complex written rules
- highly structured in nature
- being spectator-based as well as participation-based
- the need to use refined skills rather than force
- being a middle- to upper-class development
- being regionally and nationally based
- the use of sophisticated equipment and facilities.

Social reform during this period gathered momentum. The era was renowned for its attention to high morals and proper conduct, inspired by Queen Victoria and her husband, Prince Albert. The importance placed on civic conscience and social responsibility led to major developments in improving the lot of the poor. **Philanthropists**, or social reformers, emerged as influential voices. Working and living conditions of the poor were addressed, recreational facilities, such as parks and baths, began to be provided for the working classes.

Legacy for sport and recreation

Civic responsibility announced itself in the establishment of town parks by middle-class local government, council members or individual philanthropists. Reasons for the provision of parks were to improve the health of the population, discourage crime, to attract people away from alcohol, to encourage workers to participate in rational and rule-governed behaviour and to demonstrate a sense of social justice. Working men's clubs, institutes, Friendly Societies and libraries were also established in order to further the education of the working classes.

The influence of industrial patronage regarding leisure was not widespread, but some individual projects would be considered revolutionary even today. The Cadbury factory in Birmingham was proactive in improving the conditions of work and general living standards for their workers. They were the first company in England to use the half-day Saturday, and they built Bourneville Village, still in evidence today, with medical care, schools, a swimming pool and recreation grounds. They were keen on improving the fitness and health of their workers and, cynically, one might assume that they merely wanted to improve the productivity of their workforce. However, as Quakers, they also had a genuine concern for improving the lot of the poor.

Education became an issue. The need for an educated population who could work effectively under the new 'modern' production systems resulted in the introduction of compulsory state education from 1870. Up to this point, education had been the privilege of the upper classes in their elitist public schools.

Legacy for sport and recreation

The upper (and later the middle) classes developed many sports, particularly team games, via their public schools, and stressed the physical and moral benefits to be gained from participating in sport. This was a return to the Renaissance belief that the 'whole man' should be one who is intellectually, physically and spiritually developed (see Chapter 11 on the development of physical education).

The working classes in the state schools were not deemed worthy of recreational activities until much later in the twentieth century. They were to experience a tedious form of drill in an attempt to keep them disciplined, obedient, prepared for military life and healthy.

KEY WORDS

British Empire

British imperialists spread their forms of government, religion and culture, including sports, to those countries that they colonized.

The **British Empire** had expanded and was now so big that 'the sun never set on it'. The empire provided resources of raw materials for industry and markets for manufactured items. Britain exported its goods and its customs, government and religion, as well as its sporting recreations, to the rest of the world via soldiers, administrators, missionaries and so on. Overseas trade grew in importance with the expansion in manufacturing. America, or the 'New World' as it was known, was the big new destination for British goods. In 1800, nearly 60 per cent of Britain's exports crossed the Atlantic.

Legacy for sport and recreation

The British Empire allowed the import and export of sports. Polo was imported from India and cricket exported to the West Indies. The people involved in these sporting and cultural exchanges were soldiers, teachers, doctors, missionaries, engineers, clergy and so on.

KEY WORDS

Temperance movement

Restraint or moderation, especially abstinence from alcoholic drink.

The churches had expanded into the new urban areas to try to ensure that the working classes, now removed from their traditional lifestyles under the village priest and local landowner, would still be guided by religion. The church was disapproving of traditional popular recreations, such as mob football, as they were disorganized and lacked any moral learning. However, as numbers of parishioners gradually began to decline, the Church was to actively *use* rational sport to encourage attendance and instil moral codes of behaviour. In particular, they needed to attract the working classes away from the pubs. This was known as the **temperance movement**.

Legacy for sport and recreation

Now that many sports had been 'rationalized', the Church could support them as they had been civilized and could be used to instil a sense of morality in the working classes. They encouraged youth movements such as the Boys' Brigade, the Scouts and Sunday school teams. Everton and Aston Villa both started out as church teams. The churches also provided facilities such as church halls for recreation. In Birmingham, approximately a quarter of football clubs were directly connected to religious organizations between 1870 and 1885.

Muscular Christianity was an evangelical movement led by Charles Kingsley, who believed in the combination of the Christian and chivalric ideals of manliness. He believed healthy bodies were needed alongside healthy minds to serve God. However, sport was only valued for what it could achieve in moral terms.

In addition, humanitarian and religious organizations, such as the Young Men's Christian Association (YMCA), reflected the Victorian concern for the poor and needy of the period. Its aims were to develop high standards of Christian character through group activities and improve the spiritual, social and recreational life of young people. Again, this organization sought to *use* sport to achieve its aims. Through this organization came the invention of basketball and volleyball in America.

KEY WORDS

Middle class

The term was used from around the mid-eighteenth century to describe those people who were below the aristocracy in rank but above the workers.

Youth movements, such as the Boys' Brigade, the Church Lads' Brigade and the Scouts, all emerged as part of this need by the **middle class**es to 'control' the behaviour of the working classes in a period of potential social unrest. These youth organizations shared some basic similarities. They provided recreational activities for working-class youths who needed a leisure outlet, and they provided religious, moral and militaristic values, deemed important by the social elite. The militaristic element was very strong at this time as there was always the threat of war.

The Boer War took place in South Africa between 1899 and 1902, resulting in the acquisition of the Transvaal and the Orange Free State by the British Empire. Massive losses were suffered by the British troops, and this was blamed on the unfitness, lack of discipline and general poor health of the working classes.

Legacy for sport and recreation

Military drill was to provide a basis for the early experiences of school physical activity for the working classes. It was intended to raise the general health and fitness of the working classes, instil discipline and obedience, teach weapon familiarity and prepare them for the military. Even after the military content was removed (1904), drill-style school exercise was to remain for a couple more decades.

'Social class' was also a term that was being redefined during this era. Pre-industrial Britain was generally split into two main classes – upper and lower. The middle classes were to emerge as a result of the Industrial Revolution.

The middle classes emerged when entrepreneurs realized the potential to make a lot of money. Having made great fortunes through trade, the middle classes then converted this into political power in the Reform Act 1832. They were able to ensure that political decisions reflected *their* interests rather than the interests of the upper classes alone. They were striving to create a society based on merit and personal achievement rather than one based on privileged birth. They emphasized competition, thrift, prudence and self-reliance as necessary qualities for social advancement. Through education reform, schemes of civic improvement and the growth of the market, the Victorian middle classes were also influential in improving the lot of the working classes. The increasing scale of industry and overseas trade fuelled the need for banks, insurance companies, shipping and railways. The expansion of local government and increasing powers of government provided the strata of professions such as lawyers, civil servants, teachers, doctors, and so on. The age was ripe for the domination of society by the middle classes.

HOT TIPS

Governing bodies, even today, tend to be controlled by the middle/upper classes, whose values may seem to belong to a past age.

The middle classes were also the most religious of the social classes and became the new moral voice of society. A good example of the combination of political power and morality could be seen in the banning of cruel blood sports (for example, the Cruelty to Animals Act 1840), previously enjoyed by both the upper and lower classes.

Legacy for sport and recreation

The upper classes had enjoyed rational recreations, such as real tennis, for many centuries. Their recreations were characterized by having early organizational features, such as rules, and sophisticated facilities and equipment. However, the upper classes were also similar to the working classes in that they enjoyed the combination of alcohol, gambling and cruel blood sports. The upper classes often acted as patrons towards sporting events and individual performers. Today we would call them sponsors. An example would be the Duke of Cumberland acting as a patron to a working-class fighter. The fighter would fight for the name of his patron and the patron could gain financially out of a successful arrangement.

The newly emerging middle classes, who wanted to emulate the lifestyle of the upper classes, tried to disassociate themselves from the rowdy pursuits of the lower classes. The religious and moralizing middle classes were, however, suspicious of the decadence that was associated with leisure by the upper classes and wanted to formulate activities of their own that would also serve some social function and thus be of some purpose to society. Through leisure, the middle classes wanted to stabilize and transform society by the adoption of rational recreations. Sports like cricket, football and rugby began to be organized with national

Fig. 10.02 Lawn tennis was played by the middle classes

competitions such as the FA Cup. New sports were invented such as lawn tennis (Figure 10.02), acting as a substitute for real tennis, and the bicycle (the urban substitute for the horse) became a familiar sight in Britain.

With the growth of railways, people began to travel more and day trips became affordable. The administration of sport became largely the responsibility of the middle classes who used their organization skills to establish clubs and governing bodies. Governing bodies were needed as sports became more popular, so an organization to oversee the running of each sport was important. With their accumulated wealth, they were able to buy land, build facilities and establish what are now considered very British traditions such as the Wimbledon Lawn Tennis and Croquet Club.

The working classes had lost their old recreational pursuits with the advent of industrialization. Early working and living conditions in the urban areas were poor, with long hours, little free time and low wages. They were to be introduced to the rational forms of recreation by the middle classes, who imposed their own value systems on the working classes, such as teamwork, respect for rules and fair play. The rise in spectator sports, particularly football, was no coincidence with so many people in a small area needing regular and exciting entertainment.

TASK 1

1 Outline the negative and positive social factors that affected the recreational opportunities of the working classes in the nineteenth century.
2 Why did the control of sport pass from the upper classes to the middle classes in the nineteenth century?

Table 10.01 highlights some of the distinctions that can be made about the different social classes in the Victorian era.

Table 10.01

Social class	Characteristics and legacy for sport and recreation
Upper class	• Also called the aristocracy/nobility/gentry • Had ample leisure time, opportunities and choice – often termed the 'leisured class' • Role in life was to be landowners, owners, employers, officers, diplomats – that is, the leaders in society • Enjoyed cruel blood sports and the gambling and alcohol associated with leisure • Enjoyed traditional recreational activities such as field sports, cricket, real tennis • Many of these activities would have been rational in nature • Education – attended the elite public schools and were influential in developing team games for character-building qualities • Established the amateur code, which had a monetary and social class distinction. Amateurs should not be paid for participation in sport and many sports such as rowing also dictated which social classes could take part
Middle class	• Emerged as a result of the Industrial Revolution; also called the 'nouveau riche' (new rich) • Wanted to copy the lifestyle of the upper classes and disassociate themselves from the lower classes, for example lawn tennis was a substitute for real tennis, the bicycle an urban substitute for the horse • Became the moral force in society with many reforms in working conditions and the banning of cruel blood sports • Became the administrators of governing bodies, and agents and promoters of sport
Lower class	• Also called the working class • Industrial Revolution caused a major change in living and working conditions: urbanization, regimented factory work • Enjoyed popular recreations such as mob football and cock fighting until banned by the middle and upper classes • Tended to become the professionals in sport as they needed to earn money from sport in order to make a living • Women from this group of people had the least recreational opportunities of all

Industrialization was to provide new ways of defining **male and female roles**. In particular, the sense of separating male and female social roles emerged (it is important to remember, though, that these roles were also dependent on the social class these women belonged to). The female role was idealized by Queen Victoria herself as representing femininity, which was centred on the family, motherhood and respectability. She was called the 'mother of the nation'.

In the late industrial era, the female role was cast in the private sphere and the male role to the public sphere of business, commerce and politics. However, the middle-class female was also expected to work for the service of others, displaying innate moral goodness. Many women took on the role of philanthropists, actively visiting those less well off than themselves such as widows, orphans and the sick. It was from this type of work that the first feminists began to demand more rights for women. This was to take on a political mission, starting with better education and employment conditions for middle-class ladies, better wages and working conditions for working-class women, and culminating in the vote for women in the early part of the twentieth century (1917).

TASK 2

Why would working-class women experience less recreation than their male counterparts?

Legacy for sport and recreation

As female liberation emerged, the physical activities enjoyed by women began to be more active. Therefore the tight corsets and heavy materials that women had been required to wear began to change in favour of less restrictive clothing.

Working-class women had the least opportunities of all the social classes. They were expected to work *and* adopt the domestic role, so any form of leisure time was severely restricted. They were poor, with little political power, and their education was very limited.

Middle- and upper-class ladies did experience more freedom of movement than the working-class woman. The middle- and upper-class lady was gradually encouraged to demand more physical forms of recreation. Activities such as croquet were ousted by lawn tennis. Fashions began to change as more physical movement became acceptable. The girls' public schools began to copy the boys' schools in academic and sporting terms. Games like hockey, netball (a derivative of basketball from America) and tennis were acceptable activities as they adhered to dress codes, had rules and could be played in the privacy of a school, club or garden.

KEY WORDS

Amateurism

Based on the ideal that participation in sport should be for the love of it rather than for monetary gain.

HOT TIPS

For this specification, you will not be examined directly on amateurism and professionalism. However, it is useful to understand these concepts as they are integral to the development of many sports and reflect the social class distinctions of the era.

Two crucial sporting cultures were to collide in the nineteenth-century British sport scene. They were the codes of **amateurism** and professionalism. Amateurism was the dominant force in Britain, as it was the code established by the gentry in their public schools. The early amateurs were drawn from the elite social classes, hence the term 'gentleman amateur' – that is, one who is from the gentry or upper classes and who does not earn money from the sport. Amateurism was also concerned with the manner in which the sport was played. Winning alone was not considered important but *how* you performed was seen as being of equal importance. You were expected to play fairly and with respect for your opponents. Many believe that this value, still promoted in British sport today, has held us back when it comes to being hungry for success at major sporting events. It is in direct contrast to the American belief that 'winning is the most important and only thing!'

Professional sport is a much older concept than amateurism and can be traced as far back as the gladiators of Ancient Rome. Similar to a professional footballer today, these gladiators were also paid for their performances, trained seriously and provided entertainment to the masses. There are clear similarities between the societies of Ancient Greece and Rome and the first industrialized country in the nineteenth century (industrialization, effective communications, urbanization, affluent society, a population with sufficient leisure time and surplus disposable income). However, in Britain, the concept of professional sport became tainted with social class snobbery. The working classes needed to be paid to play sport, as they could not afford to take time off work without pay. In 1894, the Rugby Football Union and the Northern Union split due to the refusal of the sports authorities to allow northern players enough leisure time to compete on the same basis as players in the south. The issue of '**broken-time payments**' was to eventually lead to the professionalization of sports such as football and rugby.

TASK 3

What are the similarities between a gladiator in Ancient Rome and a professional footballer today?

Twentieth-century Britain

The Edwardian era corresponds with the relatively short reign of King Edward VII (1901–10). The Edwardian *style* broadly encompasses the years up to World War I (1914). The era was termed the 'gilded age' as the effects of industrialization were beginning to benefit many people's lives. Many might say that the ocean liner the *Titanic* epitomized the lavish excesses being enjoyed at the time.

The Edwardian era continued the advancements made in scientific and technological progress. Material novelties epitomized this new age, such as the telegraph, telephone, mass-produced typewriters, elevators and so on. The era also ushered in the first mass-produced motorcar and many domestic gadgets were invented for the home.

The new forms of sport depended on consumer goods and services such as the new leisure industries. Ordinary people realized that what had previously been the privilege of the few was now within their reach, with the growing assumption that they also had a right to leisure. Much of this depended on the availability of spare cash and the ability for the masses to pay for their pleasure.

Sport became ever more organized with bureaucracies, finances, performers, officials and spectators all becoming part of the public's imagination through the many publications devoted to sport. What began as local and regional events became national and then international affairs controlled by international committees such as FIFA in 1904.

Social consequences of World War I (1914–18) for sport and recreation

Women began to change their perceptions of themselves and the outside world as they took on many of the men's jobs during World War I, and also enjoyed the escape of the dance halls and cinema, which was to give them a glimpse of even more possibilities for their own lives. Women had contributed to the war effort both in factories and on the land. There was some relaxation of their domestic and social roles, and they emerged more independent and confident. However, working-class women were still much more restricted than men and middle-class ladies.

The establishment of the Women's League of Health and Beauty demonstrated the changes during this era, especially the increase in physical activity for women in society and the growing knowledge about the therapeutic effects of exercise. Established in 1930, the League was based on a system of exercises structured and graded to suit different needs and abilities and taught by highly trained instructors. The exercises were based on remedial health exercises and after-work classes were put on for mill workers, office and shop employees. A feature of the organization was public displays of large groups of women performing movement to music.

Anti-militarism was demonstrated in various ways. There was a mood to build a new country and a determination not to see a repeat of conflict on such a global scale again. The country returned to its lavish living amongst the upper and middle classes, and the recreations of the working classes continued to increase in variety and amount.

Changing views of children were reflected in the Syllabuses of Physical Training in the state schools. They were taking more account of children's ages and stages of development, with lessons becoming more informal than the previous drill style of teaching. More fun and play activities were being introduced with a more interactive teaching style.

Entertainment

The cinema was to take over from the church and the pub as meeting the needs of ordinary people – it was cheap, entertaining, sociable and educational. Broadcasting via the wireless dominated almost every home, and the peak audience went into the millions and also caused a growth in home-based entertainment. The development in the motorcar trade gave many people a chance to escape to new environments under their own steam as well as the coach trips, which could collect people on their street corners and give a sense of community at the same time. Travel firms catering for low-income groups thrived at this time. In the 1930s, some 7 million people went to Blackpool, and the seaside resorts were becoming even more popular. This trend in holidaymaking was also made popular by the private agreements between firms and workers for 'holidays with pay', which would be covered by legislation by 1938. So a major shift in social thinking had occurred. Before World War I, it became recognized that all workers had the right to a holiday – by the late 1930s, it was recognized through legislation that everyone had a right to 'holidays with pay'. Outdoor recreational activities, as an opportunity to enjoy the countryside and fresh air, became a national pastime, also made popular by the success of the Scout movement and similar organizations. Organizations increased to cope with the growing numbers of walkers, cyclists, climbers and campers. Football continued to thrive even in the worst hit depression areas of Britain and many players were drawn from these areas.

Commercialisation

HOT TIPS

Sport was becoming more organized, commercialized, defined by social class and of national importance.

The greatest change in the 1950s (following World War II) was the unprecedented consumer power throughout all levels of society. The increase in wages, the proliferation of domestic hardware and the opportunities for hire purchase led to the time when 'people had never had it so good'. The television set was to further transform the leisure interests of a nation. It was to provide a relatively cheap source of entertainment, education and leisure. It was also blamed for a decline in church attendance, cinemas and even attendance at football matches. Major sporting events, such as the Olympic Games and World Cup soccer, could be watched by hundreds of millions. Individual sports were becoming more popular than they had been, such as golf and tennis, and many sports were becoming multi-million pound businesses, (motorcyclists and racing drivers included), the majority of the money coming from advertising, sponsorship and TV coverage rather than gate receipts as in the past.

The growth in municipal facilities allowed more people to participate purely for the enjoyment factor and many people were prepared to spend vast amounts of money for their children to experience more expensive sports. Although commercialization of sport is often criticized, it has also provided a more varied cultural diet for the mass of the population. The need to win has pervaded all sports, particularly at the highest levels, as the prize for success became so lucrative. The fortunes of cricket reflect these changes. The organizers accepted the need for a change in attitude in favour of the new commercial interests – the traditional three-day matches have given way to shorter, more exciting contests with financial backing coming from the big banks.

Table 10.02 summarizes the major points of each era.

The history of football

It is a useful exercise to trace the history of certain sports and understand the influence that changes in society had on their development. Football is a classic example of a traditional working-class popular recreation being

Table 10.02

Early nineteenth century (c.1800–30)	Late nineteenth century (c.1870–1900)	Early twentieth century (c.1900–30)	Mid-twentieth century (c.1930–60)	Late twentieth century to present day (1960 onwards)
• Rural • Agricultural • Population live in countryside • Two social classes: upper and lower/working • Education for upper class only in public/private schools • Sport mainly in form of 'popular' recreation: limited rules and organization, for example, mob football	• Industrialization • Factory work/poor conditions (72 hour week/low pay) • Emergence of middle class through ability to make money through trade • Education for working classes • State school education began in 1870 • Sport became rationalized via public schools: developed rules and structure • Amateur code strictly defined for upper and middle classes (do not get paid for sport and winning not as important as how you play) • Professional: working-class people needed to earn money • Strict divide between the two classes	• Increase in technology • Communications • Improving work conditions (less hours of work/more pay) • Trade unions/Labour Party • World War I (1914–18) • More international competition • England dominating world in sport • Professional sport increasing	• Commercialization • World War II (1939–45) • 1930s was economic depression • Lessening division between amateur/professional • 'Open' competitions • Professional sport took over from amateur sport • England losing dominance • Other countries catching up and taking winning more seriously	• Globalization • More people spectating than participating • Media/satellite • Professional sport has more status than amateur sport

HOT TIPS

You will be learning much more than the history of football – you will also gain an insight into Victorian and twentieth-century society.

transformed into a rational, rule-bound, disciplined activity, believed to possess the qualities that would bring society together in a common aim.

Read the following account of the history of football and pay particular attention to the developments occurring in society, then attempt the questions at the end.

Popular or mob version

The game that flourished in the British Isles from the eighth to the nineteenth centuries had a considerable variety of local and regional versions, which were subsequently to form the present-day sports of association football and rugby football. At this stage of the game's development, the term 'popular recreation' is used to suggest they were initially disorganized, violent, more spontaneous and usually played by an indefinite number of players. Frequently, the games took the form of a heated contest between whole village communities or townships – through streets, village squares, across fields, hedges, fences and streams. Kicking was allowed, as in fact was almost everything else.

It is certain that in many cases pagan customs, especially fertility rites, played a major role. These games were played only occasionally, such as holy days, as these were the times when the lower classes enjoyed some free time.

Shrovetide football, as it was called, belonged in the 'mob football' category, where the number of players was unlimited and the rules were fairly vague (for example, according to an ancient handbook from Workington in England, any means could be employed to get the ball to its target with the exception of murder and manslaughter!). The repeated unsuccessful intervention of the authorities shows how powerless they were to restrict it in spite of their condemnation and threats of severe punishment.

Reasons for the disapproval of authorities

- With the spread of Puritanism, 'frivolous' amusements (and sport happened to be classified as such) constituted a violation of peace on the Sabbath. Football remained a taboo on the Sabbath for some time.
- Resentment of football was mainly for practical reasons. The game was regarded as a public disturbance that resulted in damage to property; for example, in Manchester in 1608, football was banned because so many windows had been smashed.
- An industrialized society required a disciplined workforce who was punctual and fit for work. The excesses of mob football resulted in many injuries and time off work.

Rationalization of football

The game remained essentially rough, violent and disorganized. A change did not come about until the beginning of the nineteenth century when a game previously played by lower-class 'village boys' was taken into the public schools by the sons of the gentry. In this new environment of unlimited and unsupervised free time, it was possible to make innovations and refinements to the game. This can be referred to as the technical development of games, where the skills, tactics, facilities and general organization of the game developed.

KEY WORDS

Codification

The systematic organization of laws or rules into one recognized system or code.

Games cult

Intense interest and devotion to the pursuit of team games by boys within their public schools.

Each school developed its own adaptation and, at times, these varied considerably. At this point in time, the public schools could only play inter-house competitions, as all schools did not recognize the same rules. Inter-school matches could not take place until **codification** had occurred via the universities.

All these early styles were given a great boost when it was recognized in educational circles that football could actually be beneficial educationally. The Clarendon Commission, a government report on public schools in the 1860s, formally recognized the educational value of team games. What is more, it was accepted that it also constituted a useful distraction from less desirable occupations such as heavy drinking and gambling.

A new attitude began to permeate the game, eventually leading to a '**games cult**' in public schools. This materialized when it was observed how well the team game served to encourage such fine character building qualities as loyalty, selflessness, co-operation, subordination and deference to the team spirit. Games became an integral part of the school curriculum. A more organized form of football matched the concept of athleticism (physical endeavour with moral integrity), a movement developed in public schools, and Muscular Christianity (healthy bodies and minds to serve God), a movement developed in society. As sports became rationalized, developing Sunday school teams and church youth movements became acceptable, particularly as a tool in making the Church appear attractive to the young. The moral benefits that could be gained from observing 'rule-governed' activities were stressed rather than 'sport for sport's sake'.

The birth of the governing body for football – the Football Association – occurred on 26 October 1863. Only eight years after its foundation, the Football Association already had 50 member clubs. The first football competition in the world was started in the same year – the FA Cup, which preceded the League Championship by seventeen years.

The rational game of football was introduced to the working classes via the churches, schools and workplace. In the industrial heartlands, football was to be reclaimed by the working classes and was to be called 'the game of the people'. They began to make broken-time payments, leading to the eventual professionalizing of the game. The southern amateurs were to eventually be eclipsed by the northern professionals. Similarly to today, whenever a sport becomes professional, training methods and the importance given to winning led to rapidly improving standards of performance.

International matches were being staged in Great Britain before football had hardly been heard of in Europe. The first was played in 1872 and was contested by England and Scotland.

This sudden boom of organized football, accompanied by staggering crowds of spectators, brought with it certain problems with which other countries were not confronted until much later on. It was professionalism. This practice grew rapidly and the Football Association found itself obliged to legalize professionalism as early as 1885.

The spread of football outside Great Britain, mainly due to the British influence abroad, started slowly, but it soon gathered momentum and the game spread rapidly to all parts of the world. This international football community grew steadily, although it sometimes met with obstacles and setbacks. In 1912, 21 national associations were already affiliated to the *Fédération Internationale de Football Association* (FIFA). By 1925, the number had increased to 36. In 1930, the year of the first World Cup, it was 41; in 1938, 51, and in 1950, after the interval caused by World War II, the number had reached 73. At present, after the 2000 Ordinary FIFA Congress, FIFA has 204 members in every part of the world.

The maximum wage was abolished in 1961 after George Eastham challenged Newcastle United's right to refuse him a transfer in a court of law. The 'retain and transfer' system had previously existed unchallenged and now a player had the right to decide his own destiny. It was time for market forces to rule.

TASK 4

1 Suggest three characteristics of mob football.
2 What social and economic changes led to the rationalization of football?
3 How did the public schools contribute to the technical development of games?
4 What values did the public schools bring to the game of football?
5 Why was the Football Association formed in 1863?

TASK 5

Research the history of cricket, lawn tennis and/or rugby football, paying attention to the social factors influencing their development.

Revise as you go!

1 Which social class was mostly involved in popular recreation?
2 What kind of football was an example of popular recreation?
3 Why did popular recreation decline?
4 Give three characteristics of rational recreation.
5 Give three reasons to account for the type of leisure the upper classes enjoyed in the nineteenth century.
6 Which social group devised the concept of amateurism in the nineteenth century?
7 Why did professional football become so popular in the nineteenth century?
8 What does 'YMCA' stand for?
9 What effect did the middle classes have on sport and recreation in the nineteenth century?
10 Why did working-class women have the least recreational opportunities in nineteenth-century society?
11 The Victorian era was a period of social reform. What were the intentions of the numerous Factory Acts during this time?
12 Which factors caused organized sport to expand rapidly during the period 1901–18?

Chapter 11: The development of physical education

Learning outcomes

By the end of this chapter you should be able to:

- understand the development of physical education from the nineteenth century to the present day
- appreciate the legacy of the nineteenth-century public schools in their rationalizing of mob games and creation of an educational context for team games
- know about athleticism and Muscular Christianity with their concepts of character building, loyalty and leadership
- outline the role of the sixth form and social control
- trace the development of state school physical activity, from drill to physical training to physical education, and understand the rationale behind the changes
- compare the Syllabuses of Physical Training, particularly the early syllabuses of 1909 and 1919, with the last syllabus in 1933
- understand how the post-1950 publication of *Moving and Growing* influenced the present-day scene in terms of child-centred learning through the movement approach and greater curriculum breadth
- use knowledge of the past to help you appreciate the current situation with the National Curriculum – its structure, objectives and reasons for being
- understand the role of government through a century of educational changes, particularly the level of government control over education.

KEY WORDS

Public school
A private, independent, fee-paying school.

HOT TIPS

It is important to understand who the schools were catering for, their characteristics and overall purpose.

If you have already read the section on the development of football (page xx), you will already have gained some knowledge of the nineteenth-century public schools.

Introduction

In this chapter we will begin to study the development of physical education from a chronological viewpoint, which means we will firstly look at the legacy of the nineteenth-century **public school**s. These schools were established well before any state schooling was thought of and is therefore a reasonable place to begin our study of physical education.

Public schools

Public schools have a long tradition in Britain dating back to the original nine schools of Eton, Harrow, Rugby, Charterhouse, St Paul's, Winchester, Merchant Taylors', Westminster and Shrewsbury. These schools were very prestigious and only catered for the upper classes in Victorian society, that is, those that could afford to send their sons there and who had a social standing of the highest calibre.

During the nineteenth century, the middle classes emerged with their new found wealth and desire to emulate the lifestyles of the upper classes. They were not welcomed in the established gentry schools and were to build their own copies, which were called proprietary colleges, such as Marlborough and Clifton.

- **Aims**

The nineteenth-century public schools were aiming to educate the future leaders of society in their roles as politicians, lawyers, doctors and so on. Leadership skills, as well as the behaviour befitting a gentleman, were considered vital ingredients in the boys' education. Through education, the boys were taught respect for social order and prepared to serve their country in whatever capacity was required of them.

- **Characteristics**

These schools for the upper and middle classes were very prestigious establishments. They were fee-paying and therefore elitist, as only a small section of society could afford to send their sons to them. They were institutions run on a hierarchical structure with the prefects or sixth form having control over the younger boys. They were single sex, firstly for the sons of the gentry and later, for their daughters. As there were only a few schools, they were often a long way from the boys' homes and the boys had to board. The boys would leave home at an early age and would have been institutionalized for many years during term time. This institutional lifestyle was to have a profound impact on the characters of the boys as they learnt their place in the hierarchical structure. The older boys would become prefects in the sixth form and would have younger boys – fags – to serve them. The bullying that arose from this situation could be harsh and frightening.

- **Physical activities**

Originally, the boys had many unsupervised afternoons and often caused problems in local areas as they trespassed on local landowners' property, engaged in poaching and gambling and were generally out of the control of the masters/teachers. The authorities disapproved of many of the boys' activities, as they took place off school grounds, had no moral qualities and brought the school's reputation into disrepute. The boys participated in many types of physical activities such as swimming, cross-country running, fighting, racket games and so on. However, team games would become their dominant recreational activity for a number of reasons, not least because the schools were under pressure from the government to control the behaviour of the boys. A government report in 1864, the Clarendon Commission, recognized the educational value of team games.

- **Technical development of games**

The boys arriving from their villages would bring versions of mob games and country pursuits, such as coursing and fishing, with them and would participate regularly in their spare time. The mob games were often violent and disorderly; they had few rules as they were played by the working classes in society. The masters realized the potential of these games in channelling the boys' energies and in keeping them on the school grounds. The schools would only allow the mob versions to be played if they were given rules. Mob football, played by the working classes in their villages, was now to change forever:

- it was played regularly
- it was given rules
- boundaries were reduced
- the number of players was restricted
- the equipment and facilities became more sophisticated
- a division of labour was introduced with positional roles
- tactical and strategic play evolved
- leadership roles in the form of captain were highly respected
- a competition structure was devised, initially through the house system
- individual school rules gave way to nationally recognized rules (codification).

Many of the schools developed their own unique games, mostly as a result of the architectural features of their own schools and, for many, the traditions are retained as a testament to their heritage.

> **Account of the Eton wall game**
> It is not known exactly when the Eton wall game was first played, but the first recorded game was in 1766. The first of the big St Andrew's Day matches – between the Collegers and the Oppidans – was probably in 1844. The rules must obviously have been more or less agreed by then, but they were not actually printed and published until five years later.
>
> The rules have been revised from time to time since 1849, but the game has remained essentially the same. The field of play is a fairly narrow strip, about five metres wide, running alongside a not quite straight brick wall, built in 1717, and about 110 metres from end to end. As in all forms of football, each side tries to get the ball down to the far end and then score. Players are not allowed to handle the ball, not allowed to let any part of their bodies except feet and hands touch the ground, not allowed to strike or hold their opponents, and there are also exceedingly strict 'offside' rules (no passing back and no playing in front); apart from that, almost anything goes.

KEY WORDS

Social control
Process whereby society seeks to ensure conformity to the dominant norms and values of that society

Blues
Term used at Oxford and Cambridge universities where sport performers were awarded a 'colour' for playing in the university team. In the nineteenth century, 'blues' often returned to their old schools to assist in the coaching of sporting activities.

A striking feature of the early organization of the games in public schools was that the boys organized the activities themselves. This was called '**self-government**' and gave the boys many organizational skills, which they would use later on in life. Games committees were set up by the boys. The hierarchical structure amongst the boys also allowed the prefects to organize the younger boys and could be seen as a form of **social control**. Initially, the masters had little to do with the organization and it was only later that **blues** would be recruited as valuable members of staff in helping the school achieve notable victories on the field of play. By this time, the games cult had taken over and success on the sports field would be used by headmasters in order to impress future parents. Fixtures were reported in the press and the 'sports day' became a public relations exercise to the 'old boys', parents and governors. The headmasters began to support the increasing use of sport by employing blues from universities who could help coach the teams as well as providing facilities, time and funds, in fact very similar to a headmaster today.

TASK 1

Make a list of moral qualities we believe are learnt through team games.

Moral qualities began to be assigned to team games in the nineteenth-century public schools. We have already stated how the government wanted the boys' activities to be more closely supervised and orderly. At the same time, in society, many changes were taking place, especially the civilizing and disciplining of the working classes. The middle and upper classes were also needed to be seen to display higher moral qualities. Thomas Arnold, the head of Rugby School, only encouraged team games for the moral qualities he thought the boys could gain from participating in the activities. He did not revere games for their own sake, only for the purpose they could serve. He believed the moral qualities of teamwork, loyalty, bravery, courage, decision-making and gentlemanly conduct could be acquired through team games. The individual was not as important as the team and winning should be sought in a sporting manner. Winning was to become more important later on and many people began to feel that the cult of athleticism had gone too far.

HOT TIPS

In the nineteenth century, the appreciation of a healthy lifestyle was more important than the homage to fitness that we pay today.

Athleticism (see Table 11.01) was a movement that began in the public schools that was devoted to the combination of physical endeavour with moral integrity. This movement ran parallel to the Muscular Christianity movement, amateurism and Olympism. All these concepts embraced the physical and moral benefits of participation in rational sporting activities. They have been the legacy of British sport in which we play down the importance of winning and instead stress that how you take part is more important. These were very much the values of the middle and upper classes in the nineteenth century and reflected a lifestyle of ease and few monetary worries.

Table 11.01 Athleticism

Physical endeavour	Activities	Moral integrity
• Appreciation of health and fitness	• Rugby	• Sportsmanship
• Toughen up an indulgent society	• Football	• Teamwork
• Competitive in a competitive society	• Cricket	• Honour/loyalty
• Combat tendency to over-study	• Racquets	• Leadership/response to leadership
		• The high status held by the elite games players

TASK 2

How would the nineteenth-century rational game of rugby football match the concept of athleticism?

HOT TIPS

If you are asked to match the concept of athleticism to a specific activity, you need to say what the similarities are; for example, teamwork. The converse could be required, for example, how would gymnastics not reflect the values of athleticism?

Muscular Christianity (see Table 11.02) was a movement begun by Charles Kingsley in the nineteenth century. It was an evangelical movement combining the Christian and chivalric ideals of manliness. It included the belief that healthy bodies were needed alongside healthy minds in order to serve God. The muscular Christians only supported rational activities, that is, those activities that were governed by rules and codes of behaviour.

Table 11.02 Comparison of atheleticism and muscular Christianity

Athleticism	Muscular Christianity
• Manliness/physical robustness	• Working for a team/loyalty to the cause
• Pursuit of physical endeavour/effort/striving	• Conforming to the rules/principle of fair play
• Appreciating the value of healthy exercise/fitness	• Playing honourably more important than winning
• Accepting the discipline of rule-regulated activity	• Use of 'God-given' abilities
• Moral integrity	• Performance dedicated to God

HOT TIPS

In the nineteenth century, the combination of the physical and moral was of paramount importance.

What has been the legacy of the nineteenth-century public schools? We still believe today in teaching team games for their character-building qualities and believe learning how to be competitive is still an important part of modern life. Many schools adopt a competitive fixtures afternoon as well as house systems, and many have established their own traditions of excellence.

KEY WORDS

Melting pot

The different public school versions of the games came together at the universities where a national interpretation of rules was produced.

Table 11.03 Effects of the public schools and universities on the development of sports

Public schools	Spread of athleticism into society	Universities
• Village games brought to schools	'Old boys' as they left school took on various positions as:	• A **melting pot** to the individual school rules
• Played regularly in free time	• officers in the military – spread games to the troops	• Rules codified
• Individual school rules linked to unique architectural features of the schools	• employers – spread games to their employees via factory teams and provision of time and facilities	• Technical developments made to sports
• House competitions	• clergy – spread games to their parishioners such as Sunday school teams	• Improved standards of performance
• Codified rules		• New activities developed
• Inter-school fixtures	• teachers to the pupils	
• Blues as teachers	• engineers/diplomats and so on across the British Empire	

State school education

Table 11.04 Development of state school education and physical activities

Dates	Developments in state schooling	Physical activities
Pre-1870	No formal state education – some patchy church provision	
1870	Forster Education Act – foundations of state education laid	Drill training linked to Swedish gymnastics
1899–1902	Boer War	Military drill to be introduced via the Model Course
1902–04	War Office exercises	The Model Course
1904/1909/1919	**Centralized** government control of physical activity in state schools	Early Syllabuses of Physical Training
1933	Last centralized Syllabus of Physical Training	Content more varied
1944	Butler Education Act	More of a recreational focus for schools
1952	Influence of **child-centred** learning in primary schools	*Moving and Growing* – publication for primary schools
1988	Education Reform Act National Curriculum introduced	Wider range of activities to be taught with attainment levels

KEY WORDS

Centralized

To draw under central control – the government directs policy across a country to seek some uniformity.

Child-centred

Basing a programme of study around a child's physical, cognitive, social and emotional needs.

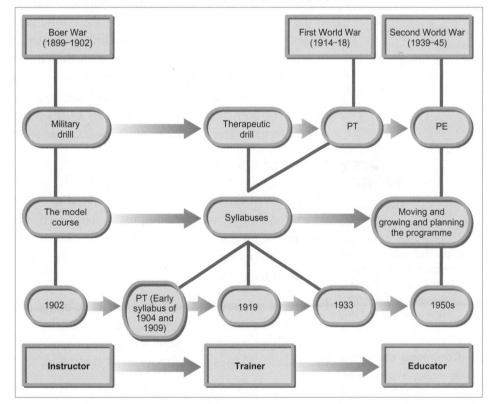

Fig. 11.01 Twentieth-century development in state elementary schools
Text used by permission of Sarah van Wely.

Prior to 1870, the working classes had no formal education other than that provided by some parishes. With the introduction of the Education Act 1870, it was soon to become compulsory for all children to attend a state school. This was met with mixed feelings – it was not immediately popular with the working classes as the children would no longer be working and they would lose vital income.

- **Aims**

The purpose of the state schools was to provide an education for the working classes. There were various reasons for this. Many social reformers and philanthropists had worked hard to secure a better lifestyle for the working classes and keep young children away from unsafe factory work, and employers were increasingly needing a more disciplined and educated workforce. However, the working classes needed to acquire basic skills – the three Rs (reading, writing and arithmetic), and the fourth R would be religious education, which was an important part of state education for many years. It was a way of instilling moral values, espoused by the middle classes, as church attendances were falling. The working classes were going to be the workers, obeying commands from their employers, therefore discipline and obedience were important values for them to learn rather than the leadership and decision-making skills that were being promoted in the public schools for the middle and upper classes.

- **Characteristics**

Experiences for the working-class children in state schools were very different to those of the sons of the gentry in their public schools. Small, cramped spaces with no recreational facilities imposed restrictions on the activities they could offer. This was combined with the philosophy that the working classes at the latter end of the nineteenth century would have no need of recreation. These schools were built in local areas, were day schools and catered for both sexes. Most age groups were taught together. These schools were also to be free of charge, in stark contrast to the public schools.

KEY WORDS

Therapeutic

A term relating to curative practices to maintain health. This was a popular term in the nineteenth century when linked to exercise and the poor health of the working classes.

Command-obey style

Teaching style in which the teacher adopts an authoritarian manner, making all the decisions with no input from the group.

- **Physical activities**

Swedish gymnastics formed the basis of early state school physical activity. The Board of Education favoured the Swedish variety over the German style, which required gymnastic equipment. The Swedish system was based on **therapeutic** principles and on the scientific knowledge of the body at the time. The exercises were free standing and free flowing and taught in an instructional style.

Following the Boer War (1899–1902), the heavy losses suffered by Britain were blamed on Swedish gymnastics for not being rigorous enough – physically or mentally. There was a need to increase the health and fitness of the working classes and impose strict discipline.

Swedish gymnastics was therefore replaced by the Model Course in 1902, which were military drill-style exercises taken directly from the War Office. However, they took no account of the children's needs and were also taught by non-commissioned officers (NCOs). These were low-ranking officers who were unpopular with the teachers. The children were taught in a **command-obey style** and the exercises were mainly free standing, static, and the only equipment required were sticks or staves as dummy weapons in order to teach weapon familiarity.

Important points/background information
- Military needs became more powerful than educational theory.
- A backward step educationally with Swedish drill, innovation and a therapeutic approach abandoned.
- Condemned by progressives and supporters of the Swedish system.
- Girls and boys instructed together.
- Failed to cater for different ages and/or genders.
- Children treated as soldiers.
- Taught by army NCOs (or teachers who had been trained by them).
- Dull and repetitive – but cheap.
- Large numbers in small spaces.
- Set against backdrop of poor diets, bad housing and other forms of social deprivation.
- It lowered the status of the subject.

Influences
- Imposed as a result of Britain's poor performance in the **Boer War.**
- Produced and imposed by **Colonel Fox** of the War Office (not Education Department).

Massed drill in the school yard around 1902.

Also note
❝It is important therefore that the short time claimed for physical training should be devoted wholly to useful exercises. No part of that time should be wasted on what is merely spectacular or entertaining, but every exercise should have its peculiar purpose and value in a complete system framed to develop all parts of the body. (*Model Course of Physical Training*, 1902)❞

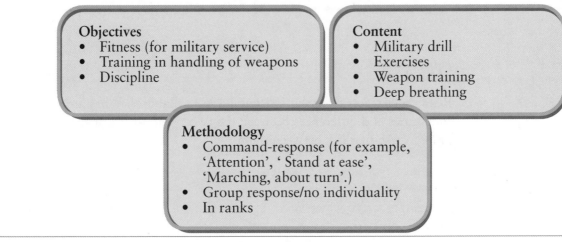

Objectives
- Fitness (for military service)
- Training in handling of weapons
- Discipline

Content
- Military drill
- Exercises
- Weapon training
- Deep breathing

Methodology
- Command-response (for example, 'Attention', ' Stand at ease', 'Marching, about turn'.)
- Group response/no individuality
- In ranks

Fig. 11.02 The Model Course, 1902
Text used by permission of Sarah van Wely.

TASK 5

Why would the command-obey style of teaching be considered suitable for state school children?

From Table 11.04 (page 183), you will see that the Model Course only lasted two years (1902–04). This was because it had no educational focus, did not cater for children's needs and was questionable in its intention of improving the health and fitness of the children. The exercises were mainly static and dull.

Syllabuses of Physical Training

HOT TIPS

You will not need to know details of the syllabuses but be prepared to outline the main differences between the early syllabuses and the last one in 1933.

The Model Course was to be replaced by the Syllabuses of Physical Training in 1904, 1909, 1919 and 1933. They sought to stress the physical and educative effects of sporting activities. However, who was going to teach physical training? The non-commissioned officers were no longer being used in the schools and the basic class teacher had no experience in teaching physical training. The government therefore needed to produce a prescriptive syllabus that a teacher could follow quite easily. Also, radical changes to the content and teaching style would not occur overnight. Schools still had limited facilities and the working classes were still required to be obedient. Changes would happen gradually over a number of years. Therefore the style of teaching was still similar to drill but without the military content.

Last Syllabus, 1933

KEY WORDS

Rudolf Laban

Text to follow

By now, there was more free movement, more creativity and some group work. Children were increasingly encouraged to use their imagination and there was a greater focus on the development of skills. There was growing interaction between the teachers and pupils and the influence of specialist teachers trained in the techniques of Rudolf Laban was being felt.

TASK 4

Read the extracts from the 1919 and 1933 syllabuses. What are the similarities and differences between the two syllabuses? List three difference/similarities between them.

Important points/background information
- Revisions of the 1902 Model Course.
- School medical service established within the Board of Education in 1908, 'which identified the necessity of raising the general standard of physical health among the children of the poor' (H. L. Fisher, House of Commons, 1918).
- A compromise between military drill and Swedish exercises.
- 1909 – local authorities required to train teachers to deliver the syllabuses.
- Emphasis on exercise in the open air and the use of suitable clothing.
- Still large numbers and poor facilities.

Influences
- Dr George Newman appointed as Chief Medical Officer within the Board of Education.
- As a medical man, he was interested in the health giving/therapeutic effects of exercise.

The early 1900s

Also note

❮ The purpose of physical training is not to produce gymnasts, but to promote and encourage the health and development of the body. ❯ (Dr George Newman)

Objectives
- 1909 – therapeutic effects of exercise (with emphasis on respiration, circulation, posture)
- Obedience
- Discipline
- Enjoyment
- Alertness, decision-making, control of mind over body

Content
- 1909 – more Swedish in character with recreative aspects to relieve dullness, tedium and monotony of former lesson
- Dancing steps/simple games
- Danish and rhythmic swinging exercises

Methodology
- 1904 – 109 'tables' of exercises for teachers to follow
- 1909 – reduced to 71 'tables'
- Still formal
- Still in ranks with marching and 'free-standing' exercises
- Still unison response to commands
- A kinder approach by teachers
- Some freedom of choice for teachers

Fig. 11.03 Early syllabuses of physical training (PT), 1904 and 1909
Text used by permission of Sarah van Wely.

Important points/background information
- Set against the huge loss of life in World War I and huge loss of life in post-war flu epidemic.
- The syllabus was progressive in terms of its broader content and child-centred appoach.

Influences
- Dr George Newman still influential and eager to fight off accusations that PT was to blame for the lack of fitness of the working class.
- Newman also stressed the benefits of recreative activities for the rehabilitation of injured soldiers.
- The Fisher Education Act 1918 promoted holiday and school camps, school playing fields and school swimming baths.

The style of free standing exercises still recommended in the 1919 syllabus.

Also note
- The first 'child-centred' syllabus.
- Broader content than 1902/1904/1909.
- But some older teachers stayed with their old ways.

Objectives
- Enjoyment and play for the under 7s
- Therapeutic work for the over 7s

Content
- The exercises and 'positions' the same as 1909
- Special section of games for the under 7s
- Not less than half the lesson on 'general activity exercises' – active free movement, including small games and dancing

Methodology
- More freedom for teachers and pupils
- Less formality

Fig. 11.04 The syllabus of physical training, 1919

Text used by permission of Sarah van Wely.

Important points/background information
- The industrial depression of the 1930s left many of the working class unemployed (no state benefits were yet available).
- A watershed between the syllabuses of the past and the physical education of the future.
- This syllabus had one section for the under elevens and one for the over elevens.

Influences
- The Hadow Report of 1926 identified the need to differentiate between ages for physical training.
- Dr George Newman – this was the last syllabus to be published under his direction.

Syllabus of physical training
1933

Emphasis on skills and posture.

Also note
- A detailed, high quality and highly respected syllabus.
- Still set out in a series of 'tables' from which teachers planned their lessons.
- 'The ultimate test by which every system of physical training should be judged [is] to be found in the posture and general carriage of the children' (1933 syllabus).
- Newman stated that good nourishment, effective medical inspection and treatment and hygienic surroundings were all necessary for good health as well as 'a comprehensive system of physical training … for the normal healthy development of the body [and] for the correction of inherent or acquired defects.'

Objectives
- Physical fitness
- Therapeutic results
- Good physique
- Good posture
- Development of mind and body (holistic aims)

Content
- Athletics, gymnastic and games skills
- Group work

Methodology
- Still direct style for the majority of the lesson
- Some **decentralised** parts to the lesson
- Group work/tasks throughout
- Encouragement of special clothing/kit
- 5 × 20-minute lesson a week recommended
- Used many schools' newly built gymnasia
- Outdoor lessons recommended for health benefits

Fig. 11.05 The syllabus of physical training, 1933
Text used by permission of Sarah van Wely.

Influence of World War I and World War II

HOT TIPS

You will not be directly examined on the effects of World War II, but it is useful to understand the legacy it was to have on the development of physical education in succeeding years.

World War I made an impact with growing appreciation of the value of recreational activities in boosting the morale of the troops, and there was a widespread belief that the country should not become involved in any more wars.

World War II saw the destruction of some schools and the growing influence of female teachers as many male teachers enlisted. The apparatus that was brought into schools following the war was a direct result of the commando training that had taken place during the war. Troops needed to engage in a more mobile style of fighting and to be able to solve problems. The educational value of this type of activity was recognized and different styles of teaching were to emerge in order to develop children in a more positive way, with a recognition of their physical, mental, social and emotional needs. This was reflected in the publication *Moving and Growing*.

The publication *Moving and Growing* in 1952 was produced by the Education Department as a guideline for primary schools. Primary school teachers were not trained specifically in physical education. The apparatus was brought in following World War II to encourage a problem-solving approach to physical activity. The term 'physical education' had now evolved, giving it a very different emphasis from the earlier term 'physical training'. Immediately, it suggests that there was now a belief that the mind needed to be involved as well as the body. This was combined with the movement approach from the Centres of Dance to develop:

KEY WORDS

Heuristic

Serves to discover or reach an understanding of something through exploratory work or trial and error. The problem has open-ended possibilities rather than pre-determined goals set by adults; therefore a sense of success is more likely to occur.

Educational gymnastics

Children given a stimulus use gymnastic skills to answer a task according to their own ability.

- exploratory work
- problem-solving
- creativity
- skill-based work
- other activities such as dance, movement, swimming and national dances.

These developments reflected changes in educational thinking. There was now a more child-centred approach, with teachers being able to show initiative and autonomy. The teaching style had changed from a command-obey style to a more **heuristic** or guidance style of teaching whereby the children are given a stimulus and they respond through movement within their own capabilities. This was particularly true in **educational gymnastics** and dance. In the early 1980s, there was also a similar movement in the teaching of games, where children were encouraged to make up their own games, devise their own rules and so on.

TASK 5

Describe the changing roles of the child and the teacher from 1900 to 1950.

Important points/background information
- The (Butler) Education Act 1944 aimed to ensure equality of educational opportunity.
- It also required local authorities to provide playing fields for all schools.
- School leaving age was raised to fifteen years.
- These syllabuses should be viewed in the context of overall expansion of physical activities in schools.
- Intended to replace the under elevens section of the 1933 syllabus.

Influences
- The Second World War, which required 'thinking' soldiers, and the subsequent perceived need for increasingly 'thinking' children.
- Assault course obstacle equipment influenced apparatus design.
- Modern educational dance methods influenced the creative/movement approach.
- An experiment in Halifax, which rehabilitated children with disabilities by encouraging individual interpretation of **open tasks**, with no pre-set rhythm or timing. This influenced the problem-solving approach.

An apparatus lesson in the 1950s

Also note
- The extensive post-war re-building programme lead to an expansion of facilities.

Objectives
- Physical, social and cognitive skills
- Variety of experiences
- Enjoyment
- Personal satisfaction
- Increased involvement for all

Content
- Agility exercises; gymnastics, dance and games skills
- Swimming
- Movement to music

Methodology
- Child-centred and enjoyment orientated
- Progressive
- Teacher guidance rather than direction
- Problem-solving/creative/exploratory/discovery
- Individual interpretation of tasks
- Using full apparatus (cave, ropes, bars, boxes, mats, and so on)

Fig. 11.06 *Moving and Growing* (1952) and *Planning the Programme* (1954)

Text used by permission of Sarah van Wely.

Recreative focus

KEY WORDS

Decentralized

The dispersal of power away from the centre towards outlying areas. It is a system of government that is organized into smaller units with more autonomy.

For the last decades of the twentieth century there were radical changes to be made to the physical activities the children at state schools experienced. The Butler Education Act 1944 required local authorities to provide for recreational sporting facilities within their schools. This was a very different philosophy to the one held at the beginning of the twentieth century, which believed the working classes had no need for recreation. The secondary school teacher was now fully trained and was therefore no longer dependent on following a syllabus drawn up centrally. Physical education teachers were to experience about 40 years of a **decentralized** system where they had their own autonomy and could choose their own physical education programme.

TASK 6

What are the advantages and disadvantages of a decentralized system of physical education? List two of each.

Present-day physical education

By the end of the 1980s, the government of the time introduced the National Curriculum. This was because the government wanted:

- more control of education
- more teacher accountability
- national standards set for education
- a wider range of activities to be taught.

This represented a return to a centralized approach towards education. All state schools now follow set guidelines about set subjects to teach, which are inspected by OFSTED.

TASK 7

What are the advantages and disadvantages of a centralized approach towards education?

Physical education continues to be a compulsory subject that pupils must follow from the ages of five to sixteen. The government must consider physical education to be an important subject, so what are the aims of physical education? Through physical education, children should be able to:

- achieve physical competence and confidence
- perform in a range of activities

KEY WORDS

Critical performer

Children should be encouraged to observe and be able to analyse physical activities in a knowledgeable way.

- achieve physical skilfulness
- gain knowledge of the body in action
- become a 'critical performer'
- learn competitiveness, creativity; face up to challenges
- learn how to plan, perform and evaluate
- discover their abilities, aptitudes and make choices for lifelong learning.

TASK 8

1 Consider the aims above against the Model Course (1902–04) and the early Syllabuses of Physical Training (1904, 1909).

2 Explain, using examples, how you have acquired these qualities through your physical education experiences. An example might be, 'I have learnt to plan and perform a ten-bounce trampoline routine.'

Key concepts of the National Curriculum

- **Therapeutic functions**

One of the main aims of the National Curriculum for physical education is to raise awareness in children of the need for a healthy lifestyle. Modern life tends to encourage children to be more sedentary; active play has been reduced in favour of the television and computer games. Increased safety concerns have led to children not walking to school as much as earlier generations and the fast food culture is leading to an increasing problem of obesity.

- **Creativity**

Since the middle of the twentieth century, children have been required by educationalists to be more creative and imaginative in their physical education lessons. With the advent of the National Curriculum, this has been given even more importance as it is also assessed more formally.

- **Recreational breadth**

During the twentieth century, the range of physical activities taught in schools has gradually increased. The National Curriculum has made this a more formal requirement in trying to combat the potential problem of teachers only teaching a few activities. Schools have developed more facilities, greater use has been made of community facilities and since the 1970s there was an explicit policy of educating people to use their leisure time effectively. The general idea is that the more activities you experience, the more likely you are to find one you enjoy and carry on into later life.

- **Critical performer**

The National Curriculum aims to provide people with knowledge of other roles in sport other than just the performer. Such roles as officiating, coaching, spectating, leadership roles and so on encourage children to appreciate physical activities in many different ways.

Range of activities

The current aims of physical education can be taught through a range of physical activities. Too much concentration on one activity would not provide a balanced physical development. The National Curriculum classifications are:

- games (invasion, striking and fielding, net/wall)
- athletic activities
- swimming
- gymnastics
- dance
- outdoor and adventurous activities.

What do we mean by a broad and balanced physical education curriculum? A school cannot possibly offer every sport available but there should be a balance of activities that are team and individual, competitive and non-competitive. The activities can be selected from different categories of sports (Table 11.05).

Table 11.05 Categories of sport

Invasion	Net/wall	Striking/fielding	Target	Movement
Football	Tennis	Cricket	Golf	Gymnastics
Netball	Badminton	Rounders	Bowls	Dance
Basketball	Table tennis	Softball		Trampolining
Hockey	Volleyball			Athletics
				Swimming

Structure of the National Curriculum

There are four key stages with eight levels of attainment.

Primary school

- Key Stage 1 (5–7 years)

Pupils are required to study three areas: gymnastics, games and dance. Pupils need to develop simple skills and eventually sequences of movement independently and then with a partner. Pupils should be taught about changes that occur to their bodies as they exercise and to recognize the short-term effects of exercise on the body.

- Key Stage 2 (7–11 years)

Six areas could be studied: games, gymnastics, dance are compulsory: plus two others from athletic activities, outdoor and adventurous activities, and swimming and water safety. Pupils need to improve motor skills and co-ordination, develop more complex patterns of movement, sustain energetic activity and understand the effects of exercise.

The class teacher in the primary school is not usually a physical education specialist although specialist help is usually sought for swimming. In recent years, many national governing bodies are beginning to tap into the primary school as a result of lottery funding. Governing bodies, such as the All

England Netball Association, have the money to send in coaches to initiate interest within the schools. Governing bodies need to highlight in their policies and plans how they intend to increase participation at the grass roots level of sport if they are to access extra lottery funding. These initiatives are often an option for schools, but, nevertheless, they do increase the range of activities offered at school and raise the awareness of sport amongst young children. This is the stage when children are learning the fundamental motor skills they will require in more specific sporting situations and therefore it is vital that they receive the best teaching possible. The TOP programme, run by the Youth Sports Trust, and specialist Sports Colleges, with their school sport co-ordinators, are contributing to the experiences offered at primary schools.

TASK 9

Outline the variety of physical activity experiences available to primary school children today.

Secondary education
- Key Stage 3 (11–14 years)

Games plus three other areas; one must be gymnastics or dance. Pupils need to refine motor skills, undertake more complex movements, learn rules and tactics and how to recover after activity.

- Key Stage 4 (14–16 years)

Two out of the six areas need to be studied. Pupils should be prepared to plan, undertake and evaluate a safe health-promoting exercise programme and show understanding of principles involved.

TASK 10

Access the DfES website, (go to www.heinemann.co.uk/hotlinks, insert the express code 9300P and click on this topic), and make yourself aware of the general requirements for each key stage of the National Curriculum.

Assessment in physical education

Each key stage has an end of key stage description and eight levels of attainment. When writing a report, teachers need to record pupils' planning, performing and evaluation. The teacher needs to indicate whether the pupil is working beyond, at the level or towards the end of key stage description.

Everyone recognizes the need for assessment but some teachers are concerned that the amount of assessment or testing can be overdone (Table 11.06).

Attainment targets are set for the four key stages where children are assessed on their knowledge, skills and understanding involved in the areas of activity experienced. The purpose of attainment targets is to set some general expectations of what children should be able to accomplish by the end of each stage.

Table 11.06

Advantages of assessment	Disadvantages of assessment
• Clear objectives and goals to reach • Gives incentives/rewards and motivation to improve • Improves quality of teaching • Gives recognition to good teachers	• Too much time on testing and not participating • Tests are mainly subjective • Not every child can achieve the highest levels • Can demotivate teachers and children due to unfair comparisons • Too much pressure – takes away the fun element

- **Level 1**

Pupils copy, repeat and explore simple skills and actions with basic control and co-ordination. They start to link these skills and actions in ways that suit the activities. They describe and comment on their own and others' actions. They talk about how to exercise safely and how their bodies feel during an activity.

- **Level 4**

Pupils link skills, techniques and ideas and apply them accurately and appropriately. Their performance shows precision, control and fluency, and that they understand tactics and composition. They compare and comment on skills, techniques and ideas used in their own and others' work, and use this understanding to improve their performance. They explain and apply basic safety principles in preparing for exercise. They describe what effects exercise has on their bodies and how it is valuable to their fitness and health.

- **Level 8**

Pupils consistently distinguish and apply advanced skills, techniques and ideas, showing high standards of precision, control, fluency and originality. Drawing on what they know of the principles of advanced tactics or composition, they apply these principles with proficiency and flair in their own and others' work. They adapt it appropriately in response to changing circumstances and other performers. They evaluate their own and others' work, showing that they understand the impact of skills, strategy and tactics or composition, and fitness on the quality and effectiveness of performance. They plan ways in which their own and others' performance could be improved. They create action plans and ways of monitoring improvement. They use their knowledge of health and fitness to plan and evaluate their own and others' exercise and activity programme.

As well as the core curriculum lessons, children are also offered many other sporting experiences whilst at school.

'Extra-curricular activities' is the term given to the optional activities offered in schools during lunchtime and after school. They offer purely recreational experiences as well as competitive fixtures. Another term for this is 'school sport' and this should be viewed differently to physical education, which refers to the compulsory core lessons. There is an overlap between them but their central focus is different. The hope is that physical education will provide the building blocks that the extra-curricular programmes can enhance and extend a child's interest and aptitude. One problem is that extra-curricular activities rely on the goodwill of teachers.

In the 1980s, there was a decline in the extra-curricular opportunities offered to children in the state school sector. Many factors affected the drop in competitive school sport such as:

- teacher strikes based on contractual hours reduced teachers' goodwill
- financial pressures of running fixtures
- the competing leisure and employment options of teenagers
- the anti-competitive lobby.

In the UK, we have traditionally kept physical education and school sport separate, believing them to serve different aims. There is a growing belief today that these two strands should be brought closer together and many initiatives are taking place to try and achieve this such as the Physical Education and School Sport Links Strategy (PESSCLS) and Sports College status being given to some schools.

TASK 11

1 Consider activities that you have taken part in competitively and decide what benefits you have gained from them.
2 What problems can competitive sport produce for some people?

Current government policies

Sports Colleges

Sports Colleges are part of the specialist schools programme run by the Department for Education and Skills (DfES). As of September 2003, there are 228 designated Sports Colleges with a government target of at least 400 by the end of 2005. They will have an important role in helping to deliver the government's 'Plan for Sport' (Figure 11.07): 'They will become important hub sites for school and community sport, providing high quality opportunities for all young people in their neighbourhood.' (Richard Caborn – Minister for Sport.)

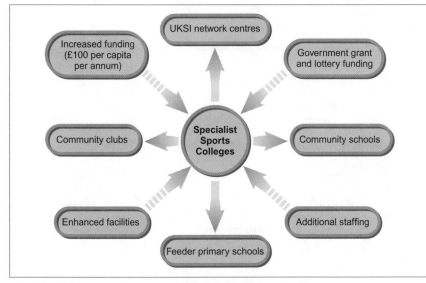

Fig. 11.07 Inputs and outputs of specialist Sports Colleges

Text used by permission of Sarah van Wely.

School sport co-ordinators

By 2006, there should be 3200 school sport co-ordinators working across families of schools with 18,000 primary link teachers. The following model (Figure 11.08) illustrates the way a typical school sport co-ordinator (SSCo) partnership might work. The partnership around a Sports College starts with an average of four schools, ultimately growing to eight schools. Each partnership receives a grant of up to £270,000 a year. This helps pay for the full-time partnership development manager (PDM).

The primary link teacher (PLT) is located within each of the primary/specialist schools within the partnership with a remit to improve PE and school sport within the primary school. They have twelve days a year to act as link teachers.

The school sport co-ordinator partnership is based around families of schools with a team made up of a partnership development manager (PDM), SSCo and PLT. Their role is to enhance opportunities for young people to experience different sports, access high quality coaching and engage in competition. They are released two days a week.

The partnership development manager is usually located within a Sports College and manages the development of the partnership and the links with other PE and sport organizations.

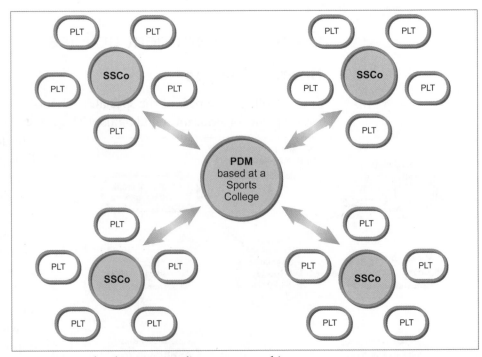

Fig. 11.08 A school sport co-ordinator partnership
Text used by permission of Sarah van Wely.

The overall aim of the partnership is to ensure children spend a minimum of two hours a week on high quality PE and school sport. Six strategic objectives have been set:

- strategic planning – develop and implement a PE/sport strategy
- primary liaison – develop links particularly between Key Stages 2 and 3
- out of school hours – provide enhanced opportunities for all pupils
- school to community – increase participation in community sport
- coaching and leadership – provide opportunities in leadership, coaching and officiating for senior pupils, teachers and other adults
- raising standards – raise standards of pupil achievement.

TASK 12

What would be the advantages of attending a school that has been granted Sport College status?

The Physical Education and School Sport Links Strategy (PESScLS)

This is a current government policy aiming for 'high quality physical education and sport' (see Chapter 12). Above all, it demonstrates the increasing trend towards developing strong links between schools and local clubs (Table 11.07). It is part of the school sport co-ordinators partnership, and the overriding aim is to give all children in school the minimum of two hours high quality sport and physical education a week.

What does the government think high quality sport and physical education can contribute to individual children and society? The following points are summarized from the government's document 'Learning through Physical Education and Sport'.

Characteristics of high quality physical education and sport:
- pupils who show a strong commitment to making PE and sport an important and valuable part of their lives
- know and understand what they are trying to achieve
- understand how PE and sport contribute to a healthy lifestyle
- have the confidence to get involved
- develop the necessary skills and be in control of their movements
- respond effectively to a range of different competitive, creative and challenging type activities, as individuals and in groups
- think clearly and make appropriate decisions
- show a desire to improve and achieve
- have the stamina, suppleness and strength to keep going
- enjoy physical education and school and community sport.

Why is the government so keen to promote high quality physical education and sport?

Table 11.07 The FA school to club links programme

Opportunities	Description
FA Charter Standard Schools Programme	Involves primary, middle, secondary and special schools, independent and state, required as part of the criteria for all schools to form a partnership with a local charter standard club for boys and girls
FA Charter Standard Development Club	Requires clubs who have met the development criteria (minimum of five teams) to create a partnership with a local school or schools as part of their football development plan
FA Charter Standard Community Clubs	Requires clubs (minimum ten teams, male and female) to form schools to club links and appoint a voluntary schools liaison officer
FA TOP Sport Football Community Programme	Targets young people aged 7–11 who are less likely to be participating in football for their school due to more limited opportunities and helps them move onto Charter Standard Club
Active Sports Girls Football Programme	The Active Sports Programme is a fundamental part of the FA's strategy for the development of girls' football. The framework includes a school to club link scheme for 10–16 year olds called 'Kick Start'
FA Soccability Community Programme	This is an educational programme designed as part of the FA TOP Sport Football Programme to assist young people with disabilities to participate in football

TASK 13

Research another national governing body and its response to the government's strategy of developing school and club links.

The 'age' issue

The fall in sports participation with age is worrying because individuals reduce their chances of maintaining health and agility and being able to live independently into their old age. Research shows that people who are exposed to a wide range of sporting activities in their youth are more likely to continue to participate throughout their lives – the 'sports literacy' effect. People who are in the older age groups in the 1990s were more likely to be 'sports literate' than those who were in the equivalent age groups in the 1970s.

 KEY WORDS

Post-school gap
The drop in sport participation when young adults leave full time education

There is a dramatic drop in participation once young people leave school. This drop is higher in the UK than in a number of other European countries. This drop in participation can be called 'the post-school gap' (see Table 11.08) and has concerned the government and sporting institutions for many decades.

There have been calls for more lifelong activities to be encouraged at schools, as these appear to be the activities that this age group are attracted to. Sustaining a broader choice at school is likely to support lifelong learning.

Table 11.08 The post-school gap

Reasons for the post-school gap	Solutions to the post-school gap
• Physical education is no longer compulsory	• Improve links between schools and clubs
• Young adults have many competing leisure interests	• Instil knowledge of the need for a healthy lifestyle
• Facilities are no longer as accessible or free to use	• Concessionary rates
• Traditionally poor links between schools and clubs	• Youth sections at clubs
• Less leisure time as full-time work and increasing domestic responsibilities take hold	• Promote recreational sports as well as the competitive element

Lifelong learning is a government policy that aims to enable people to be occupied in activities that will enrich their lives, as well as that of the community, for a very long time. Activities such as golf, bowls, swimming and so on are sporting activities that people can continue with for the rest of their lives. Traditionally, the British physical education programme has consisted of a diet of team games, and yet research suggests these activities are not successful in retaining people's interest at a participation level as they get older. Is there a point to be made for encouraging other sporting activities in schools that people could continue with for longer? Since the 1970s, schools did begin to branch out and offer other activities, sometimes using community facilities in an attempt to foster in young people the opportunities available in their wider community.

Why can golf be a lifelong sport?
• It can be played at any age.
• It is physically active with health benefits.
• The unique handicap system allows people of any gender, ability and age to compete with each other.
• It is a very sociable game.
• It can be played recreationally and competitively.
• A range of municipal and private facilities make it accessible for everyone.
• It possesses character building qualities of honesty, integrity and fairness.
• It has a positive media image of elite performers.
• It is a global sport.

If this youth section drops out of society the social consequences are costly. Sport is seen as one way of including them in positive activities, channelling their energies, making them less likely to resort to drugs, alcohol and so on. Sport can help them acquire new skills and help integrate them into wider society.

Schools have been challenging the idea of only teaching the traditional activities and with the help of national governing bodies they are trying to introduce different sports into their curriculum. Adaptations in equipment and the development of mini games have meant more activities are suitable to be taught in schools.

TASK 14

Discuss the suggestion that 'schools should become the nursery of sporting talent'. NB: Remember to give both sides of the argument.

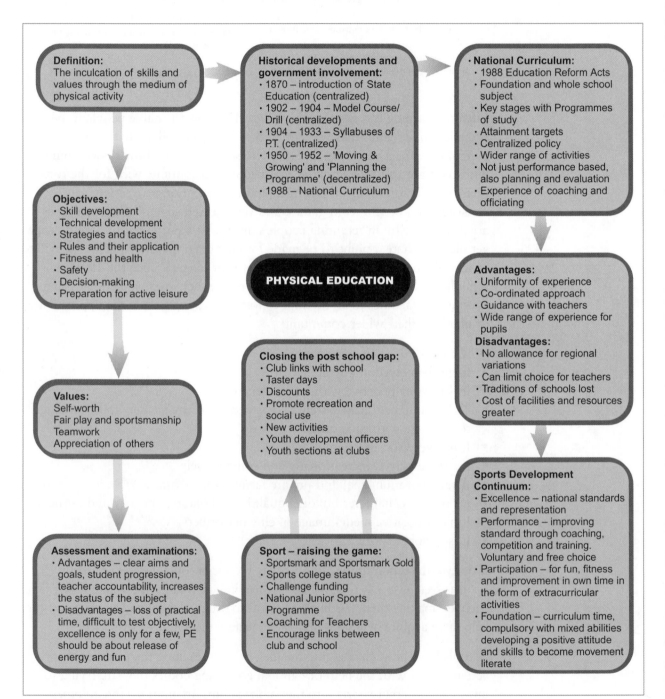

Fig. 11.09 Developments in physical education

Revise as you go!

1 What were the characteristics of sport in the nineteenth-century English public schools?

2 How did the technical development of games occur in the public schools?

3 How did the public schools help influence the spread of sports into wider society?

4 Why were team games so highly valued by the public schools?

5 What does the term 'self-government' mean with reference to the organization of team games in the public schools?

6 Suggest three reasons why games such as cricket acted as a form of social control for the boys in the public schools.

7 What is meant by the term 'athleticism'?

8 How did the cult of athleticism help the boys become leaders in society?

9 What was the effect of the universities on the development of sport in the nineteenth century?

10 What is meant by the term 'codified' or 'codification'?

11 What is meant by the term 'blues' and what was the influence of the blues on sport?

12 Name three characteristics of physical education in the early state schools.

13 Why did team games take longer to appear in state schools than in public schools?

14 What was the effect of the Boer War (1899–1902) on activities in state schools?

15 What were the three main aims of the Model Course?

16 Give three characteristics of military drill.

17 Why was there a need for Syllabuses of Physical Training?

18 What was the role of the teacher in the movement approach?

19 What skills were encouraged in the movement approach?

20 What does the term 'child-centred' mean?

21 Give three differences between the content of a physical training class in 1906 and a physical education lesson in 1953.

22 Give three differences between the lesson objectives of a physical training class in 1906 and a physical education lesson in 1953.

23 Give three main aims of physical education today.

24 How many key stages are there in the National Curriculum?

25 What roles, other than as a performer, does the National Curriculum require pupils to perform?

Chapter 12: The administration and organization of sport in the United Kingdom

Learning outcomes

By the end of this chapter you should be able to:

- understand the role of central government and the degree of central control in the administration of sport
- understand the tradition of local authority provision for sport and physical recreation as a public service
- understand the central government policies of 'best value' and their impact on local authority provision for sport and physical activity
- understand the effects of joint funding and management of local facilities
- understand the comparison of provision for sport and physical recreation between the public, private and voluntary sectors
- understand the influence of national bodies such as Sport England and the British Sports Trust as well as current national policies for participation in physical recreation and sport.

KEY WORDS

Administration

The involvement of government at local, regional, national and international levels. Administrative tasks include governing sport, making decisions and creating and distributing finances and resources.

Grass roots

The essential roots of learning sporting skills at the foundation and participation level of sport.

Introduction

For this specification, you need to focus on the **administration** of physical recreation and sport at the participation or **grass roots** level. It is the A2 specification that concentrates on high performance sport.

Participation pyramid

Foundation level – the introduction to basic sport skills; mostly via the physical education programme in schools.

Participation level – the individual participates out of choice; extends an initial interest in an activity; participates for fun and to develop skills; this may be evidenced by participating in extra-curricular activities in schools or joining a sports club.

Performance level – at high club or regional standard; commitment in training and perfecting skills.

Excellence level – can be reached in terms of a personal achievement; elite is the level to which only a few aspire.

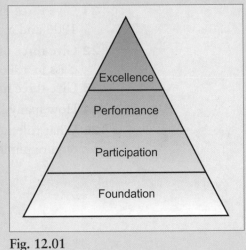

Fig. 12.01

For the majority of the twentieth century, there was very little legislation covering sport and this was some indication of the low priority given to sport by consecutive UK governments. This is because sport developed in the UK from the grass roots level upwards rather than as part of a government's **policy**. However, there was a shift in government thinking in the latter decades of the twentieth century, showing the UK government beginning to take more notice of sport, its function within society and the benefits it could have for local communities and the nation as a whole.

The structures for administering and delivering sport in the UK are very complex, as they have evolved over a century and a half, in a rather ad hoc fashion. In other countries, where sport developed later and where governments saw its potential, there tended to be more government control from an earlier stage and more uniformity in their structures and policies. We would call this a centralized system. In the UK, we have a more decentralized system, which is good for allowing regions to adapt policies suitable to their own needs but has led to a situation where many organizations involved in sport policy tend to have similar and sometimes competing roles. Recently, there has been a trend towards trying to simplify the bureaucracy and delineate the roles of various organizations.

Administration of sport and active recreation in the UK

Broadly speaking, there are four main sectors responsible for the delivery of sport and physical activity/recreation:
- local government (public sector provision)
- education (schools, further education (FE) and higher education (HE))
- voluntary sector (clubs and national governing bodies)
- private sector.

Key organizations involved in sport in England (taken from 'Game Plan' – DCMS, 2002)

National (government):
- *Department of Culture, Media and Sport* (DCMS)
- Other government departments such as DfES – Department for Education and Skills (responsible for funding physical education and school sport)

National (non-government):
- UK Sport
- UK Sports Institutes
- *Sport England*
- English Institute of Sport (EIS)
- *National governing bodies* (NGBs)
- National sports organizations including Youth Sports Trust (YST), Central Council of Physical Recreation (CCPR), *British Sports Trust (now known as Sports Leaders UK)*, SportsCoach UK

Regional:

- Sport England's Regional Offices (directed by Sport England's central office)
- Regional cultural consortia (bring together the activities of the DCMS in the regions – sport as part of overall culture)
- Nine regional sports boards (RSB) bring together key regional sports stakeholders to provide a voice for sport in the region
- Government offices (each has a DCMS representative with sport included as part of DCMS policies)
- Regional Federations of Sport and Recreation bring together representatives of governing bodies and other national sports organizations at regional and county level
- County partnerships
- National governing bodies (NGBs) at regional and county level

Local:

- *Local authorities*
- NGB at local level
- *Local sports councils*
- *Local sports clubs and associations*
- *Private health and fitness clubs*
- Further and higher education institutions/schools (private and state)

Points for consideration

- Central government, through the Department for Culture, Media and Sport (DCMS), is responsible for the overall development of sports policy in England as laid out in 'A Sporting Future for All' – the government's national vision for sport outlined in 2001. The DCMS takes the lead on decisions about the allocation of exchequer funds. 'Game Plan' (2002) is the strategic implementation of the vision set out in 2001.
- There are four sports councils (Sport England, SportScotland, the Sports Council for Wales and the Sports Council for Northern Ireland) in the UK, which form the link between government and sports organizations, and they distribute government and lottery funding. The four home countries each have their own remit to set different sport policies.
- National sports organizations are independent of government and represent different interest groups. The most notable for your purpose of study is the British Sports Trust.
- Each sport has at least one national governing body, which oversees rules and competitions for their own sport. The NGB also delivers funds with a focus on coaches, officials and administrators. There are over 300 governing bodies for the 112 sports recognized in the UK. Sometimes there are specific subsets within sports (such as women or specialities). This can lead to internal competition for funding and resources.
- Local authorities are the biggest key providers for sport and recreation, yet it is not one of their statutory duties. Provision for sport and recreation is permissive rather than mandatory – that means they can

HOT TIPS

Whilst it is important that you have an overall idea of the number and level of organizations involved in sport development, for the purpose of revision, you need to focus on those organizations outlined in the learning objectives and italicized above.

choose what level of provision they provide. They work in partnership with the voluntary and private sectors providing opportunities through their sport development officers (SDO) and teams. Recently, sport has been used as a vehicle for delivering wider community development issues, such as health, employment and reduction in crime. It reflects the government's policy of 'joined-up thinking'. In two-tier areas, the district council is responsible for sport, with the county responsible for education and overall strategic planning.

- The voluntary-run local sports clubs, affiliated to their own national governing body, provide the most opportunities at participation levels, that is, the non-high performance levels of sport. It is estimated that currently there are some 110,000 voluntary sport clubs in the UK, but recent research suggests this number has declined since 1996 by about 40,000.

Funding for sport and physical activity

Sport and physical recreation are funded from a variety of sources, the government and local authorities (or public sector) being a major contributor, with the voluntary sector making a significant unpaid contribution. The private sector, another chief contributor, is increasing its role, and television and sponsorship, though mainly directed at football and Formula 1, continue to make an impact.

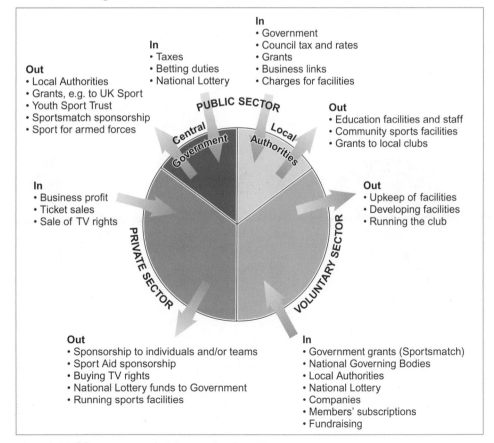

Fig. 12.02 Three sectors fund sport in the UK
Text used by permission of Sarah van Wely.

HOT TIPS

A frequent mistake made by students in the examination is to assume that the government is responsible for local sports facilities when they are in fact the responsibility of the local authority.

KEY WORDS

Funding for sport

Sum of money set aside for the purpose of sport; can be obtained from a variety of sources including individuals, commercial organizations such as companies, and national government.

HOT TIPS

Be prepared to justify or discuss the spending of lottery money on sport.

Three important points emerge:

- the local authorities (public sector) bear the brunt of providing for sport and physical activity
- actual public sector spending on sport and physical activity is often higher than quoted
- although very substantial, local authority expenditure has remained relatively stable with a large proportion going to indoor sports.

One fact is undeniable – lottery funding in the last decade has significantly increased the amount of **funding for sport**, combined with increases in exchequer/government funding and TV rights. Perhaps an important point to note is that as lottery sales appear to be decreasing (they reached a peak in 1997/8), government funding may prove to be crucial in the next few years.

The voluntary sector holds up the grass roots delivery with a network of 110,000 community amateur sports clubs run by 1.5 million volunteers. The private sector has grown dramatically with almost 3 million people belonging to private fitness clubs, compared to 2.4 million members of public health and fitness centres. Could this provide an alternative to public provision in the future? If so, what about the people who clearly could not afford the high membership fees charged by private clubs?

In conclusion:

- the organizational framework could be reformed
- the funding arrangements are fragmented and need simplifying.

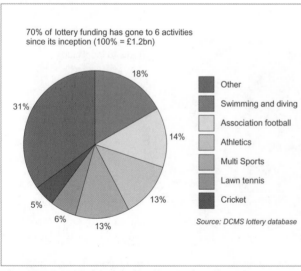

Fig. 12.03 How lottery funding is distributed among sports

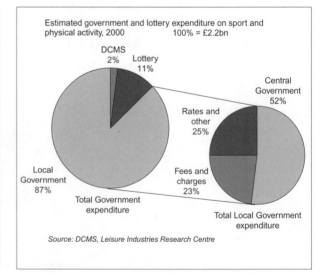

Fig. 12.04 Government and lottery expenditure on sport

Reasons for national government involvement in sport

There are different reasons for governments becoming involved in sport policies.

- Political indoctrination: using sport to influence the beliefs of a nation, for example the 1936 Berlin Olympics when Hitler used the Olympics as a showcase for Aryan superiority.
- Labour function: using sport to create healthy and productive workers, for example use of military drill in the nineteenth-century state schools.
- National prestige: the 'feel good' factor a nation experiences following success at international sport.
- Socializing or nationalizing function: the values learnt from participating in sport can help produce valuable citizens who respect the social order and are loyal/patriotic to the state.
- Individualizing function: the individual becomes a happier and successful person through achieving in sport.
- International goodwill: countries can come together in sporting competition and this helps to keep open avenues of communication that may be lost politically.
- Military function: a healthy population is more likely to be able to defend the country when required.
- Economic function: sport is now big business and leisure is a boom industry; the government receives more revenue from sport than it actually gives to sport.
- Legislative function: laws sometimes have to be passed regarding sport, such as safety issues, spectator violence as well as direct sport policies.

Key government policies impacting on sport and physical activity

Since the last decade of the twentieth century, there have been three major policies regarding sport by consecutive governments. They show clearly that governments want more control of sport.

- Sport: Raising the Game, 1995
- A Sporting Future for All, 2001 (the government's vision). This policy sets out the government's vision for sport in the twentieth-first century and highlights the importance of co-ordinating sport between schools, local clubs and organizations.
- Game Plan, 2002 (action plan for the delivery of the vision). Game Plan is the *implementation* of 'A Sporting Future for All'. It is a strategy for delivering the government's 'Sport and Physical Activity Objectives' (2002). The recommendations in the Game Plan are:
  - developing the UK's sport and physical activity culture
  - enhancing international success

○ improving our approach to mega events and major sporting facilities
○ improving our organizational structures for delivering sport and physical activity.

Equity in sport: The government wants everybody to have the opportunity to participate in sporting activities, regardless of age, sex, race or disability. The basic principle of equity is being applied to all centrally funded schemes. Social inclusion for under-represented groups is an important part of community sport policy. The groups the government prioritize are: children in schools, people with disabilities or special needs, people from ethnic minority groups and women.

Facilities: Local authorities are the providers of sport and recreation facilities as they are best placed to make decisions about the direction of taxpayers' money. The government has recently introduced new protection to prevent the unnecessary sale of school playing fields. Local authorities must conduct an assessment of the playing fields and the needs of their communities before considering any application to sell a playing field. It is Sport England's policy to object to proposals by local authorities concerning any planning applications unless there are exceptional circumstances.

Health: The government's overall objective is to increase participation levels of all people to ensure that society generally achieves the minimum levels of physical activity necessary for maintaining health. A key aim is to ensure young people continue to be active beyond the statutory school leaving age.

Local authorities

 KEY WORDS

Leisure services

Includes sport, arts, museums, parks and recreation.

Best value

A key government policy (Local Government Act 1999) that requires local authorities and any other related organizations to consider the best value for money they can provide as well as considering the value of the experiences they offer.

Although the responsibility to deliver sporting opportunities is a non-statutory requirement, the government is placing a stronger emphasis on the key role that culture, sport and tourism can play in improving people's quality of life, and how it has the potential to impact upon the wider social, economic and environmental agendas. For this reason, it states that investment in sport is a necessity for local authorities. The government has highlighted the need for local authorities (LAs), as the largest providers of sporting opportunities, to encourage people to lead healthy, active lifestyles, particularly young people. Any local authority improvement plan needs to address priorities for their area and **leisure services** will be subject to scrutiny through the government's '**best value**' process. The purpose of such a plan is to provide strategic direction for the provision of sport in the region. It also identifies key issues and sets a framework for managing performance.

TASK 1

Write to your local sport development officer, asking for details of their aims for sporting and recreational provision. They are usually based within the Leisure Services Department of the borough council.

Sports development

The sports development process that local authorities are involved in can be defined as enhancing 'opportunities for people of all ages, degrees of interest and levels of ability to take part, get better and excel in their chosen sport' (Eady, 1993). Sports development is proactive, planned and with achievable outcomes; concerned with change, expansion and growth; relevant to local needs; enables others to provide opportunities; partnership-based and raises awareness that equal opportunities require an enormous effort if sport opportunities for all are to be realized.

KEY WORDS

Regeneration

The positive transformation of a place, whether residential, commercial or open space, that has previously displayed symptoms of physical, social and/or economic decline.

The key organizations that have produced policy documents which will influence the planning process for local authorities are the government, through the Strategy Unit, the Department for Culture, Media and Sport, and Sport England. The key messages from these policies are:
- the important health benefits of active participation in sport
- the strong 'feel good' factor brought about by sporting success
- the importance of young people taking part in sport, in and out of school, and maintaining this participation
- the positive impact sport has on local communities and **regeneration** areas.

Best value

'Best value' is a key government policy (Local Government Act 1999) that requires local authorities and any other related organizations to consider the best value for money they can provide as well as considering the value of the experiences they offer. Sport England has worked with local authorities to improve sport through facility development, raising standards of management, sports development initiatives, events and campaigns. Together they balance national objectives and priorities with those at local level. Best value put simply is about:
- finding out what people want and expect
- setting standards that match expectations
- delivering services to these standards
- measuring and demonstrating successful service delivery
- reviewing expectations, standards, delivery and success.

The document 'The Value of Sport' (1999) poses the challenge – Why invest in sport? It demonstrates that sport can make a difference to people's lives and to their communities. It emphasizes that for every pound spent on sport there are multiple returns in:
- improved health
- reduced crime
- economic regeneration
- improved employment opportunities.

Sport impacts on a whole range of corporate policy issues – local authorities need to highlight this in visible and tangible ways in order to secure funding:
- sustainable communities
- anti-poverty
- job creation
- environmental protection

- equity and equality
- community safety
- social and economic regeneration
- inward investment
- lifelong learning
- crime prevention
- healthy lifestyles
- social cohesion
- community development.

'Regeneration is not simply about bricks and mortar. It is about the physical, social and economic well-being of an area; it is about the quality of life in our neighbourhoods.' (Towns and cities: Partners in urban renewal)

What does value mean?

The word 'value' is used a lot in relation to sport, but what does it mean? The value of sport should not be underestimated in terms of the social, economic and environmental benefits to be gained by individuals, communities or even the country. Residents of any local area place a high level of expectation on the availability of a range of good quality, accessible and affordable sporting opportunities. The range of leisure activities and opportunities is increasingly seen as an important indicator of the quality of life in an area. A local population will often judge a council's performance by the leisure facilities they have provided. In particular, sport has the potential to:

- encourage those who feel excluded from society to access a wide range of services and facilities, creating a renewed sense of purpose, helping to bring people together and provide a common identity
- contribute to personal development through the enhancement of new skills, social interaction and well-being
- deter people from anti-social behaviour, allowing them to channel and challenge offending behaviour in a non-threatening environment
- improve health by keeping people physically active and promoting the health benefits associated with exercise
- create employment opportunities, which help to improve the economy
- advance young people's development by instilling self-belief and a sense of achievement.

Development plans

TASK 2

Imagine you work for the local authority and need to prepare a development plan for sport. What factors would you have to consider?

Numerous factors influence sports development, such as:
- economic: the wealth of the community, that is, the average socio-economic grade of the majority of the population
- cultural: for example, the local ethnic mix and historical traditions

- geographical: for example, is it a rural or urban population?
- political influences: the leanings of the elected council/historical investment in sports services
- facilities available: from the education and private sectors and so on
- aims/plans of other groups/work with existing partnerships.

Local authorities have, for many years, been working hard to maximize the use of existing facilities as well as building new facilities to be used by schools and the community. The initial scheme in the 1970s started with the dual-use policy whereby a local school's facilities could be used by a local community after school, at weekends and in the school holidays (Table 12.01). This was then superseded to some extent by the term 'joint provision', or joint funding, which was a more sophisticated approach. These facilities usually have a centre manager who co-ordinates the use of the facility and the costs can be shared between authorities.

Table 12.01 Strengths and weaknesses of dual-use facilities

Strengths	Weaknesses
- Community base - Links with schools - Shared costs - Guaranteed usage	- Limited access for public - Image/awareness - Different needs for school and public

TASK 3

1 What does 'non-statutory' mean in relation to a local authority's responsibility in delivering sport opportunities?
2 What objectives would a local borough council have in terms of leisure provision in its local area?
3 What advantages are there to a local authority developing a strategic plan for leisure provision?
4 What is the value of sport to local residents in a local community?
5 How could the make-up of a population affect leisure provision?

Local provision of leisure

We have stated that local provision for leisure comes from three main areas:
- public (via the local authority)
- private (from businesses aiming to make a profit)
- voluntary (from the grass roots of local clubs).

They each have their different characteristics (see Tables 12.02 and 12.03), but a local community is dependent on all three contributing.

Table 12.02 Characteristics of each sector

Public (for example, local leisure centre)	Private (for example, private fitness centre)	Voluntary (for example, local netball club)
• Business operations run by local authorities • Trading on set prices/charges according to a pre-set budget • Managed by local authority employees • May involve subsidies as a matter of policy/council tax or equivalent	• Privately owned registered companies • Trading on normal profit/loss/self-financed • Managed by owners and their employees • Must operate and survive in open market/make a profit/compete • Funds from membership fees	• Business operations owned by members • Possibly on trust/charity basis: trading on normal profit/loss/breakeven • Managed by members committees/may employ staff • Financed by members' fees, fundraising, sponsorship

Table 12.03 Objectives of each sector

Public	Private	Voluntary
• Provides a service for the local community • Tends to be more affordable than the private sector • Social impact on health, employment and occupying population in positive activities	• Aims to make a profit for the owner • Can cater for a more exclusive and wealthier clientele	• Provides for grass roots of sport • Tries to increase participation in their sport

TASK 4

Conduct a survey of your local area and try to determine the number and types of leisure facilities available for use by the local community. You might like to visit the Sport England website when researching your answer. Go to www.heinemann.co.uk/hotlinks, insert the express code 9300P click on this topic.

Sport England

Sport England has a Royal Charter, which means it should be free from political control but still accountable for its actions. It is the government-funded agency responsible for providing the strategic lead for sport in England in order to deliver the government's objectives. It is also a distributor of the lottery sports fund. The Sport England mission is to make England an active and successful sporting nation.

Its role is to:
- be the strategic lead for sport in England
- make focused investments through partners
- provide advice, support and knowledge to partners and customers
- influence the decision-makers and public opinion on sport.

Its objectives are to:
- start – increase participation in sport in order to improve the health of the nation, with a focus on priority groups
- stay – retain people in sport and active recreation through an effective network of clubs, sports facilities and coaches, volunteers and competitive opportunities
- succeed – achieve sporting success at every level
- ensure internal efficiency – that we operate and allocate our resources with maximum effectiveness.

Active Sports programme

This is a scheme co-ordinated by Sport England based on four policy headings:
- active schools – forms the foundation
- active communities – looks at breaking down the barriers to participation and considers equity issues
- active sports – links participation to excellence such as participation in the Millennium Youth Games
- World Class England – operates four programmes of 'World Class Start', 'World Class Potential', 'World Class Performance' and 'World Class Events'.

They are meant to act as building blocks and are not necessarily linear, as shown by Figure 12.05. They also complement the participation pyramid of foundation, participation, performance and excellence (page xx). The majority of the funding will come from the National Lottery and there will be a strengthening of the regional set-up via local authorities. There will be a framework around all experiences available to potential participants such as the National Junior Sports Programme, Sportsmark and Coaching for Teachers.

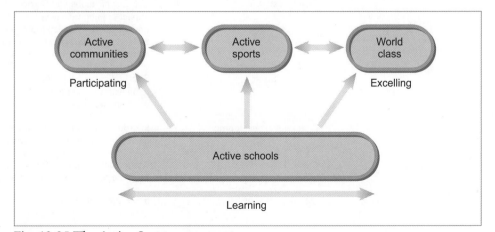

Fig. 12.05 The Active Sports programme

Sportsmark and Activemark

These awards are given to schools, secondary schools and primary schools respectively, for showing good provision for sport and physical education. Sportsmark and Activemark are currently being revamped and a new Sports Partnership Mark is to be introduced because:

- the awards were developed some time ago when little other investment was being made into school sport
- the government is now making investment into PE and school sport, and is delivering the national school sport strategy.

KEY WORDS

High quality PE and school sport

'High quality PE and school sport produces young people with the skills, understanding, desire and commitment to continue to improve and achieve in a range of PE, sport and health-enhancing physical activities in line with their abilities.' (DfES website)

Physical Education, School Sport and Club Links Strategy (PESSCLS)

PESSCLS is a joint DCMS/DfES initiative to implement a national strategy for PE and school sport. The aim is to enhance the take-up of sporting opportunities of 5 to 16 year olds so that the percentage of school children in England who spend a minimum of two hours each week on **high quality PE and school sport** within and beyond the curriculum increases.

Table 12.04 The eight components of the PESSCLS

Specialist Sports Colleges (see also Chapter 11)	A specialist system is being created in which every secondary school has its own special ethos and works with others to spread best practice and raise standards
School sport partnerships	Families of schools that come together to enhance sporting opportunities for all. They are made up of one specialist Sports College, eight secondary schools and approximately 45 primary or specialist schools
Gifted and talented	Part of a wider strategy to improve gifted and talented education. Aims to improve quality of teaching, coaching and learning, and raise aspirations, which will improve performance, motivation and self-esteem. Young people with potential will be encouraged to join junior sports clubs and develop links between NGBs and school
QCA investigation	The Qualifications and Curriculum Authority is investigating the impact of 'high quality sport and PE' on schools that have undertaken the project. Many schools have seen wider benefits to the school including better attendance, better behaviour, positive attitudes and higher self-esteem
Step into Sport	Sport relies on 1.5 million volunteer officials, coaches, administrators and managers. Step into Sport encourages children and young people to lead and volunteer
Professional development	In order to deliver high quality PE and sport, teachers and other professionals need training and to be able to draw on resources
Club links	To increase the proportion of children guided into affiliated clubs from the school sport co-ordinator partnerships
Swimming	It is a statutory requirement that 80 per cent of children should be able to swim 25 metres by the end of Key Stage 2

PE and sport in schools, both within and beyond the curriculum, can improve:

- pupil concentration, commitment and self-esteem, leading to higher attendance and better behaviour and attainment
- fitness levels: active children are less likely to be obese and more likely to pursue sporting activities as adults, thereby reducing the likelihood of coronary heart disease, diabetes and some forms of cancer
- success in international competitions by ensuring that talented young sports people have a clear pathway to elite sport and competitions whatever their circumstances.

The project has eight sub-delivery programmes (see Table 12.04) and is closely linked with a separate project to implement the recommendations of the Coaching Task Force.

National governing bodies

HOT TIPS

For this specification, you only need to know the historical development of governing bodies (see Chapter 13) and their policies for ensuring equity in sport (see Chapter 13).

A national governing body is responsible for its own sport, overseeing competitions and ensuring internationally agreed rules are adhered to. The NGB then affiliates to the International Sport Federation (ISF). An example would be the FA and FIFA. In the past, NGBs in the UK have been very independent, but nowadays, as they become more dependent on lottery funding, they have to demonstrate that they are meeting some of the core objectives of the government.

Sports Leaders UK (new operating name of the British Sports Trust)

Sports Leaders UK believes it needs to provide the opportunity and motivation for anyone to make a meaningful contribution to their local community. It aims to achieve this through the nationally recognized qualification of the Sports Leader Awards, whereby people can learn essential skills, such as working with and organizing others, as well as motivational, communication and teamwork skills.

Following a recent two-year £2.38 million government grant to encourage further participation in volunteering, particularly amongst young people, the British Sports Trust, organizers of the Sports Leader Awards Scheme, is now keen to further develop its partnerships with organizations and groups working with young people aged 14–19. The grant is part of the £7 million Step into Sport initiative, which will see the British Sports Trust, the Youth Sport Trust and Sport England teaming up to help train a new generation of volunteer coaches, mainly aged 14–19. The project aims to create around 60,000 young coaches and a further 8000 adult coaches and officials.

- The Junior Sports Leader Award: for 14–16 year olds and is taught mainly in schools within the National Curriculum for physical education at Key

Stage 4. The award develops a young person's skills in organizing activities, planning, communicating and motivating.

- The Community Sports Leader Award: for those aged 16 years and over, this popular award is taught in schools, colleges, youth clubs, prisons, and sports and leisure centres nationwide.
- The Higher Sports Leader Award: builds on the skills gained through the Community Sports Leader Award to equip people to lead specific community groups such as older people, people with disabilities and primary school children. The award includes units in event management, first aid, sports development and obtaining a coaching award.
- Basic Expedition Leader Award: for those interested in the outdoors and builds the ability to organize safe expeditions and overnight camps.

Core values:
- Developing leadership – teaching people the ability to organize activities, to lead, motivate and communicate with groups.
- Developing skills for life – helping people reach their true potential.
- Providing a stepping-stone to employment – offering a qualification to get started.
- Encouraging volunteering in communities – motivating others to organize safe sporting activities in their communities.
- Reducing youth crime – young people engaging in positive activities.
- Supporting more active, healthier communities – by providing sports leaders to organize a range of physical activity sessions.

Youth Sports Trust

Much mention has already been made of this organization. It is becoming a key player in all the government's strategies for grass roots sport. Its mission is to support the education and development of all young people through physical education and sport in order that they can experience and enjoy PE and sport through a quality introduction at their own level of development. The teaching, coaching and resources should be of the best quality possible and healthy competition should help develop a healthy lifestyle so everyone can achieve their potential. The YST is also involved in supporting and developing the specialist Sports Colleges and school sport co-ordinators initiatives.

The YST has developed a series of linked and progressive schemes – the TOP programmes, from eighteen months to eighteen years. Key features of the programme are:
- resource cards
- child-friendly equipment
- quality training for teachers and deliverers.

Other projects the YST is involved with are:
- inclusion of young disabled people
- encouraging more teenage girls to take part

- tackling social exclusion within primary schools through playground development
- supporting gifted and talented young sports people.

Revise as you go!

1. What does DCMS stand for and what is its role in relation to sport?
2. What is meant by a decentralized administration and what are the advantages and disadvantages of this set-up?
3. Give three reasons why national governments will become involved in sport.
4. What does 'centralized' mean?
5. Why should the UK government want to spend large sums of money on sport in local communities?
6. The British Sports Trust delivers four Sport Leader Awards. What are they?
7. What are the core elements of the active sports programme run by Sport England?
8. Give three functions of a governing body of sport.
9. Give two features of the Sportsmark policy.
10. What occurs when a school is given Sports College status?
11. What is meant by the public sector?
12. Give two factors that explain what is meant by the voluntary sector.
13. Give two key features of the private sector in relation to leisure provision.
14. State three points to explain 'best value'.
15. Explain what the following terms signify: active schools, active communities, active sports.

Chapter 13: Equal opportunities in the participation of physical recreation and sport

Learning outcomes

By the end of this chapter you should be able to:
- understand the effectiveness of government and national governing body policies in achieving equal opportunities in active recreation and sport for a variety of social groups
- understand the effect of social class on opportunities for participation, particularly low socio-economic groups
- understand ethnic preferences and implications for participation
- understand the effect of gender and sexism on participation
- understand the effect of disability on opportunities for participation
- understand the role of the Women's Sport Foundation and Disability Sport England.

Introduction

HOT TIPS

You will not need to know specific figures but you may need to interpret similar sources of data and account for the findings of each.

HOT TIPS

The focus or target groups in this specification are:
- ethnic minority groups
- women
- disabled
- youth 16-24
- low socio-economic groups

Module 2 of the AS course studies factors that have influenced how certain people have been able to maximize their opportunities for participating in active recreation and how others have experienced many more restrictions on their participation. Although we can safely say that opportunities for the majority of the population have improved over the last century, there are still unacceptable levels of inequalities experienced by certain groups. This chapter is going to explore these issues further, focusing on participation levels in active recreation rather than high level sport.

In the government's mission for sport, Game Plan, figures have been produced under the title, 'Where are we now? The state of sport today.' It might be useful to begin with some facts and figures to appreciate the reality of the situation.

- The quality and quantity of participation in sport and physical activity in the UK is lower than it could be, and levels have not changed significantly over recent years.
- For sport, only 47 per cent of the UK population participate in sport more than twelve times a year, compared to 70 per cent in Sweden and almost 80 per cent in Finland.
- For physical activity, only 32 per cent of adults in England take 30 minutes of moderate exercise five times a week, compared to 57 per cent of Australians and 70 per cent of Finns.
- Young white males are most likely to take part in sport and physical activity, and the most disadvantaged groups least likely.
- Participation falls dramatically after leaving school and continues to drop with age.

- The more active in sport and physical activity you are at a young age, the more likely you are to continue to participate throughout your life.
- The levels of participation in the UK are lower than those in Scandinavia, but so is the regularity and quality of that participation.

If we need to increase participation in sport and active recreation across the population, then there is a particular need to target specific groups who are below the national average. These can be called focus, priority or target groups.

It would appear that the group with the highest participation rates come from the white, male, middle-class section of society. This would also be the group we would call the 'dominant group', as they have the most access to employment, decision-making and control of the major social institutions such as the law, education, media and so on. This group traditionally could be seen to protect its own position, for example by establishing laws or membership clauses, or having in place discriminatory practices that will limit the opportunities of other groups, usually based on prejudicial attitudes.

It would appear that groups with the lowest participation rates in active recreation are from the same groups that have been identified as most likely to suffer from social exclusion:

- ethnic background
- females
- disability
- demographics/rural areas/inner cities.
- youth
- age
- low income

KEY WORDS

Discrimination

To make a distinction: to give unfair treatment especially because of prejudice.

Social exclusion

A shorthand term for what can happen when people or areas suffer from a combination of linked problems such as unemployment, poor skills, low incomes, unfair discrimination, poor housing, high crime, bad health and family breakdown.

The question could be posed – so what? If people *prefer* not to participate, why should the government and national sport organizations feel any sense of obligation to change their minds and habits?

As a society, there is a definite belief that sport is good for people: it provides enjoyment, contributes to health. As part of a wider social policy, it can help reduce crime levels and increase educational attainment; it can create a sense of pride in community and country.

It is more likely that some sections of the population do not participate as much as others due to fewer opportunities and traditional **discrimination**, and therefore have not had the same opportunities to make informed decisions as to whether they would like to participate in active recreation or not.

Social exclusion

The **Social Exclusion** Unit was set up by the government in 1997, with a broad remit to 'reduce social exclusion by finding joined-up solutions to interconnected problems'. The government has invested funds in trying to tackle the economic causes of exclusion and attempting to improve people's lifestyles by creating opportunities for them to develop their education and skills.

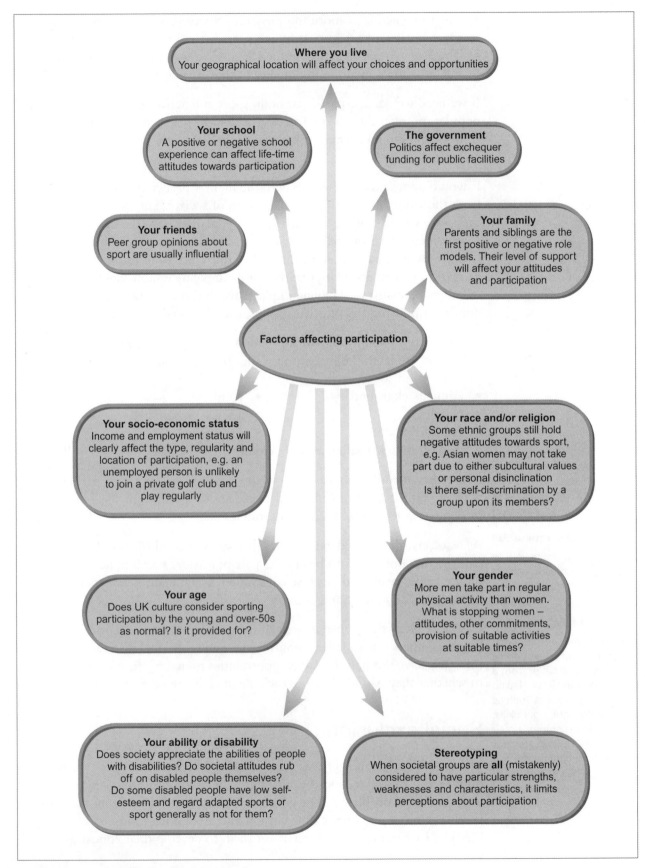

Fig. 13.01 Factors affecting participation in sport
Text used by permission of Sarah van Wely.

KEY WORDS

Social mobility

Movement of individuals up or down the social class structure.

The term 'joined-up solutions' refers to the government's belief in recent decades that many social policies inter-relate and affect each other. It involves developing working partnerships amongst different organizations. In previous years, there may have been a policy for health and a separate one for employment and reducing crime. Nowadays, the government recognizes that these social issues often inter-relate and separate policies are a false economy.

Social mobility

When subordinate groups are discriminated against, their opportunities for **social mobility** and participation in a variety of sports can be limited.

Social mobility has increased throughout the twentieth century. The middle class expanded whilst the working class declined in size, reflecting structural changes in society and the economy as a result of economic growth. However, in recent decades, the improved opportunities enjoyed by greater numbers of children have begun to slow down and have halted in some cases. This is due to the contraction in skilled manual work in the early 1980s and a slower growth in the number of professional and managerial jobs.

Table 13.01 Cost of social exclusion

Cost to the individual	Cost to the taxpayer	Cost to the economy
• Individuals not realizing their educational potential • Higher risk of unemployment • Poorer physical health • Crime and fear of crime affect the most deprived communities	• Expenditure in 2001/02 totalled £30.7 billion in income support, housing benefit and so on • Cost of school exclusions estimated at £406 million • A report calculated that if one in ten young offenders received effective early intervention, the annual saving would be in excess of £100 million	• A lack of skilled workers, resulting in a productivity gap between the UK and its international competitors • Lack of customers – low income reduces the nation's spending power

TASK 1

1 How could participating in sport improve the quality of life for an individual who suffers from social exclusion?
2 Why should a government be concerned about a number of citizens being socially excluded?

Table 13.02 Constraints and exclusion in sport and leisure DCMS

Group excluded	Youth			Poor/ unemployed	Women	Older people	Ethnic minority	People disabled/ learn diff.
Constraint/exclusion factor	Child	Young people	Young delinq.					
Structural factors								
Poor physical/social environment	✔	✔	✔✔	✔✔	✔	✔	✔✔	✔
Poor facilities/community capacity	✔	✔	✔✔	✔✔	✔	✔	✔	✔✔
Poor support network	✔	✔	✔✔	✔✔	✔	✔	✔	✔✔
Poor transport	✔✔	✔✔	✔✔	✔✔	✔✔	✔✔	✔	✔✔
Managers' policies and attitudes	✔	✔	✔✔	✔✔	✔	✔	✔✔	✔✔
Labelling by society	✔	✔	✔✔✔	✔	✔	✔	✔✔	✔✔
Lack of time structure	✔	✔	✔✔	✔✔		✔		✔
Lack of income	✔	✔	✔✔	✔✔✔	✔	✔✔	✔	✔✔
Lack of skills/personal and social capital	✔	✔	✔✔✔	✔✔✔	✔	✔	✔✔	✔✔
Fears for safety	✔✔	✔✔	✔✔	✔✔	✔✔✔	✔✔✔✔	✔✔	✔✔
Powerlessness	✔✔	✔✔	✔✔✔	✔✔	✔✔	✔✔	✔✔✔✔	✔✔
Poor self/body image	✔	✔	✔✔	✔✔	✔	✔	✔✔	✔✔

The number of ✔ signs shows the severity of particular constraints for particular groups

Any sporting policies will need to take account of these trends in order to tackle social exclusion. The National Strategy for Neighbourhood Renewal is an important part of the government's plan to build socially inclusive communities. All local authorities have a remit to lower 'worklessness' and crime, improve skills, health and housing, and to narrow the gap that exists between the most deprived areas and the rest of the country.

Table 13.03 General barriers to participation in sport

Attitudes	Access	Programme
• Stereotyping	• Facilities	• Range of activities
• Lack of confidence	• Times of opening	• Inappropriate for ability
• Lack of self-motivation	• Transport	• Inappropriate for delivery style
• Image of sport	• Lack of information	• Quality of provision
• Family/personal relationships	• Official procedures	• Too competitive
• Cultural norms	• Fees	• Not enough fun
• Lack of interest	• Lack of childcare facilities	
• Too competitive	• Lifestyle	
	• Health	
	• Education	
	• Socio-economic status	
	• Other competing activities	

Socio-economic groups

KEY WORDS

Gender

Used by sociologists to describe the cultural and social attributes of men and women, which are manifested in masculinity and feminity.

Subculture

An identifiable group within society whose members share common values and have similar behaviour patterns.

Not surprisingly, participation rates in sport varies across social groups, as Figure 13.02 below shows. Furthermore, the link between **gender** and social class appears to be increasingly significant when looking at participation rates.

Generally, individuals from the lower socio-economic groups have poorer health and mortality rates that those in the other groups, therefore the health benefits of participation in physical activity are particularly important for this group. This group is very likely to suffer from social exclusion as they have less power, less opportunities for decision-making, less disposable income and so on. This can affect what they can afford to do and the quality of life they can expect. The 'working-class **subculture**' can also affect how this group may adapt to what can be middle-class sporting environments. The values that are transferred through the generations can still alienate some people who have been brought up with different values to that of the dominant culture. Feelings of inadequacy, low self-esteem, isolation from major social institutions are all factors that make this group difficult to mobilize.

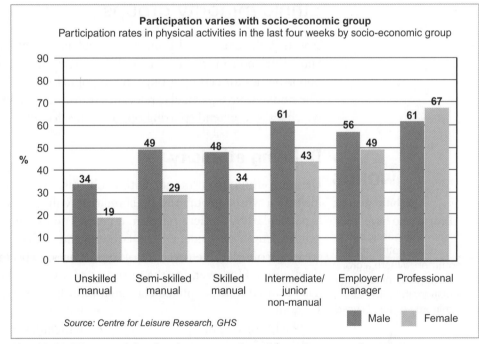

Fig. 13.02 How participation in sport varies with socio-economic group

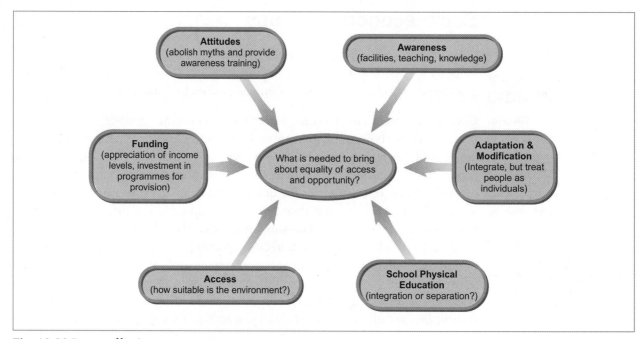

Fig. 13.03 Issues affecting access to sport

Ethnic minority groups

'Sports Participation and Ethnicity in England, 1999/2000' was a survey by Sport England to better understand the extent and causes of inequity in sporting opportunities for certain groups in the population and ways to overcome them. The findings have particular relevance to the active communities programme, which aims to extend sporting opportunities for all.

KEY WORDS

Ethnic groups

People who have racial, religious, linguistic and/or certain other traits in common. Where a group forms a minority in a population, the term 'ethnic minority group' is used.

HOT TIPS

For the purpose of this specification, ethnic minority groups refer to those people residing in the UK. Many students mistakenly refer to these groups as if they still lived in another country.

Defining ethnicity

Defining ethnicity is fraught with problems, as it is almost impossible to identify a whole group and presume they will have similar experiences. This is particularly so where religion, culture, values, language, generation, age, gender, length of residency in a country and nationality all play a part in creating considerable diversity of experiences, expectations, way of life and behaviours. However, for the purposes of a national quantitative survey, it has required that people be classified into these 'broad **ethnic groups**':

- White
- Black Caribbean
- Black African
- Black other
- Indian
- Pakistani
- Bangladeshi
- Chinese
- None of these (17 per cent) became 'Other'.

The findings of the survey showed that for ethnic minority groups, the overall participation rate in sport is 40 per cent compared to 46 per cent national average. Only the 'Black other' group (60 per cent) has participation rates higher than the population as a whole. Black Caribbean, Chinese, Pakistani and Bangladeshi were lower than the national average. These figures were similar for women from the same groups. However, the

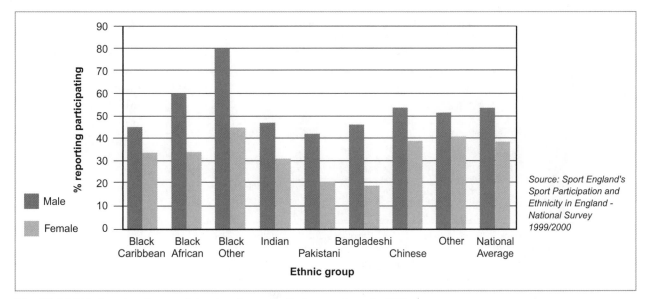

Source: Sport England's
Sport Participation and
Ethnicity in England -
National Survey
1999/2000

Fig. 13.04 Ethnic minority participation is generally lower than the UK average

gap between men's and women's participation is greater amongst ethnic minority groups than it is in the population as a whole.

Reasons for low participation rates

Reasons given for constraining factors in participation are similar to the population as a whole, for example work/study demands, home and family responsibilities, lack of money, laziness and so on, but some also quoted negative experiences in sport due to ethnicity. These instances were higher for the 'Black other' men and less relevant for the Chinese section of the population. Indian (31 per cent), Pakistani (21 per cent) and Bangladeshi (19 per cent) women in particular have a lower involvement in sport than the national female average of 39 per cent.

Sporting patterns are also different for different ethnic groups, for example participation rates in football amongst all ethnic groups is higher than the national average, whereas for swimming it is lower.

Within a multi-cultural population, sport needs to be sensitive to the barriers that impact on these groups and provide types of activities that appeal to them within environments that are accessible and welcoming. So what activities are popular with ethnic minority groups?

Ethnic preferences

There are a number of instances where sports have relatively high levels of participation amongst certain ethnic minority groups. These include:
- weight training amongst Black males
- running/jogging amongst Black other males and Black Africans, which is higher than general male population
- badminton by Chinese men
- cricket by Pakistani, Black other and Indian
- basketball amongst Black Caribbean and Black African.

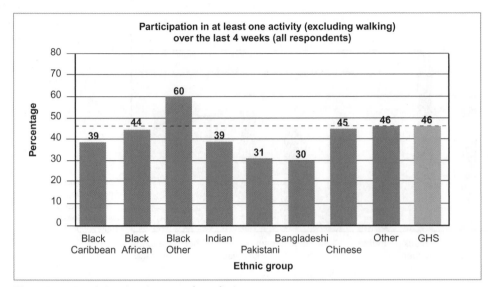

Fig. 13.05 Participation in sport by ethnic groups

TASK 2

Why do you think cricket is popular amongst the Pakistani and Indian communities?

An important result of the survey is the complexity of the whole issue. There is considerable variation in the levels of participation between different ethnic groups, between men and women and between different sports. The results also challenge the stereotypical view that suggests that low levels of participation in sport by certain groups are more a reflection of culture and choice rather than other constraints such as provision, affordability and access.

The issue of racial discrimination was touched on and although the results were variable, at its highest, as many as one in five said that they had had a negative experience in sport related to their ethnicity. This should be a concern of policy makers.

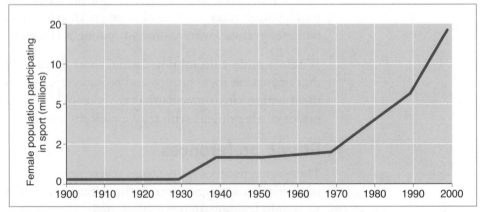

Fig. 13.06 Number of women participating in sport and physical activity over the last 100 years

KEY WORDS

Racism

A set of ideas or beliefs based on the assumption that races have distinct characteristics determined by hereditary factors endowing some races with an intrinsic superiority and others with inferiority.

Stereotype

A standardized image or concept shared by members of a social group. Behaviour traits are associated with particular types of individuals. They are usually negative images related to race and gender.

Self-fulfilling prophecy

By making a prediction that those in positions of influence will act as though the prediction were already true. For example, a teacher may believe a black child is more likely to succeed at sport and will provide more encouragement for those types of activities. It is likely the child will be more successful at sport given the greater opportunities provided.

Table 13.04 Examples of racism in sport

Stacking	Refers to the disproportionate concentration of ethnic minorities in certain positions in a sports team, based on the **stereotype** that they are more valued for their physical skills than for their decision-making qualities. An example would be placing black players in outfield positions in baseball
Centrality	According to Grusky's theory of centrality, this restricts ethnic minority groups from more central positions, which are based on co-ordinative tasks, requiring decision-making and social interaction
Labelling	An approach that focuses on the way in which agents of social control, such as teachers, attach stigmatizing stereotypes to particular groups of people. These can then have a **self-fulfilling prophecy**. An example can be a teacher having lower educational expectations of black children compared to white children, or girls compared to boys in the field of sport. Children take these expectations on board and behave accordingly – the implication being that the prediction was always true
Channelling	The idea that teachers and coaches will channel children from ethnic minority groups into certain sports that they feel they are most likely to succeed in. It can also involve them channelling them into sport rather than down the academic route
Attitudes/prejudice	Opinion, bias or judgement formed without due consideration of facts or arguments. For example, certain types of people are sometimes not made to feel welcome in a sports centre
Racist attacks	If someone is attacked, physically or verbally, and feels they were targeted because of the colour of their skin, this constitutes a racist attack

Solutions to the lower participation rates from ethnic minority groups

- Sport policies that are sensitive to and respectful of other cultures – this can mean providing single-sex sessions for Muslim women, changing facilities and physical educational programmes in schools.
- Use of policy planning, race relations advisors and customer care.
- Information should be available about sport provision in a local area.
- Clubs should be supported but integration not forced.
- People from ethnic minorities from the local communities to be trained as sport leaders and sport development officers.
- Greater media coverage to raise awareness of ethnic minority sports and role models.
- Campaigns to eliminate racism.

Kick it Out is football's anti-racism campaign. The brand name of the campaign – Let's Kick Racism out of Football – was established by the Commission for Racial Equality and the Professional Footballers' Association (PFA) in 1993. Kick it Out works throughout the football, educational and community sectors to challenge racism and work for positive change. The campaign is supported and funded by the game's governing bodies including the players' union (the PFA), the FA Premier League, the Football Association and the Football Foundation.

Internationally, Kick it Out plays a leading role in the Football Against Racism in Europe (FARE) network and has been cited as an example of good practice by the European governing body UEFA, the world governing body FIFA, the Council of Europe, the European Commission, European parliamentarians and the British Council.

Female participation

Statistics show that for most sport and physical activity, participation is higher amongst men. Swimming and keep fit/yoga are notable exceptions.

Changing trends in female participation can be difficult to track fully due to a lack of up-to-date comparable data. Using the information contained in the 1996 General Household Survey, however, it appears that participation rates are relatively static, with modest increases in some activities (see Figure 13.07).

Those are the statistics – we now need to account for them.

Reasons for lower female participation rates in active recreation

KEY WORDS

Femininity

Characteristics associated with being a woman.

- Domestic role: women still bear the greater burden of domestic work, reducing the time they have for leisure.
- Social stereotyping: society is still less less positive about female sport participation in comparison to males. This is because the characteristics associated with sport tend to match society's view of masculinity rather than **femininity**. Examples are being competitive, assertive, achievement orientated and so on.

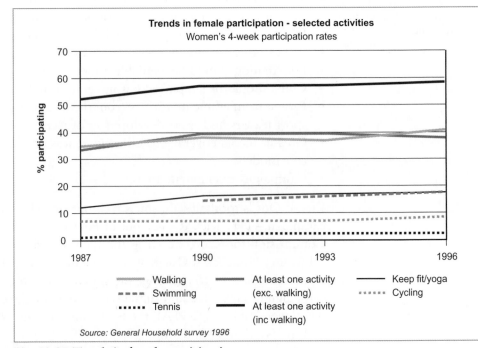

Trends in female participation - selected activities
Women's 4-week participation rates

Legend:
- Walking
- Swimming
- Tennis
- At least one activity (exc. walking)
- At least one activity (inc walking)
- Keep fit/yoga
- Cycling

Source: General Household survey 1996

Fig. 13.07 Trends in female participation

- Sport traditionally the preserve of males: sport was established and controlled by men and this led to situations where women were actively discouraged from participating in sport.
- Less media coverage: there has traditionally been less media coverage of female sport. This does not raise the profile of women's sport and there are fewer role models for women to aspire to.
- Traditionally less money and power: women generally earn less money than men and occupy fewer positions of power in society and in the workplace, and consequently in sporting institutions where decisions are made.
- **Sexism:** discrimination can be overt, as in legislation and club membership clauses, and also covert, as in society's more negative attitudes towards female participation.
- Evidence of inequalities in sporting opportunities: unequal provision of facilities, less variety of activities – women have had to fight long and hard to be allowed to participate in some sports such as football, boxing and rugby. There are fewer female coaches/administrators, restricted club access and lack of effective childcare.

KEY WORDS

Sexism

The belief that one sex is inferior to the other, and is most often directed towards women.

Solutions to low participation rates

- Equal opportunities: the feminist movement began at the beginning of the twentieth century with the suffragettes and women's rights. It gathered momentum when women won the right to vote in 1917. Women have fought for equal rights since this time. In the present day, organizations, such as national governing bodies, must create and deliver **equal opportunity** policies following the Sex Discrimination Act 1975 and in line with government policies. The Women's Sport Foundation has been established to raise the awareness of inequalities in female sporting provision and provides guidelines for organizations involving female sport participation.
- More facilities for women: facilities should be made accessible to women offering women-only sessions where appropriate and combined with more effective childcare facilities.
- Better links between schools and clubs: the drop in participation amongst young women when they leave education is dramatic. This has serious consequences for later participation in sport and their general health. The government is determined to improve links between schools and clubs to help lower this 'post-school gap'.
- Media coverage: more and better quality media coverage of female sport should help to widen women's horizons and promote positive images of women. This should create positive role models for women to aspire to.
- Health-related activities: women are very interested in activities that are geared towards improving their general health and conditioning activities for toning the body. Women should be aware of all the possibilities in their area and the health benefits of sport participation should be promoted.

KEY WORDS

Equal opportunity

The principle and practice of providing all people with the same chance to participate, in this context, in recreational and sporting activities.

Sex means the biological aspect of a person, either female or male. Gender roles refer to what different societies and cultures attribute as appropriate behaviour for that sex. Gender roles therefore carry social expectations that can be very difficult to fight against. These can vary from culture to culture and can change over time within a culture. An example would be the contrast between the ideal image of a woman in the UK and the old Eastern bloc ideal image of a woman. In the latter, they appreciated the strong woman who could do heavy manual work, and this is also emphasized in the popularity of female shot putters. In this country, we have revered the dainty and delicate female, one who is physically slim and emotionally vulnerable. In modern-day sport, this means that sports such as tennis, gymnastics and so on receive more social acceptance than sports requiring more 'masculine' orientated features.

TASK 4

1 Make a list of the characteristics you associate with the terms 'femininity' and 'masculinity'.
2 Now list the words you feel demonstrate the ability to succeed in sport.
3 Which gender role is the sporting success model most similar to?

Historically, sport was always seen as a male preserve as they developed and controlled sports whilst women have had to fight hard to achieve similar opportunities. This immediately suggests that men discriminated against women and there are many instances of this, one notable example being the banning of female football by the Football Association in 1921. Many reasons given for these limitations or restrictions have been based on medical grounds and the idealistic image of femininity, which was strengthened in the nineteenth century. This led to many stereotypes and myths developing, particularly regarding the medical problems women would encounter if they participated in sport too strenuously. These myths existed well into the twentieth century.

In the present day, opportunities for women to participate in sport have increased greatly due to greater independence via more disposable income and transport, availability of more sports, clubs and competitions, more media coverage and women in positions of responsibility in sport organizations. Also, all organizations have to face the responsibility for improving opportunities for women as part of their social and legal responsibility.

Sex Discrimination Act 1975

This act made sex discrimination unlawful in employment, training, education and the provision of goods, facilities and services, that is, a female should be treated in the same way as a male in similar circumstances. However, competitive sport is excluded by Section 44 of the Act. Separate competitions for men and women are allowed where 'the physical strength, stamina or physique puts her at a disadvantage to the average man'.

Successful appeals have been made where discrimination has occurred towards female referees. Private sports clubs can also legally discriminate under Sections 29 and 34 of the Act.

The Women's Sport Foundation

The Women's Sports Foundation (for further information please go to www.heinemann.co.uk/hotlinks, insert express code 9300P and click on this topic) is the UK's leading organization dedicated to improving and promoting opportunities for women and girls in sport and physical activity. They are committed to improving, increasing and promoting opportunities for women and girls – in all roles and at all levels – in sport, fitness and physical activity through advocacy, information, education, research and training. They campaign for change at all levels of sport through raising awareness and influencing policy.

It was originally set up in 1984 by women working in sport who were concerned about the lack of sport and recreation opportunities for women and girls, and the low representation of women in sports coaching, sports management and the sports media. WSF became a registered charity and company limited by guarantee in 1997.

- At present, the Women's Sports Foundation is funded primarily by Sport England.
- They have a quarterly newsletter – *Women in Sport*.
- They also receive a small amount of additional income via other grants, donations and supporter subscriptions for the magazine and information resources.

Since 1984, the Women's Sports Foundation has been involved in a variety of projects to promote women's sport. These have included:

- the Women's Sports Foundation Awards for Girls and Young Women
- training for Britain's top sportswomen on working with the media, attracting sports sponsorship, employment opportunities in sport and recreation, and receiving benefits from sports science support
- the National Action Plan for Women's and Girls' Sport and Physical Activity (1999–2001)
- Women into High Performance Coaching Project
- Women Get Set Go: a personal development course intended to provide a springboard for women into sports leadership, whether as coaches, administrators or officials
- production of a variety of women and sport resources including posters, information packs, photographic exhibitions and fact sheets.

The factor that seems to have the greatest impact on female participation is the growing emphasis placed on health and fitness and the toned, slim stereotypical female form.

TASK 5

Fig. 13.08

Fig. 13.09

Why is aerobics considered more socially acceptable than body building for women?

Football is the number one sport for girls and women. There are now 61,000 women competing in clubs affiliated to the Football Association, and there is also a similar increase in the number of girls' football teams, which are developing within schools. There are 40,000 more under-14 girls playing at school than ten years ago. One problem holding back the number of girls taking up the sport, however, is the lack of career prospects. There are still only approximately nineteen England-based professional players. The FA has put in place a series of initiatives to increase opportunities.

- In 1997, it launched its Talent Development Plan for Women's Football.
- Establishment of 42 Centres of Excellence to develop 10–16 year olds.
- Nineteen Women's Football Academies – 16 years and over.
- In 2001, the National Women's Player Development Centre was launched in Loughborough University – for the most promising.

Disability and participation in active recreation and sport

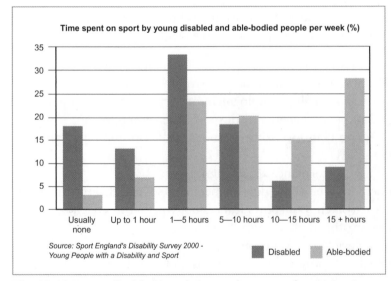

Time spent on sport by young disabled and able-bodied people per week (%)

Source: Sport England's Disability Survey 2000 - Young People with a Disability and Sport

Disabled | Able-bodied

Fig. 13.10 Young disabled people have a low rate of participation in sport

A national survey by Sport England (2000) revealed lower levels of participation in sport among the young disabled compared with the rest of the population (see Figure 13.10). The most popular sports for the young disabled are horse riding and swimming, where participation levels are higher than in the overall population of younger people. However, these are sports that tend to organize events specifically for people with disabilities. Participation in other sports alongside the non-disabled is low.

'Disability sport' is a term used to suggest a more positive approach towards the participation in sport of disabled people. It includes people with a physical, sensory or mental impairment. The term 'disability' is used when impairment adversely affects performance. Other terms used are handicapped sport, sports for the disabled, adapted sport, wheelchair sport and deaf sport. Competitive sports have either been designed specifically for the disabled, such as goalball for the blind (see below), or have been modified such as volleyball and wheelchair basketball and tennis.

Goalball is a three-a-side game. The aim is to score a goal by rolling the ball along the floor into your opponent's goal. All players wear eyeshades to ensure that everyone is equal when it comes to visual perception. The features of the game that enable visually impaired people to play include:
- the ball has a bell inside
- the playing court has tactile markings.

Internationally, goalball is played in 87 countries, is a paralympic sport and has European and World Championships. In Britain, the British Blind Sport (BBS) is the organization that is responsible for the sport.

Adapted sports

Although there are a number of sports that have been developed specifically for disabled people, the majority of disabled people participate in mainstream sports. If a sport is adapted, it is essential that the activity is recognizable as the original sport it is being associated with.

Adaptations may be needed for one disabled person and not for another. For example, in tennis, wheelchair users are allowed to let the ball bounce twice before playing it, whereas for the non-wheelchair user tennis player who is deaf, this would not be permitted.

Sports can be adapted by changing aspects such as the rules, equipment, role of players, environment playing area, time or duration. The following are examples of adaptations needed for two specific sports.
- Wheelchair basketball: the rules, height of the ring and court size are identical. The only adaptation is in the dribble rule: two pushes and one bounce replaces the 'bouncing whilst travelling' rule in ambulant basketball.
- Swimming: some technique rules can be more flexible for some classifications and visually impaired people may need a tap on the head to let them know they are nearing the end of the lane.

TASK 6

1 In groups, research different sports that have been adapted for disabled people. Remember to consider outdoor and adventurous activities.
2 Consider a game of rounders. Discuss how this game could be adapted for children with disabilities.

KEY WORDS

Inclusiveness

Inclusiveness recognizes diversity of needs and does not necessarily mean integration or segregation.

Inclusiveness

There have been many improvements in trying to integrate disabled people into mainstream sport as well as recognizing in some instances that segregation is the more appropriate option. The key word is **inclusiveness,**

KEY WORDS

Integration

The act of incorporating individuals into mainstream society.

Segregated activity

To set or be set apart from the main group.

Classification

An attempt to group sports competitors to enable fair competition.

which is a belief or philosophy that all people should have their needs, abilities and aspirations recognized, understood and met within a supportive environment. Inclusiveness does not only include people with disabilities, but also those who may suffer difficult social or economic circumstances, such as people from low socio-economic backgrounds. We have already made mention of the government's policies to challenge social exclusion. An inclusive approach is being developed by:

- putting the individual at the centre of its policies
- recognizing and supporting diversity by striving to meet the widest range of needs
- seeking to achieve the best 'match' between provision and the needs of the individual
- providing staff training and development
- liaising with other relevant organizations and fostering 'joined-up thinking'.

Integration in this context relates to the able-bodied and the disabled taking part together in the same activity at the same time, whilst **segregated activity** means people with disabilities participating among themselves. There are

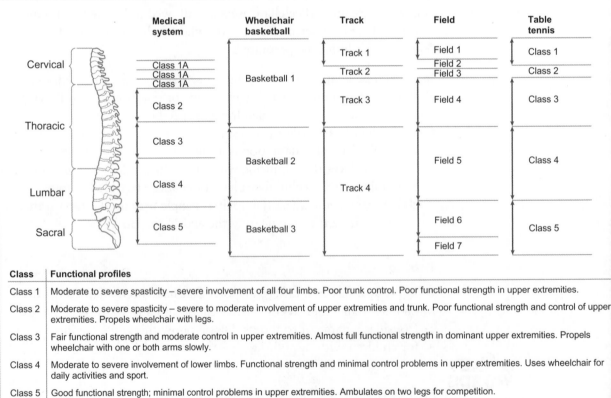

Class	Functional profiles
Class 1	Moderate to severe spasticity – severe involvement of all four limbs. Poor trunk control. Poor functional strength in upper extremities.
Class 2	Moderate to severe spasticity – severe to moderate involvement of upper extremities and trunk. Poor functional strength and control of upper extremities. Propels wheelchair with legs.
Class 3	Fair functional strength and moderate control in upper extremities. Almost full functional strength in dominant upper extremities. Propels wheelchair with one or both arms slowly.
Class 4	Moderate to severe involvement of lower limbs. Functional strength and minimal control problems in upper extremities. Uses wheelchair for daily activities and sport.
Class 5	Good functional strength; minimal control problems in upper extremities. Ambulates on two legs for competition.
Class 6	Moderate to severe involvement of all four extremities and trunk; walks without aids. May use assistive devices for track events.
Class 7	Moderate to minimal hemiplagia. Good functional ability is non-affected side. Walks without aids.
Class 8	Minimally affected hemiplegic or monoplegic. Minimal co-ordination problems. Good balance and is able to run and jump freely.

Note: 1–4 wheelchair for competition, 5–8 ambulatory for competition.

Fig. 13.11 Disability groupings

advantages and disadvantages with each approach. With integration, the disabled participant may not be able to participate fully and the able-bodied players may find it unchallenging. Safety issues would have to be addressed. However, it can help the disabled person feel more included in society and can help raise their self-esteem when they achieve success. Segregation, on the other hand, reinforces the notion of being different to the rest of society but could be the best option in some cases. Participants may actually achieve more in this environment.

Functional **classification** is an integrated classification system that places emphasis on sport performance by disability groupings rather than by specific disability (Figure 13.11). This has enabled disability sport to move on from its rehabilitation base to developing elite competitive sport.

How can opportunities for people with disabilities be improved?

Various organizations such as Sport England, Disability Sport England, the English Federation of Disability Sport, local authorities and national governing bodies have supported and implemented various projects aimed at improving opportunities. However, there is a need for greater co-ordination of policies:

- raising awareness amongst the disabled about opportunities already available
- raising awareness amongst the general public about disability issues
- specialist training programmes for staff who will be involved
- making access to and within facilities more manageable
- adapting even more sports.

Disability Sport England

The aims of Disability Sport England are to:

- provide opportunities for disabled people to participate in sport
- promote the benefits of sport and physical recreation by disabled people
- support organizations in providing sporting opportunities for disabled people
- educate and make people aware of the sporting abilities of disabled people
- enhance the image, awareness and understanding of disability sport
- encourage disabled people to play an active role in the development of their sport.

The following seven National Disability Sports Organizations are recognized by Sport England:

- British Amputees and Les Autres Sports Association
- British Blind Sport
- UK Deaf Sport
- British Wheelchair Sports Foundation
- Cerebral Palsy Sport
- Disability Sport England
- English Sports Association for People with Learning Disabilities.

National governing bodies

Many national governing bodies have been required to democratize their sport. This means to open sport up to all sections of society. One example is the Lawn Tennis Association, which has developed inner city tennis schemes. How can national governing bodies of sport try to achieve equity in sporting opportunities for the priority groups?

They need to develop specific policies to specific target groups via community projects and in particular need to meet government policies such as 'best value' and neighbourhood regeneration if they are to receive much needed lottery funding. They also need to target funding at the grass roots level of sport and elite sport as they each serve the needs of the other. Attempts need to be made to make facilities accessible/affordable/attractive (the three 'A's), but this alone is not enough.

Changes in the structural aspects such as admission fees, membership clauses and cost all need to be considered. Attitudes within the sport need to change with positive campaigns to get rid of discrimination. They need to raise awareness through publicity and advertising. Active participation is important but national governing bodies also need to make sure their employment opportunities within the institutions are not restrictive in terms of colour/race/ethnic origin and so on. Much has already been said about the value of having more people from these sections of society in decision-making positions and the role models they create for others.

TASK 7

Choose a governing body and try to discover what policies it has regarding equity issues. You may find websites a useful source of information. An example could be the Lawn Tennis Association and the Football Association.

Revise as you go!

1 Explain the term 'discrimination' with reference to sport participation.
2 What does the term 'stereotyping' mean and how does it affect participation in sport?
3 What is a target or priority group?
4 Name three target groups identified by Sport England.
5 What is 'upward social mobility' when referring to successful sport participation?
6 How can positive sporting role models be influential in society?
7 What is meant by 'inclusion' with reference to sport participation?
8 What are the three main aims of Sport England?
9 Outline the difference between integrated and segregated sport.

10 Explain the term 'adapted' sport.

11 What is the role of Disability Sport England (DSE) in relation to participation in physical recreation?

12 Suggest barriers disabled people may face when participating in a sport.

13 State three strategies that a sports club may introduce to attract more disabled people.

14 Give two advantages of integrated sport.

15 Give two advantages of segregated sport.

16 Explain the term 'sexism'.

17 Suggest three barriers women may face when participating in sport.

18 State three strategies a sports club may introduce to attract more women to participate.

19 In what way is sport exempt from the Sex Discrimination Act?

20 Give three possible reasons why females participate less than males in sporting activities.

21 What is the role of the Women's Sport Foundation in terms of participation in physical recreation and sport?

22 How could the media help to promote women in sport?

23 Explain the term 'racism'.

24 Suggest three barriers ethnic minority groups face in relation to participation in sport.

25 Suggest three strategies a sports club could introduce to attract more people from ethnic minority groups.

26 What does the term 'stacking' mean?

27 Suggest two reasons why there are fewer coaches and managers from ethnic minority groups in the professional game of football in the UK.

Chapter 14: Exploring the different concepts of physical performance

Learning outcomes

By the end of this chapter you should be able to:
- outline the characteristics and objectives of play: its relationship with recreation and the difference between child play and adult play
- understand the characteristics of recreation and the recreative, educative and escapist objectives
- identify the characteristics of Leisure: the function it serves for individuals and society, and its relationship with recreation; the terms 'active' and 'purposeful' leisure
- outline the objectives, values and characteristics of sport; understand the principles of the subcategories of competitive sport – athletic, gymnastic and game
- explore the concept of physical education with its physical, social and intellectual objectives; appreciate the cultural, educational and social values associated with physical education
- highlight the specific nature of outdoor and adventurous activities as they occur in outdoor education and outdoor recreation; identify the characteristics and values associated with the natural environment, particularly risk and safety, challenge and adventure; understand the development of outdoor activities as competitive sport
- analyse activities using the structural, strategic, technical, physiological and psychological model.

Introduction

KEY WORDS

Physical education

The instilling of skills and values through the medium of physical activity in an educational setting.

Play

When someone 'plays', they engage in an activity for personal amusement.

In everyday life, we use terms such as play, leisure, recreation, sport, **physical education** and so on often interchangeably. At this stage in your learning, it is necessary to adopt a more analytical approach and to try and tease out the characteristics that make each concept unique, and yet also appreciate the inter-relationship existing between them. You are not required to learn specific definitions or theories but you need to be able to explain them using your own words.

For each concept, we need to clarify the following points:
- the structure of the activity: the level or sophistication of its organization
- the motivation: the reasons people engage in the activity
- the benefits: what people gain from participating in the activity.

Many students find this part of the specification difficult to grasp, so we are going to try and begin at the start of it all – **play**. Play is the first experience

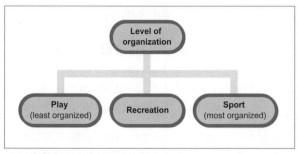

Fig. 14.01 Level of organization increases from play to sport

we have as young children learning basic physical skills. We will then move on to recreation, which is slightly more organized than play but not as organized as sport, which will be the third concept we will examine (see Figure 14.01). For each concept, you will be asked to draw from your own experiences to help you understand the relevance of this unit.

Play

Play is one of the first types of activity we engage in as young children. As such it can be viewed as a natural development of children and may appear a useful and logical starting point in understanding the differing concepts of physical activity.

HOT TIPS

You need to be prepared to:

• explain definitions
• compare across concepts
• analyse data sources such as diagrams.

Many theories have been developed in an attempt to explain the value of play for the individual child and for society. The psychologist Piaget (1962) was very influential in determining how we consider play in the modern era. He proposed that play develops alongside children's cognitive development. He identified:

• *mastery play* – play that allows the child to develop muscle control in order to feel a sense of control over the physical environment. In this context, play can be viewed as helping in the physical development of children. From early on, the child needs to make an impact on its environment and early play is often physical, concerned with sensory or motor co-ordination.

• *symbolic play* – occurs in the second stage, involving the child in make-believe and pretend play. This can also involve mimicry, whereby the child tries to make sense of their world by taking on the role of others. This can be called 'role rehearsal'. Examples of popular games would be 'mummies and daddies' and 'doctors and nurses'. When adults 'play', they tend to want to escape from the real world and forget the stresses of life, but children use play to 'master their world'.

KEY WORDS

Competition

The very nature of competition is to aim to achieve what another is aiming to achieve at the same time before they do.

• *rule-bound play* – as the child begins to develop cognitively, it engages in activities whereby the child learns to develop structured activities from which they can experience more enjoyment from **competition** and achievement. In children's play there are no pre-set rules. Each play situation starts afresh or spontaneously, with children making up their own rules, modifying them and also officiating themselves. This gives them control over their play group and encourages decision-making and independence. It is very important that the play group adhere to the rules agreed by them. Agreement suggests levels of negotiation and compromise – social skills considered important to society.

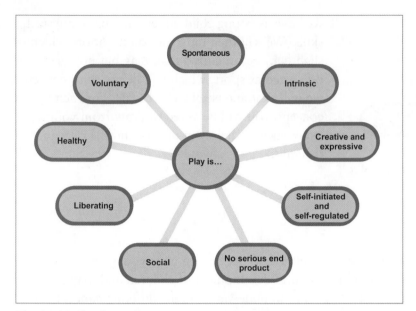

Fig. 14.02 Play is...

Play is also entered into voluntarily, that is, the children choose to play. They are not playing because it is expected of them. The true play experience comes from within the child.

Another important feature of play is that it is intrinsically motivated – this means that there is no ulterior motive for playing other than the wish to play for the enjoyment that comes from the activity. The children are developing many skills, but at a young age, they are not aware of this and this is not why they play. They just want to have fun. There are no leagues, cups or extrinsic rewards. Therefore, can play be serious? Children's play is generally accepted as being 'non-serious'. This means the outcome is not considered serious by society. Play provides a basis for 'reality' but in a safe environment, allowing for exploratory behaviour. The child, in effect, learns 'how to learn' through play, and this knowledge can be used into adulthood.

Although children experience a lot of freedom in play, there are necessarily some restrictions they face, particularly regarding safety. Adults will usually impose defined space boundaries, which they must abide by, as well as occasional time limits such as teatime, break-time and so on. Sharing equipment and space, such as a playground or garden, can also be a constraint.

HOT TIPS

When asked to explain a definition, do not re-use the words in the definition. You need to find alternative words to show your understanding. Keep a dictionary handy! Make sure you address all the key words or phrases in the definition or the ones specified in the question.

TASK 1

Using your own words, explain the following definitions of 'play'.
- 'Play is a voluntary activity, never a physical necessity or moral obligation.'
- 'Play is an activity from which you get immediate pleasure without ulterior motive.'

Other useful definitions to be aware of are:

Huizinga (1964):
'Play is a voluntary activity or occupation exercised within certain fixed rules of time and place according to rules freely accepted and absolutely binding, having its aim in itself and accompanied by a feeling of tension, joy and the consciousness that this is different from ordinary life.'

G. Torkildsen:

'Play is activity – mental, passive or active. Play is undertaken freely and is usually spontaneous. It is fun, purposeless, self-initiated and often extremely serious. Play is indulged in for its own sake; it has intrinsic value; there is innate satisfaction in the doing. Play transports the player, as it were, to a world outside his or her normal world. It can heighten arousal. It can be vivid, colourful, creative and innovative. Because the player shrugs off inhibitions and is lost in the play, it seems to be much harder for adults, with social and personal inhibitions, to really play.'

HOT TIPS

For each concept we study, you should be able to analyse them on a structural level, that is, the level of organization, as well as the attitudes of the participants.

TASK 2

From the information already covered on children's play, explain:
a) its level of organization
b) the attitudes the children bring to the play world
c) any constraints or restrictions that may occur on children's play.

Play also inter-relates with other concepts. For example, there is a relationship between play and physical education, and between play and recreation.

Play and physical education

If a teacher wanted to consider the value play has for children, there are certain aspects they could incorporate into a lesson such as:
- giving children some choice in terms of activity or equipment
- allowing them to make up their own games and routines
- use of mini games or adapted games rather than full-sized games
- instilling an element of fun.

Play and recreation

We tend to use the term 'play' when referring to young children. We do not often use the term in relation to adults. Equally, we do not use the term 'recreation' when referring to young children, probably because recreation is connected with a break from the world of work, which does not involve children. However, when adults *are* at play, we generally use the term 'recreation'. It immediately suggests that recreation and play have *shared characteristics*, but because adults are involved, there will be some differences. One of the common characteristics would be their primary motive being intrinsic and both would be undertaken voluntarily.

Recreation

In the modern day, recreation tends to be valued for its own sake and is viewed as an important aspect of life for individuals and society. The following definition attempts to highlight the main features of recreation:

R. Krauss (1971):

'Recreation consists of activities or experiences carried on in leisure, usually chosen voluntarily by the participant – either because of satisfaction, pleasure or creative enrichment derived, or because he perceives certain personal or social gains to be gained from them. It may also be perceived as the process of participation, or as the emotional state derived from the involvement.'

However, in the past, certain religious groups, particularly the Puritans in the sixteenth century, have actively discouraged recreational activities believing them to be a sinful waste of time.

With the advent of industrialization in the nineteenth century, recreation was seen to have positive qualities. Recreation actually means 'to restore to health', so, by allowing recreation, people's energies for work were restored and they became more productive (for more information, see Chapter 10).

When work patterns became regulated, leisure time became woven into people's lives. There was a need to provide for that time and create opportunities for recreational activities in order to create an orderly society with individuals who could appreciate rule-governed behaviour (see Chapter 11). The potential for trouble, with hordes of working-class people unoccupied during their leisure time, was something the middle-class authorities needed to be aware of and cater for.

 KEY WORDS

Socialization

The term given to the process of individuals learning the cultural norms and values of their society.

Primary socialization

Occurs through the immediate family group from birth to approximately three years.

Secondary socialization

Occurs as the child interacts with wider socializing agents such as school.

People in positions of power felt that society had an obligation to provide recreational facilities. As it was the middle and upper classes who had the resources to do this, they would be providing for activities *they* approved of. This could be seen as a form of social control, as people's energies could be controlled through recreational and sporting activities, keeping them content and giving them fewer reasons for becoming rebellious. This also allowed the transmission of middle-class values, such as respect for rules, into wider society. Recreation must also be seen as a means of **socialization**. This means citizens are provided with acceptable activities to participate in. They are, therefore, learning behaviour patterns acceptable to society such as adhering to rules, etiquette and so on. People initially learn cultural values through the family (**primary socialization**) in the early years, and play in very young children would be reflective of their family's values. However, as children move into the wider world, such as nursery, school, libraries, clubs and so on, they may begin to learn other values (**secondary socialization**), which may or may not coincide with their family values.

Today, leisure and recreation are now a boom industry and cannot be seen as something unimportant or trivial. The amount of money involved and the political decisions made, the varying opportunities experienced by different social groups, mean we do need to consider them as important parts of our society.

KEY WORDS

Active leisure

Physically energetic recreational activities.

KEY WORDS

Structure

How something is organized: how formal the structure is or how tightly defined.

Attitude

The opinion or feelings of individuals towards an object. For example, an individual may adopt a casual or serious approach towards an activity.

Opportunity

A chance to experience something beneficial.

We have already stated that the term 'play' is used when referring to young children. However, when adults are at play, we generally use the term recreation. Earlier in the chapter we suggested that recreation and play have shared characteristics, such as their informal organization, but because adults are involved, there will be some differences, particularly in the reasons or motives for participation.

At what stage in an individual's life would we begin to use the term 'recreation'? Consider your own life. As we move into the teenage years, physical activity takes on different connotations. We have learned more formal types of sporting activities, and work patterns, through school and part-time employment, have begun to take shape. As soon as you feel your motivation for taking part in an activity is for reasons such as to make friends, increase your level of fitness or have a break from work, you are moving into the world of recreation.

Recreation itself could be passive or active. It could involve reading a book or listening to music. For our purposes, we need to concentrate on the more active type of recreation. This is what we will call 'physical recreation'. It will share the same characteristics as recreation but it should have some physical output where energy is expended. Another common term used in this instance is '**active leisure**' or 'active recreation'.

Shared characteristics of play and recreation

- Play and recreation must be entered into freely, of one's own free will. Any sense of obligation to take part means the play and recreational experience will be lessened.
- The primary motive for participating in play and recreation should be for enjoyment.
- Play and recreation are informal in their **structure**.
- Play and recreation provide a sense of well-being.
- Play and recreation develop skills – physical, cognitive, social and emotional.
- The outcome of play and recreation is non-serious.
- A casual **attitude** is adopted, as the outcome or end product is non-serious, compared to participating in sport.

Differences between play and recreation

Although intrinsic motivation is the primary aim for both play and recreation, some other motives may well become involved in the recreation process. Individuals may well use recreation to escape from the stresses of their daily lives, or view it as an **opportunity** to improve their social lives, or simply to become healthier. In terms of structure, both play and recreation are loosely organized but recreation is more organized than play. Adults tend to take part in recognized physical activities, though usually with modified rules, for example using jumpers for goalposts.

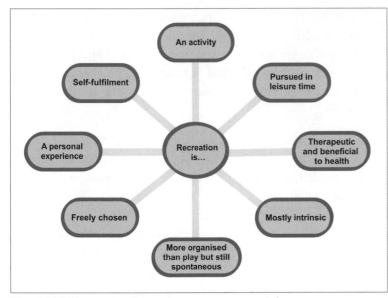

Fig. 14.03 Recreation is...

Leisure

A common phrase when studying recreation has been 'carried out in leisure time'. We now need to consider the concept of leisure. What is **leisure**? Leisure is **free time** from all other obligations such as work, including school work, domestic chores, eating, sleeping and so on. It is free time to pursue any activity of your choice (Figure 14.04). Similarly to play and recreation, leisure serves several functions for the individual and society (Table 14.01).

Table 14.01 The functions of leisure

Individual	Society
• Provides relief from stress/cathartic/relaxing	• Keeps mass of population occupied
• Promotes physical and mental well-being	• Re-creates energies for work
• Active leisure = health and fitness	• Economic benefit – leisure boom industry
• Entertainment	• Maintains cultural traditions (nationally/regionally/class based and so on)
• Self-fulfilment	• Integrates society
• Acquirement of new skills	
• Social/communication/friendships	

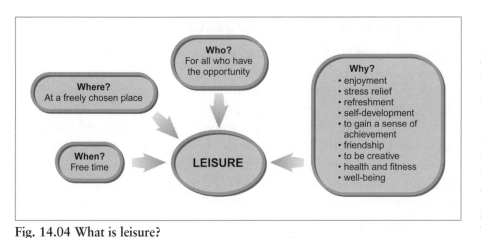

Fig. 14.04 What is leisure?

In socialist states, particularly the communist states, the term **purposeful leisure** emerged whereby it was felt that the leisure time of a population should not be left to chance but should be controlled by the state as much as possible. Certain activities were either encouraged as benefiting society or discouraged because they were considered to be harmful to their society. In a society such as the UK, there is not such a direct admission of control, but any public provision will to some extent reflect the values of the controlling group.

In the UK, leisure activities are provided by three main sectors: private, public and voluntary. Each sector makes value judgements about which activities will be made available to the general population. Traditionally, the wealthier sections of society have had more control over their recreational activities, as they are able to provide for themselves. The general public is more dependent on what is provided. Even today, if public tennis courts were not available in leisure centres or schools, many of us would not be able to play tennis. Few of us can afford a tennis court or have a garden large enough to accommodate one.

 KEY WORDS

Purposeful leisure

A term used in communist governments to suggest that the control of leisure activities is as important as work, defence and so on. For example, activities encouraging health and fitness might be encouraged, whilst more anti-social activities, such as gambling, might be prohibited.

How much time do we have for leisure?

There is no clear answer to this question. It is dependent on who you are in society and which culture you live in. In this chapter, we will concentrate on the present day and the culture of the UK, recognizing that it is a multi-cultural society.

Leisure is free time from work, so the number of hours you work, combined with the nature of your work (is it manual and active or more sedentary?) will directly influence the amount and type of leisure you wish to pursue. Our work patterns have changed since the beginning of the twentieth century, from a heavy manufacturing base to a greater service sector. Hours tend to be more flexible and work tends to be more inactive. An extreme example to illustrate this point may be the decline in shipbuilding and the increase in call centres! In the latter situation, recreation activities pursued may be more active in order to achieve some balance in life.

Unemployment is usually enforced, so this time would not be classed as true leisure as the individual has not chosen to have that time free. This might be classed as 'enforced leisure'.

Has the status of leisure increased?

Leisure has always occupied a high status in the lives of the wealthier sections of society. They have often been referred to as 'the leisured classes'. They have had the pre-requisites for leisure – free time, opportunity and choice. The lower classes have traditionally been encouraged to work and leisure has been seen as a waste of time. It took many years for the industrial working classes to earn the right to leisure. However, many people today work to enjoy a better quality of leisure time. So we could say that, whereas before leisure was viewed as a tool to recreate people's energies for work, people today use work in order to provide the means for a better quality of leisure activities.

Have the opportunities for leisure increased?

The opportunities for leisure have definitely increased since the nineteenth century, as working hours have reduced and provision for leisure has increased. Other factors have also been significant:
- increased life expectancy/better health = more energy and time for leisure
- labour-saving gadgets such as washing machines
- increase in disposable incomes
- educating for leisure in schools
- personal mobility such as cars allows more access to facilities
- more facilities
- early retirement.

Leisure time depends on who you are!

Women in our society are known to have the least amount of leisure time due to an increased role in the workplace, as well as remaining the person with the most responsibility for domestic chores. If they do not work, they will often have young children to care for, so pursuing a leisure activity can be awkward if childcare provision is either scarce or costly.

Type of leisure activity depends on who you are!

Social class can still be a significant factor. Traditionally, the terms 'high culture' and 'low culture' have been used to highlight the differences in the type of recreation activities in which different social groups are most likely to be involved (Table 14.02).

Multi-cultural societies, such as the UK, also house many different cultures with different religious beliefs, cultural traditions and customs. Different ethnic minority groups will also have varying approaches to how they occupy their leisure time (see Chapter 13).

Table 14.02 Types of leisure activities

High culture (for example polo, gymnastics)	Low culture (for example football, boxing)
• Traditionally refers to cultural pursuits of higher social classes	• Traditionally refers to cultural pursuits of lower social classes
• Reflects lifestyle of wealth, free time, privileged education, etiquette	• Reflects lifestyle of popular culture
• Activities tend to require a level of refinement and understanding	• Open to change with trends and social development (for example, skateboarding)
	• Activities tend to be easy to understand, providing entertainment value and quick excitement

TASK 5

1 Outline as many key words as you can that characterize leisure.
2 How can you distinguish between leisure and recreation?
3 What is meant by the term 'active leisure'?

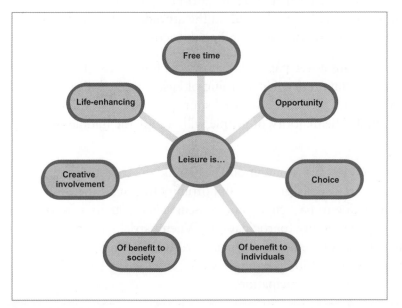

Fig. 14.05 Leisure is…

Torkildson
'Leisure can conceptually embrace the freedom of play, the recreation process and the recreation institution. Leisure can be presented as the opportunity and means for play and recreation to occur.'

Choice is a crucial element in all the three concepts covered so far. When the element of choice begins to lessen, the play, recreational and leisure experiences will begin to decline. This can become evident in situations where an individual chooses to participate in an activity and gradually becomes more involved in the organization of the activity, such as a captain or a coach. Slowly, a sense of obligation to turn up occurs and the activity can begin to feel more like a chore. The true recreational experience can begin to diminish.

At the other end of the spectrum from play is sport. Its level of organization and the motivations of participants set it apart from the previous two concepts.

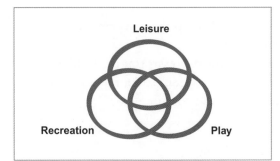

Fig. 14.06 This diagram shows the relationship that exists between play, recreation and leisure but also highlights their uniqueness

KEY WORDS

Sport

Sport

Sport is a competitive and institutionalized physical activity.

Coakley (1993):

*'**Sport** is an institutionalized, competitive activity that involves vigorous physical exertion or the use of relatively complex physical skills by individuals whose participation is motivated by a combination of intrinsic and extrinsic factors.'*

Wuest, Buscher (1991):

'Physical activities with established rules engaged in by individuals attempting to outperform their competitors.'

HOT TIPS

Be prepared to explain these definitions using your own words. Remember the earlier tip – do not use the same words but find alternatives.

Most of you will belong to or have belonged to sports clubs, either in school or locally. The best way of approaching the concept of sport is to remember your experiences as you became more involved and serious about a particular activity. What changed a recreational activity into becoming a sport?

You could be participating in the same activity as someone else, for example football, but they could be participating in sport and you could be participating in recreation. It will depend on the attitude each brings to the activity and the level of structure surrounding the activity.

HOT TIPS

The concept of sport is at the other end of the spectrum to play. Therefore, if you reverse many of the answers on sport, you would correctly answer questions on play. An example would be sport is serious, play is non-serious.

The participation pyramid (see page 204) shows the four levels of participation in ascending order. The learning of basic motor skills begins at the foundation level and the most advanced sport performers will reach the apex of the pyramid. The majority of people will occupy the middle two sections.

In physical education lessons (foundation level), children are introduced to the basic skills and are usually given the opportunity to extend their interest in the activity by opting to participate in extra-curricular activities or to join sports clubs in the community (participation). When participants begin to train to develop skills, compete under officially recognized rules, with important outcomes, we could determine they are involved in sport. This could occur at the stage of participation.

HOT TIPS

An individual may occupy the participation level in one sporting activity but the performance level in another sporting activity.

TASK 6

1 Outline where you think you are in relation to the participation pyramid in a number of sporting activities.
2 What factors have been influential in this process? You might like to consider factors such as parental influence, peer group, religious and/or cultural, access to resources, education and so on.

Characteristics of sport

When thinking about play, the first aspect we considered was the level of physical activity. Children learn to control their bodies and produce movements that are effective in helping them control and make an impact on their environment. At the level of sport, specific skills will have been mastered in order to be an effective performer. If we take a simple game involving throwing and catching, by the time a child has transferred this skill into basketball, they will need to practise until they can produce a variety of passes effectively, considering the weight and direction of the pass, dependent on the game situation. The ability to reproduce the same movement consistently and effectively is what we call skill.

Children will have moved on from the situation of making up their own rules to learning formally laid down rules, which are externally enforced by officials. This requires a level of cognitive development as well as a moral code, which allows the individual to accept the need for rules.

The aspect of choice is also important. People do choose to participate in a sport, but often extrinsic reasons can begin to dominate. They may feel an obligation to their teammates or coach; they feel an obligation to themselves to achieve the best they can, and, in the case of a professional sportsperson, the sport becomes their work!

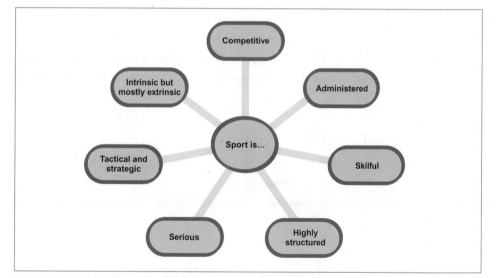

Fig. 14.07 Sport is…

People, other than the performers, are involved in the sport process. We have already mentioned rules. These have to be drawn up by an international sport federation, such as FIFA, and disseminated across the world in order that all clubs adhere to them. Officials, such as referees, linesmen, scorers and coaches, to name but a few, make up the administrative system.

Practice and training become more important as selection is often an aspect of sport. It requires individuals to prove they are better than the next person, and commitment and dedication to training will often separate the highly successful from the mediocre. At the level of recreation, a group of people can participate in a kick about in the park whatever their level of skill. This is because the outcome is not as important as if they were playing in a club match.

Sport is often structured into competitive levels and individuals can move up the levels as they improve. This could be explained by starting an activity such as gymnastics in a physical education lesson, joining a gym club to begin gymnastic awards and beginning to compete in gymnastic competitions as the skill levels increase.

TASK 7

1 What do we mean by 'skilful'?
2 How is the organization of sport different to that of recreation?
3 How might your attitude be different when representing your club to when you are having a 'kick about in the park'?

TASK 8

What is the opposite to each of the following words?

- Recreation
- Choice
- Sport
- Outcome unimportant
- Intrinsic
- Spontaneous

Benefits and problems of sport

Why do so many of us participate in sport? We must feel there is some benefit to it (Table 14.03). On the other hand, there have been many criticisms of sport (see Table 14.04). George Orwell said it was 'war minus the shooting'.

Table 14.03 Benefits of sport

Individual	Society
• Health and fitness	• Healthy society
• Socializing and making friends	• Integration of society
• Acquiring new skills	• Skills useful in life
• Cathartic/enjoyment	• More relaxed society
• Alleviates boredom	• Social control
• Provides an income	• Sport a boom industry
• Sense of achievement	• Pride in self and community

Table 14.04 Problems of sport

Individual	Society
• Take it too seriously/obsessive	• Pride – community and national
• Deviant behaviour in order to win	• Society condones deviant behaviour
• Armchair enthusiasts rather than participants	• Media encourages non-active
• Discriminatory if female, ethnic, disabled	• Popular sports receive most publicity

TASK 9

1 How can an international sport fixture be referred to as 'war minus the shooting'?
2 What counter-arguments would you give to support international sport?
3 Give three benefits of sport for the individual and society.

Values in sport

KEY WORDS

Values

The moral principles and beliefs of an individual or social group.

So far, we have looked at the characteristics and benefits of sport. What about the **values** invested in sport (Table 14.05)?

The way in which we view the world is determined by many factors. One important factor is who we are and the values we have learned from our society (socialization), and consequently whether we have accepted or rejected them.

Table 14.05 Positive and negative values in sport

Positive values of sport	Negative values of sport
Competitive: aiming to achieve what another is aiming to achieve at the same time/learn how to win and lose	Gamesmanship: bend the rules of the sport in order to gain an advantage
Sportsmanship: qualities such as fairness, respect for opponents and playing within the rules	Win at all costs: winning is the primary aim even if it means breaking the rules; it could be an intention, for example 'take him out'
Amateurism: participate in sport for the love of it and without financial gain; it is not just the winning that is important but also how you participate	Cheating: deliberately breaking the rules of the sport, for example professional foul
Assertive: goal-directed, non-aggressive behaviour in a sporting situation	Aggression: the behaviour in a sporting situation which intends to cause harm to an opponent

It is probably fairly obvious, living in our society, why most of these points are in a particular category. However, why is the term 'amateurism' in a value category at all? Is it not just a sporting term?

The values embodied in amateurism, such as fair play, the idea that taking part in sport is more important than the winning, emerged during the nineteenth century when much of sport was controlled by the upper and middle classes. This section of the population was able to engage in sporting activities for fun and enjoyment. They did not need to earn a living from sport.

Attitudes such as these take many years and sometimes generations to change. Also, it is interesting to realize that not all countries adopted this point of view. Countries such as America, a much younger country than the UK and with a less strict social class distinction, found professional sport much more in keeping with its cultural beliefs. So, values are dependent on who you are and what culture you belong to.

When analysing sport, it is also important to consider the attention given to winning.

The value of winning

The amateur code emphasized playing sport for the love of it without monetary gain. It also stressed the importance of how you play becoming almost more important than whether or not you won. Hence the terms 'fair play' and 'sportsmanship', and showing courtesy and respect for your opponent developed. The nineteenth-century amateurs enjoyed a variety of sports and the all-rounder had great status. There was honour in victory and defeat.

The very nature of professional sport is to earn money from sport and it has become a livelihood for many people. Therefore the outcome is more significant. This results in performers specializing in an activity and training hard in order to secure a victory. It also means that 'win at all costs' has become a sport ethic. Performers may take drugs, may deliberately foul and so on as the rewards for winning become ever greater.

Physical education and school sport

In this section we will concentrate on the concept of physical education. The aims of physical education are to teach:
- activity-specific skills such as throwing: that is, motor development
- fitness such as endurance: that is, physical development
- knowledge such as the rules of an activity: that is, it is cognitive
- values such as sportsmanship: that is, it is cultural.

Physical education delivers these objectives via many sports. It has become a requirement of the National Curriculum to teach a variety of activities rather than a select few. The more experiences children have, the more likely they are to continue these activities into later life. Therefore activities ranging

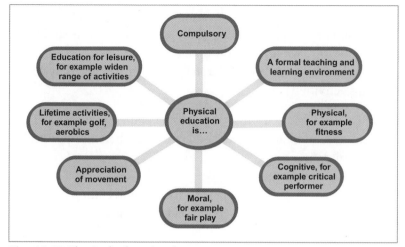

Fig. 14.08 Physical education is...

from team games, individual, competitive and non-competitive should be taught. It aims to offer a balanced physical education programme.

You will have experienced physical education throughout primary and secondary school. You have chosen to study it as an examination subject. Similar to sport, physical education is a highly structured activity: everyone knows beforehand when the lesson will take place, the duration, the nature of the activity and the number of people involved.

However, physical education also has qualities that set it apart from play, recreation and leisure.

- It lacks choice. It is compulsory! This can affect the attitudes of children taking part as it is enforced. It can often create feelings of resentment.
- Learning takes place but the educational aspect has been formalized.
- The purpose of physical education is to teach children activity-specific skills in a range of activities.
- There is a physical education teacher in authority over the children. This is quite different to play and recreation, which is mostly self-initiated and self-officiated.
- In sport, the role of the authority figure is the sports coach. (We will look at the roles of the physical education teacher and the sports coach further on in this chapter.)

Another important remit of physical education is trying to encourage children to appreciate the value of a healthy lifestyle and understanding the important role exercise plays in this. Lifetime activities are becoming central to the choice offered in school physical education programmes.

As well as being able to perform physical activities, children are also expected to be able to analyse and evaluate movement. They need to develop their critical understanding.

TASK 10

1 Conduct a survey of the types of activities your group have experienced in physical education lessons.
2 Categorize the activities under the headings: team, individual, game and movement.
3 Has your group experienced a balanced physical education programme? What might prevent a school offering a balanced programme?

KEY WORDS

School sport

The competitive, performance-orientated extra-curricular activities offered by schools, for example school netball and football teams.

HOT TIPS

It is important that you understand the significance of these terms when they appear in a question. If 'school sport' is mentioned, it will mean the extra-curricular activities: if 'physical education' is mentioned, it means the core compulsory lessons.

It is no coincidence at this stage that the word 'sport' has been used sparingly. The government is investing a lot of money into physical education *and* school sport. In the UK, we have traditionally treated these two concepts differently, believing them to have very different purposes. They merely focus on the same sporting activities.

Physical education is concerned with the needs of the child – their physical, emotional and social development. Physical education teachers use physical activities to develop children's:

- confidence and self-esteem
- physical competencies
- creativity and expressiveness
- aesthetic appreciation
- social awareness.

Table 14.06 Objectives of physical education for the child

Physical	Intellectual/cognitive	Social
• Motor development, for example co-ordination, agility and balance • Fitness • Skilfulness, for example activity-specific skills	• Appreciation of movement • Critical performer • Observation and analysis • Learning rules • Learning strategies and tactics • Problem-solving	• Teamwork and co-operation • Leadership • Communication and social skills • Trust in others • Pursue recreational activities after leaving school

School sport is more concerned with developing the children's ability to perform sporting activities and with results and performance standards. It is extra-curricular and voluntary, and is therefore an expression of the children extending their initial interest in the activity. They are given opportunities to be more competitive and experience representative sport. In some instances, its philosophy and objectives may be more similar to club sport in society than physical education. It is interesting to note that in some countries physical education and school sport are *both* compulsory.

TASK 11

1 What are the advantages and disadvantages of keeping physical education and school sport separate?
2 What physical, social and moral values can children gain from school sport?

Who teaches physical education and school sport?

In the UK, the physical education teacher is usually responsible for both physical education and school sport. This suggests that they have to adopt different roles during the school day. By analysing the role of a teacher and a sports coach, it can further our understanding of these two concepts (Table 14.07). When taking a representative school team, the physical education teacher may tend to adopt the role of a sports coach.

Table 14.07 The roles of a teacher and a coach

Role of a physical education teacher	Role of a sports coach
• Compulsory: this is a National Curriculum subject; children have to attend	• Voluntary: children will have chosen to participate
• Range of activities: the National Curriculum requires a variety of activities to be taught	• Specialism: the sport coach tends to have specialized in their activity and may coach to a higher standard
• Ability level: mixed ability classes are the norm for physical education lessons	• Ability level: performers will normally be taught according to their ability; some selection tends to occur
• Children's needs: physical, psychological and emotional needs are developed and nurtured above their performance results	• Performance: the sports coach is often measured by the progress of their performers and therefore there is a concentration on results
• Values: values such as teamwork, sportsmanship and co-operation are encouraged	• Values: values such as commitment, dedication to training and competitiveness are encouraged

Some schools face problems when they offer school sport:
- it is based on teacher goodwill
- lack of funding for transport and facilities
- pupils having competing leisure interests and part-time jobs
- risk assessment/safety considerations.

However, many people feel the benefits outweigh the disadvantages.

The government says it is committed to increasing the role of physical education and school sport. It is investing millions in trying to improve the infrastructure that will enable this to happen. However, physical educationalists might be suspicious if it appears that the traditional philosophies are being threatened and may feel that they should not be used as a 'nursery' for sporting talent. What do you think?

So far, we have contrasted physical education and school sport. What about the relationship between school sport and club sport? Many of you will already have experienced both. Are they similar or different (Table 14.08)?

Table 14.08 Contrasts between school sport and club sport

Similarities	Differences
• Participate in the same sporting activities	• Teacher in school rather than a sports coach
• Learn skills and tactics	• Conflicts between school and club expectations
• Are formally taught	• Win at all cost may be emphasized more in club sport
• Physical education teacher may adopt role of a coach	
• Still aim to be successful/win	

We can conclude by saying that:
- physical education uses sporting activities to achieve its aims
- school sport is offered as an additional experience to most children to develop levels of skill with a more competitive emphasis
- schools try to offer some link between themselves and local sports clubs – an increasingly important government policy (see Chapter 12).

Outdoor and adventurous activities

The types of activities we will be discussing in this final section are different to 'everyday' sports. They can be called outdoor pursuit activities, outdoor and adventurous activities, extreme sports or outdoor pursuit activities in the natural environment.

TASK 12

Have you ever been on an activity holiday such as PGL or participated in a school ski trip or done some rock climbing? In pairs, consider how these experiences differed from other types of sporting activity.

TASK 13

Place the following activities in their natural environment of land, air or water.

- Rock climbing
- Skiing
- Paragliding
- Scuba diving
- Canoeing
- Abseiling
- White water rafting
- Parachuting
- Rambling

Outdoor and adventurous activities became popular with the upper and middle classes in the nineteenth century. They were the group in society who were able to enjoy more leisure time, disposable income and personal transport long before the working classes had access to them. During the nineteenth century, and with the onset of industrialization, the working classes began to participate. As people began to live in cramped, polluted towns, poets such as Wordsworth provided attractive images of the countryside to which people could escape to restore their energies. This, combined with advances in communications, particularly the railways, made access to the countryside possible for working-class people.

During the twentieth century and to the present day, these activities have continued to grow in their levels of participation. People have enjoyed increasing leisure time and disposable income, and as work patterns have become more flexible and sedentary (inactive), people may seek more excitement and adrenalin rush in their recreation, as well as needing to escape from stressful jobs and lifestyles.

Traditionally, outdoor and adventurous activities would appeal to more conservative individuals wishing to take part in activities with little need for competition, as these are activities that can be participated in without rules and without opponents. In the latter half of the twentieth century, the media has portrayed these activities as fashionable and attractive to the youth culture, particularly as new sports have emerged, such as snowboarding and jet ski, often due to advances in technology. They are now fashionable pastimes with a whole new leisure industry catering for them.

Access to more isolated environments has been one of the restrictive features of these activities. This has been partly overcome by creating man-made versions, such as climbing walls and dry ski slopes, as well as the proliferation of clubs. This has introduced more people to these sports who can then practise the basic skills before actually visiting the natural environment. Personal mobility, such as cars, has become more widely available, enabling people to access more remote parts of the country. Management companies are increasingly using these types of activities in testing managers for their personal qualities such as problem-solving, team leading and so on. Apart from taking place in the natural environment, these activities are also characterized by their sense of danger or risk, which are inherent in the activities themselves.

Many of these activities can be adapted for people with special needs and disabilities, such as skiing, canoeing and so on. Society recognizes that people with special needs have as much right to enjoy these activities as anyone else and equal rights demand that governing bodies seek to ensure their sport is made more accessible. The benefits listed below are just as applicable to people with special needs. Developments in technology have also helped adaptations to take place such as specialized equipment for skiing.

There are many benefits to be gained from pursuing outdoor and adventurous activities. Some of these are:

- a sense of freedom (some of these sports can be participated in alone)
- handling risk
- leadership and response to leadership
- crucial decision-making
- appreciation of the natural environment and environmental issues
- trust in yourself/self-reliance/knowing, but also challenging your personal limits
- trust in others/teamwork
- escape from pressures of urban lifestyles
- sense of danger/adrenalin rush
- cross-curricular links in schools with geography and fieldwork studies.

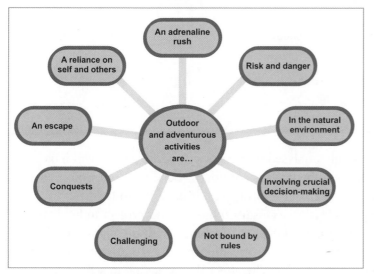

Fig. 14.09 Outdoor and adventurous activities are...

KEY WORDS

Adventure

An undertaking that involves risk and may have an unknown outcome.

Objective danger

Danger that is not under the control of the individual, such as an avalanche.

Subjective danger

Danger that is under the control of the individual, for example the careful planning of a route to avoid hazards.

TASK 14

How might an inner-city school help prepare its pupils to develop the necessary skills in a range of outdoor and adventurous activities before embarking on an adventure holiday to the natural environment?

Mortlock suggests there are four main stages of **adventure:**
- play – little challenge or risk
- adventure – individual is placed in challenging situations relative to their skill levels
- frontier adventure – individual is experienced and skilful and able to explore wilderness areas
- misadventure – something has gone wrong such as an accident.

Adventure and frontier adventure are the most desirable situations to experience.

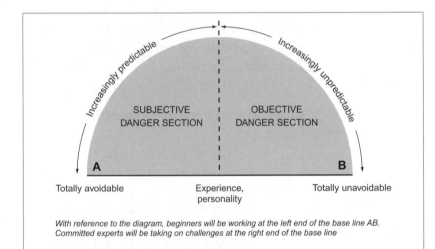

Fig. 14.10 Danger diagram

TASK 15

Consider Figure 14.10 and establish the difference between **objective danger** and **subjective danger,** and explain how this varies according to the difficulty of the challenge.

Risk is being increasingly analysed in our society. Most people will have heard the term 'risk assessment'. It is a modern social phenomenon that we are trying to eliminate all risk from our lives. It began with the best intentions of trying to avert unnecessary tragedies and protect individuals from institutional negligence. However, combined with the blame culture that is evolving and the risk of huge compensation payouts, many people feel the situation is getting out of control. The effect this is having in schools is worrying. Many teachers are beginning to withdraw their involvement in trips, as risk assessments have to be carried out in great detail and can leave them liable should anything go wrong.

Many people feel there are benefits to the individuals when learning to handle risk. We do risk assessments every day, for example when we cross a

KEY WORDS

Real risk

Risk from the environment such as a rock fall, which is beyond anyone's control.

Perceived risk

Potential risk that an individual is aware of; this adds to the sense of danger.

road we make a judgement call. Outdoor and adventurous activities provide a wealth of learning experiences in this area. **Real risk** comes from the environment such as an avalanche, flood or landslide. This should be avoided at all costs as it will most likely result in serious injury or death. With careful planning, it can be avoided to some extent, but the more experienced a performer becomes, the more likely they are to enter 'wilderness' areas where the environment becomes increasingly unpredictable. **Perceived risk** is the sense of danger or excitement the individual gets from the activity. It can be the experience of abseiling for the first time, with the anxiety and adrenalin rush, but with safety ropes the activity is under control.

Outdoor education v. outdoor recreation

KEY WORDS

Outdoor education

Outdoor and adventurous activities in the natural environment in an educational setting, for example a school ski trip.

Outdoor recreation

Outdoor and adventurous activities in the natural environment in an individual's own free time, for example a ski trip with friends.

We need to clarify the two terms **outdoor education** and **outdoor recreation**. They both involve the same type of sporting activity, that is, outdoor and adventurous activities such as canoeing, abseiling and skydiving, but the difference between the two terms is the *context* in which we may refer to them. If you have been on a school trip to participate in these activities, then the correct term would be 'outdoor education' as it has taken place in an educational setting. However, if you took part in the same activity on a weekend away with friends, then the correct term would be 'outdoor recreation' and the qualities of recreation that we have already studied would still hold true, as they are entered into voluntarily and in an individual's free time. Although learning is still taking place, it is not within an educational setting, that is, under the aegis of a school or education institution.

Table 14.09 Values of outdoor education and recreation

Educational values	Recreational values
• Appreciation of natural environment	• Free time
• Environmental/conservation issues	• Choice
• Cross-curricular/map reading	• Opportunity
• Survival skills	• Enhance quality of life/creative and participation
• Personal limits/knowledge	• Active leisure
• Teamwork/leadership	• Escape stresses of life
	• Health
	• Intrinsic
	• Sense of achievement/fulfilment

The activities outdoor education encompasses are sports such as canoeing, climbing, rafting, skiing and so on. The values they have for individuals can be very different from those of other sports. They can be competitive or non-competitive; they take place in challenging and exciting environments, which induce fear and exhilaration. They develop inter-personal skills such as self-reliance, leadership, teamwork and critical decision-making. There are strong reasons why outdoor education should be on the National Curriculum, and in even greater depth, but schools face many problems in trying to offer a valuable programme:

• an already constricted timetable

- lack of teacher specialists
- lack of funds
- accessibility to natural environments
- safety issues in a risk assessment culture.

However, there are cross-curricular links that could be made with subjects such as geography and biology fieldwork, and schools could adapt their own environments to teach the basic skills of many of these activities such as:

- use of dry ski slopes
- swimming pools for canoeing/scuba diving
- parks for orienteering
- climbing walls.

Outdoor and adventurous activities as competitive sports

We have already established that many of these activities can be participated in purely for the personal challenge but as Chris Bonnington in his book *Quest* for *Adventure* writes:

'In theory, climbing is a non-competitive sport. In practice, however, there is a very high level of competition. At its simplest level, a group of climbers bouldering almost inevitably start to compete, trying to outdo each other, to solve a climbing problem that has beaten the others … in any activity competition is a spur to progress.'

Many outdoor and adventurous activities are now institutionalized competitive activities in their own right. Figure 14.11 suggests what is required for an outdoor activity to become a competitive sport.

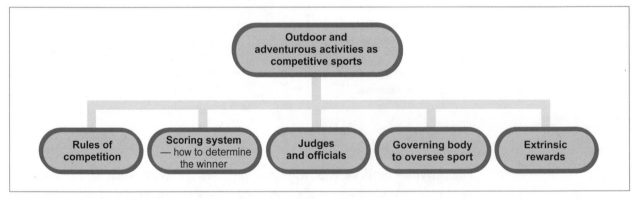

Fig. 14.11 The features of competitive outdoor activities

KEY WORDS Classification of sports

Classification
An attempt to group sports that share similar characteristics.

There are hundreds of different sporting activities. In order to help us understand the principles underlying many of them, a **classification** system has been suggested based on the National Curriculum classifications (see the chapter on development of physical education). For our purposes here, we need to understand the three subcategories of competitive sports:

- athletic
- gymnastic
- game.

KEY WORDS

Nature of the sport problem

How the winner is determined.

Objective

The collection of data without allowing personal interpretation or bias to influence the result, usually a time or distance.

Subjective

Based on individual interpretation of behaviour, action or events, usually by judges.

Each sport is categorized depending on the **nature of the sport problem**, that is, what a performer has to do in order to win. Do they score more goals? Do they execute a perfect routine? Do they have to be faster over a certain distance than their opponent?

The nature of the sport problem is the manner by which a winner is decided.

- Athletic category activities, such as ski slalom, high jump and javelin, are determined by who skied the fastest, who jumped the highest and who threw the furthest. These activities have undisputed quantitative and **objective** measurements by a stopwatch or a tape measure. Any activity where the outcome is determined by such methods would come under the athletic category.
- Gymnastic category activities, such as gymnastics, trampolining and synchronized swimming, are judged on repetitive movement patterns to set criteria, by a panel of judges. These activities rely on judges' **subjective** and qualitative opinions and can sometimes be controversial. Any activity where the outcome is determined by judges' opinions would come under the gymnastic category. It is important to realize that a 50m swimming race would come under the athletic category but synchronized swimming would come under the gymnastic category.
- Game activities can be subdivided into further categories (Table 14.10).

Table 14.10 Categories of games

Category	Description	Classification
Invasion	Where opponents invade each other's territory	For example, rugby, hockey and netball. The winner is determined by the number of goals scored
Net/wall	Where opponents are separated by a net	For example, tennis and squash. The winner is determined by the number of points scored/won
Striking and fielding	Innings games where territory is shared and teams take it in turns	For example, cricket and rounders. The winner is determined by the number of runs made by each team
Fighting	Martial arts	For example, boxing and martial arts. The winner is determined by a judge's opinion. However, we would not class it as a gymnastic activity as the opponents are involved in a contest and are reacting to each other's moves
Target	Accuracy of aiming at a target	For example, golf and archery. The winner is determined by the accuracy of hitting a target

HOT TIPS

As long as you understand the principles upon which the sports are categorized, you should be able to apply knowledge across any sport.

TASK 16

For each category below, think of at least two activities that would share the same 'nature of the sport problem'.

- Athletic
- Gymnastic
- Invasion game
- Fighting game

- Net/wall game
- Target game
- Striking and fielding game

Analysis of activities

The specification requires you to be able to analyse different sporting activities. Any sporting activity can be analysed using the model in Table 14.11.

Table 14.11 Analysis of sporting activities

Structural	Nature of the sport problem; scoring system; rules – complex or simple; behaviour of player – direct contact/indirect non-contact
Strategic	Tactical and planning; related to the sport problem in that you plan the most effective way of winning, for example pre-planned trampolining routine or a set play in football
Technical	Skills – whether they are open or closed skills; whether technical competence is crucial to the outcome, for example in football, as long as the ball hits the back of the net, the technique is not considered but in gymnastics the technical competence is crucial
Physical	Body conditions required for success; may depend on performer's role in the sport and the requirements of the sport itself
Psychological	Mental preparation; assertive/aggressive; limelight role (where all eyes are on the performer); anticipation

TASK 17

Using the example below, fill in a similar table for one activity from each category of athletic, gymnastic and game.

Table 14.12 Analysis of sprint swim racing

Structural	Athletic activity involving no direct physical contact/interference from other competitors; simple rule structure defined: time over distance, legal means of starting, swimming, turning and finishing
Strategic	Little strategic demand (essentially flat out from start to finish); have to read wall for approach turns
Technical	Little variety required. One stroke plus relevant start and turn technique only; closed skills – emphasis lies in the control of the stroke – maximum power; high level of technical perfection and consistency in a skill
Physical	Highly specific anaerobic and strength requirements, implying demanding physical training programmes
Psychological	Individual involvement; limelight role; competitive stress potential; need to 'shut out' other information and concentrate on technique; cope with demands of long, 'stimulus poor' training regimes

Revise as you go!

1 Why can play be spontaneous?

2 What motivates children to play?

3 What is physical recreation also known as?

4 State three characteristics of physical recreation.

5 What are the three main pre-requisites of leisure?

6 How can work affect leisure?

7 What does the term 'institutionalized' mean when referring to sport?

8 Give three characteristics of sport.

9 What physical objectives does physical education have?

10 What personal qualities does physical education encourage in children's development?

11 What types of activities are included in the terms 'outdoor education', 'outdoor recreation' and 'outdoor and adventurous activities'?

12 What is the difference between outdoor education and outdoor recreation?

13 Name three subcategories of games.

End of Unit 2 Questions

Unit 2: Socio-cultural and historical effects on participation in physical activity and their influence on performance

1 Historically, the Church has had a variable attitude towards sport.
a) During the latter part of the nineteenth and early part of the twentieth centuries, the Church gave positive support to sport.
  i) How was this support shown and how was it linked to the public schools? **(3 marks)**
  ii) Why did the Church adopt a positive attitude towards sport at this time? **(5 marks)**
b) Our work-leisure patterns affect our participation in sport and leisure. How might the move from an industrial (manufacturing) based economy to a knowledge (service) based economy affect our work-leisure patterns? **(5 marks)**
(Q3a, c, January 2001)

2 Many sports have undergone dramatic changes since the middle of the nineteenth century.
a) Mob football was an example of popular recreation. What were the characteristics of mob games? **(3 marks)**
b) What social factors caused mob games to develop into their rational form? **(5 marks)**
(Q2, May 2004)

3 At the beginning of the twentieth century, the extent and nature of a person's participation in sport were influenced by their social class and gender.
a) Describe the differences in the sports played and the roles undertaken by the upper/middle classes and the working class. Illustrate your answer with examples **(5 marks)**
b) Discuss the reasons why people from the working class had fewer opportunities to participate than those from the upper and middle classes. **(4 marks)**
c) Why were women discouraged from taking part in many competitive sports at the beginning of the twentieth century? **(3 marks)**
(Q2, January 2004)

4 From the middle of the nineteenth century, modern sports have gained in popularity.
a) The development of modern sport began in the English public schools.
  i) Describe how sport was developed by the English public schools. **(4 marks)**
  ii) What were the reasons for these developments? **(5 marks)**

b) During the late nineteenth century, church organizations promoted sport among their local communities. What was their purpose for doing this and how was it achieved? **(3 marks)**
(Q3, January 2004)

5 During the nineteenth and early twentieth centuries, very clear distinctions were maintained between social classes in terms of their participation in sport and physical activity.

a) With reference to sporting activities, explain how such distinctions were maintained. **(3 marks)**

b) Between 1860 and 1900, many national governing bodies for sport were formed in England. Explain why these governing bodies were formed. **(3 marks)**
(Q4, January 2003)

6 Sport England has initiated a number of policies designed to develop competitive sport in schools. Discuss, with examples, the effect that these policies may have on school sport and physical education. **(6 marks)**
(January 2001)

7 National sports organizations, such as Sport England, have devised schemes to introduce children to sport and to develop their talents. Using examples, explain how such schemes help to achieve these aims **(5 marks)**
(Q2e, January 2003)

8 Our modern society believes that we should try to achieve equality of opportunity for all. In physical education and sport, this may be taken to mean opportunities to participate and then develop one's abilities.

a) Sport England is committed to improving opportunities in sport through its 'Active Communities' programme.

   i) In what way may this and other local or national government initiatives improve opportunities in local communities? **(3 marks)**

   ii) Sport England also believes that active participation in sport can provide 'value' for an individual or a community. In what ways can sport do this? **(3 marks)**
(Q4a, June 2001)

Unit 3: Coursework

Chapter 15: Planning, performing and evaluating a Personal Exercise Programme (PEP)

Learning outcomes

By the end of this chapter you should be able to:
- understand the structure of the PEP and how the marks are awarded
- explain each area of the PEP and its requirements
- keep a clear and accurate record of your training and justify the reasons for your actions.

Introduction

The Personal Exercise Programme (PEP) is probably the first chance in the course for you to combine some theoretical knowledge with practical activity. The completion of the PEP may seem to take a while but it can be very rewarding, not only in terms of the marks achieved but the personal satisfaction of developing a clear understanding of how a structured training programme is used to improve performance. If you follow the advice outlined in this chapter correctly, not only will your fitness levels hopefully improve, albeit slightly, but in the majority of cases so will your performance in your chosen practical activity.

The work completed in this section should overlap with the theoretical aspects covered in the physiology and psychology lessons. The key to achieving good marks in the PEP involves justification of your decisions and actions, being realistic in your targets, and completing accurate records of training sessions and specific modifications.

Structure of the PEP

The Personal Exercise Programme is divided into three main sections and further subdivided, as shown on Figure 15.01.

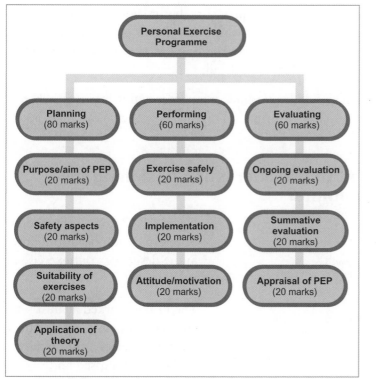

Fig. 15.01 The structure of the PEP

The aim of the Personal Exercise Programme is not, as many students assume, to change your level of fitness dramatically within a limited space of time. A large number of students will already be competing at high levels and any improvement expected will be minimal. As a result, there are no marks for improvement.

Its purpose is to allow you to demonstrate your ability to apply various theoretical aspects of the course and construct a structured training regime for a specific activity. A major difference to similar coursework at GCSE level is the requirement to justify the reasons for implementing the programme and evaluating the sessions completed in more depth. If you train regularly and your training regime is set by your coach, the PEP may be incorporated into the existing schedule. It should not be seen to interfere with any form of ongoing training or periodized programme, but to complement it.

However, if your programme is set and modified by a coach, you must still complete all the relevant sections fully and justify why different theoretical aspects have been applied. Whilst many students follow a schedule set by their coach, they cannot access the marks available in the planning and evaluation sections if they do not clearly justify the reasons for their actions.

The specification criteria require you to use only one training method or exercise activity. If you already train seriously for a specific activity, you may well incorporate several methods into your regime. This information is useful to record in a diary but there is no need to explain in detail each method of training – limit the planning section to one method only. There are no additional marks for outlining more than one type of exercise activity. There are four training methods from which to select, as shown in Figure 15.02.

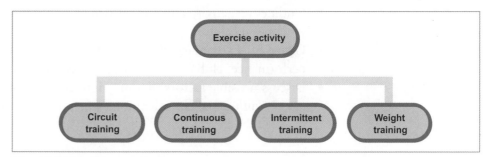

Fig. 15.02 Training methods

The length of time to follow the PEP may vary, but it should last ideally a minimum of six weeks, completing at least two sessions per week. Although many students may complete more than this number, this is the amount that should be written up and evaluated in detail.

The following section should be read in conjunction with Chapter 4, where you will find all the required information on the components of fitness and fitness testing.

What do I need to consider when designing my exercise programme?

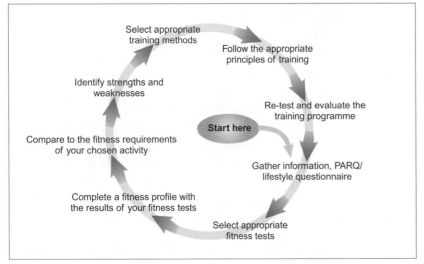

Fig. 15.03 Designing an exercise programme

Figure 15.03 gives a suggestion of the steps you need to follow in the design of your exercise programme.

The PEP is marked against set criteria and within each section certain elements must be fully explained, discussed and justified. Outlined below are a series of suggested questions that need to be answered within each section and an explanation of what may be included for each one.

Planning the programme

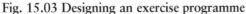

Section 1: Purpose/aim of the programme in relation to prior fitness and performance levels

- *What sport/activity is the PEP designed for?*
- *What is your current level of performance?*
- *Are there any health or injury problems that need to be considered?*

Advice

- Limit your training to one sport/activity.
- Outline the activity and any particular position, event and so on in which you may specialize.
- Give a brief summary of how often you participate, current standard of performance, club involvement, representative honours and so on.
- Discuss possible factors that may hinder the training programme or which may be influential considerations when devising the schedule.

- *What are the fitness/ability requirements of the activity and why?*
- *Are there specific requirements for your specialist position and/or event?*

Advice

- Outline both the health- and skill-related components of fitness required. Expand your explanation to include specific examples of when they are needed during performance.
- Discuss any particularly relevant factors, for example reaction time for a sprinter or explosive leg power for a basketball player.
- Comment about your strengths and weaknesses during performance, both general and skill-related.

- *What fitness tests were completed and why?*
- *Were the tests valid and reliable?*
- *How do the fitness results compare to national averages?*

Advice

- The criteria only require the outlining of tests actually linked to your specific aims. However, it may be useful to include the results from all tests completed as it helps to illustrate how the aims have been constructed.
- Explain in detail the procedures for the tests linked to the aims and discuss their validity, reliability and suitability with reference to the chosen activity.
- Most of the completed tests will be standard tests as outlined in the textbook, but it is possible to include others if they are deemed suitable. You may wish to devise and include your own skill-specific tests.
- If possible, use data from national averages as a basis for the construction of your aims. If these are unavailable, try to use data from school/college students.

- *What are the overall aims of the PEP?*
- *What are the specific aims of the PEP?*
- *Have specific targets been set which are measurable?*

Advice

- Explain how you intend to complete the PEP in terms of number of sessions per week, facilities used and so on.
- Clearly state the aims for both fitness and skill development. Do not give vague targets such as 'improve stamina' or 'better passing'. Remember the targets have to be evaluated at the end of the PEP.

Refer to Unit 1, Section 1 for detailed information regarding physical abilities, fitness requirements and fitness testing methods.

Section 2: Awareness of safety aspects/equipment/physical/physiological

- *What does the warm up involve and why?*
- *Are there any sport-specific related stretches?*
- *What does the cool down involve and why?*

Advice

- Explain the structure of the warm up and the benefits gained from its completion.
- Outline the exercises, the muscles involved and the type of stretching. Diagrams may be useful to aid your explanation.
- Discuss the benefits specific exercises may have on your sporting performance.
- Explain the structure of the cool down and the benefits gained from its completion.

- *What safety issues need to be considered to ensure the selected training method is completed without injury?*
- *How are the specific techniques/exercises completed correctly?*
- *What safety considerations need to be considered regarding the facilities and equipment?*

Advice

- Discuss general safety considerations for the training method such as exercise selection and order, dehydration, recovery periods and so on.
- Explain clearly how exercises are completed correctly. Again, diagrams may aid clarity.
- Outline checks that need to be performed on equipment and facilities, such as slippery surfaces, weights collars, benches and so on.

- *Are there any personal factors that need to be considered?*

Advice

- Discuss issues such as age, gender, illness, physical condition, recovery from injury and anything else you feel may be of concern during training sessions.

Why should I perform a warm up and a cool down?

Warm ups and cool downs are among the most important of all principles of training. They should be performed not only to prepare the body for exercise but also to prevent injury and undue muscle soreness and discomfort following exercise. Table 15.01 highlights some of the key benefits of warm ups and cool downs.

How should I structure my warm up?

Your warm up should consist of three distinct phases.

- Stage 1 – the pulse raiser

A five to ten minute period of light continuous exercise such as jogging or skipping. This will increase heart rate and body temperature and help redistribute blood to the working muscles.

- Stage 2 – stretching activity

Once the muscles are warm, stretching activities can follow. Stretches should aim to take the muscles through their full range and each should be held for a minimum of fifteen seconds. It may be necessary to replicate movements from the activity that follows to ensure that the muscles are fully prepared. A triple jumper, for example, may perform some bounding type activities

Table 15.01 Importance of warm ups and cool downs

Warm ups	Cool downs
• Improves oxygen delivery to the muscles due to an increase in heart rate and dilation of blood vessels through the release of adrenaline and the vascular shunt mechanism	• Maintains cardiorespiratory functioning, which helps to speed up the recovery process
• Increases venous return and therefore stroke volume through the action of the skeletal muscle pump	• Keeps capillaries and other blood vessels dilated, enabling the muscles to be flushed through with oxygen-rich blood, which helps to remove fatiguing by-products such as lactic acid and carbon dioxide, which can act on our pain receptors
• Increased temperature reduces the viscosity of the blood, improving blood flow to the working muscles	• Maintains the venous return mechanism, thereby preventing blood pooling in the veins, which can cause dizziness if the exercise is stopped abruptly
• Increased muscle temperatures improve the elasticity of muscle fibres, which can lead to a greater force and speed of contraction	• It can help minimize the muscular pain associated with DOMS (delayed onset of muscle soreness), which occurs 24–48 hours following exercise
• Increased muscle temperature facilitates enzyme activity, which ensures a readily available supply of energy to the muscles	
• Increased speed of nerve impulse transmission means that we become more alert, which can help us perform skills better	

- Stage 3 – skill-related practices

The focus of this third phase of the warm up should be some kind of skills-related practice to improve the co-ordination of the neuromuscular system. This might include shooting baskets in basketball, practising tumble turns in swimming or practising team plays such as corner kicks in football.

Section 3: Suitability/purpose of exercise/techniques used to improve fitness and skills

- *What methods of training are suitable to develop the specified aims and why?*
- *What do these forms of training involve?*
- *Which method of training is most suitable for the needs of the PEP?*

Advice
- Outline all the methods of training and discuss their merits and shortfalls.
- Select the most appropriate method and justify the reasons for doing so.
- Make reference to the stated aims of the PEP.
- Explain the potential benefits not only in terms of fitness but skill and performance development.

- *What specific exercises/sessions are included using the selected training method?*
- *What is the purpose of each with reference to muscle and skill development?*

Advice
- Outline each of the exercises involved and/or the type of session to be completed. Justify the reason for inclusion by outlining the potential benefits to be gained both in terms of muscle development and actual skilled performance within the selected sport/activity.

There are many different types of training. How do I know which are best suited for my exercise programme?

There are many different methods of training. Table 15.02 outlines the most common methods of training that can be used in your Personal Exercise Programme.

Table 15.02 The main benefits of the different types of training

Type of training	Brief description	Major components of fitness stressed	Example of a session
Continuous training	Low intensity rhythmic exercise that uses large muscle groups. The intensity of the training should be between 60 and 85% HR max, and the duration of the session between 30 minutes and 2 hours. Distance running, swimming and cycling are good examples of this	• Cardiorespiratory endurance • Muscular endurance	5–10K steady runs at 65% HR max
Fartlek training	A form of continuous training where the intensity or speed of the activity is varied throughout the session – from sprinting to walking. The beauty of this type of training is that it develops both aerobic and anaerobic fitness. It is ideal for games players	• Cardiorespiratory endurance • Muscular endurance • Speed	Jog at 60% HR max for 15 minutes Sprint × 50m, jog × 150m Repeat 10 times Walk for 90 seconds Jog at 70% HR max for 5 minutes Sprint × 200m Jog gently to finish
Sprint interval training	An intermittent training regime that involves periods of alternating exercise and rest. Widely used in athletics and swimming, the main benefit of this training method is its versatility, since there are many variables that can be altered in order to stress the required components of fitness. These variables include: • distance of work period • intensity of work period • the number of sets • the number of reps • duration of rest period	• Speed • Power	3 sets × 10 reps × 30m sprints (wbr) 5-minute rest between sets
Anaerobic interval training		• Speed • Power • Muscular endurance	2 sets × 4 reps × 300m runs (90 seconds rest, work relief)
Aerobic interval training		• Cardiorespiratory endurance • Muscular endurance	3 × 1000m runs (125% personal best time) Work:relief ratio = 1:1/2
Weight training	An intermittent training method that uses free weights or resistance machines to overload the body. The resistance is determined by working as a percentage of your one rep max (1RM) and the session is divided into sets and repetitions, which can be manipulated to stress the required aspect of strength	• Maximum strength • Power • Muscular endurance	**Maximum strength** Heavy weights, low reps 5 sets × 6 reps × 85% 1RM **Elastic strength** (must be rapid contractions) 3 sets × 12 reps × 75% 1RM **Strength endurance** Light weights, high reps 3 sets × 20 reps × 50% 1RM
Circuit training (Figure 15.04)	A general conditioning activity in which a series of exercises are used to work different muscle groups. Exercises can be made activity- or game-specific	• Muscular endurance • Cardiorespiratory endurance	See Figure 15.04 below. Circuit A = 8 exercises × 30 seconds Circuit B = 8 exercises × 30 seconds Circuit C = run for 4 minutes Total = 12 minutes Repeat 2 or 3 times
Plyometrics	A type of training that involves an eccentric muscle contraction followed immediately by a concentric contraction. When the quadriceps lengthen, for example when jumping down from a box top, it pre-loads the muscle and initiates the stretch reflex, which causes a rapid and forceful concentric contraction	• Power • Strength • Speed	A plyometrics circuit to include depth jumping, hopping, skipping, press-ups with claps, throwing and catching a medicine ball

Type of training	Brief description	Major components of fitness stressed	Example of a session
PNF (Proprioceptive neuromuscular facilitation)	A stretching technique that seeks to inhibit the stretch reflex that occurs when a muscle is stretched to its limit. By isometrically contracting the muscle that is being stretched (usually with the aid of a partner), the stretch reflex is diminished and a greater stretch can occur	• Flexibility	1 With the aid of a partner, stretch the muscle to its limit 2 Isometrically contract the muscle for a minimum of 6 seconds (this can be achieved through pushing against your partner) 3 Relax the muscle 4 When the stretch is performed a second time, the range of movement should have increased
SAQ (Speed, agility and quickness)	A type of training designed to improve the speed, agility and quickness of performers, particularly games players	• Speed • Agility • Power	Training activities include ladder drills, resistance drills, for example parachute runs, bungee rope runs, and plyometric drills

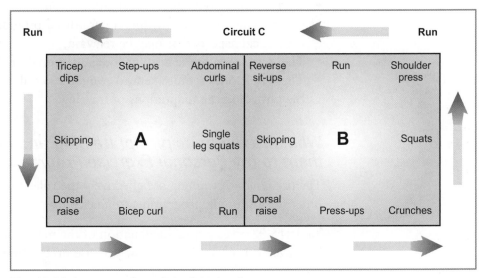

Fig. 15.04 A suggested conditioning circuit

Section 4: Appropriate application of activities within the programme in relation to theoretical areas

- *What principles of training need to be considered and how do they relate to the selected training method?*
- *Has the FITT principle been discussed (see below)?*
- *Do the planned sessions show 'progression' and 'overload'?*

Advice

- Outline briefly all the relevant principles of training and explain how they can be applied to your training method and schedule. Do not just copy sections of the textbook – apply the knowledge to your situation.
- Explain how they are intended to be utilized during the PEP. Do not worry if this has to change, it is part of the ongoing evaluation and modification process.

- *What are the workload intensities to be used and how have they been calculated?*
- *Why are the intensities at this level?*
- *How and when might they alter during the course of the PEP?*

Advice

- Outline the workload intensity. This may include, for example, the weight lifted, the intended training zone for heart rate, the exercise time, recovery periods, number of repetitions and sets and so on.
- Explain how these have been calculated and justify the reasons for doing so. Do not worry if they are actually wrong when you start training, they can be evaluated and adjusted accordingly.

- *Are there any other factors that need to be considered?*

Advice

- This section may include information about age, gender, overtraining, seasonal factors, cycles within a periodized programme and any other theoretical aspects that may be relevant.
- There is no requirement to include nutritional or dietary considerations.
- There is also no requirement to complete detailed information regarding the physiological adaptations of training.

What are the principles of training and how can I apply them to my Personal Exercise Programme?

The principles of training are effectively the rules that must be followed in order for a training programme to be effective.

Table 15.03 gives a brief explanation of the main principles of training and how each can be applied to your exercise programme.

How can I make sure that I am training at the correct intensity when I am performing continuous type training?

For aerobic type activities, such as long distance running and cycling, you can use heart rate training zones to gauge how hard you are working.

Simplified versions of this include working at a percentage of your maximum heart rate (HR max). This can be calculated by subtracting your age from the figure 220.

Maximum heart rate = 220 – age

For a 16 year old, this would be:

HR max = 220 – 16
HR max = 204bpm

Depending upon the intensity of training required, a lower or higher percentage of this maximum heart rate can be used. Some guidelines are

Table 15.03 Applying the principles of training

Principle of training	Explanation	Application
Specificity	All training must be relevant to the activity or sport. For example, a cyclist must perform most of their training on a bike. There is, of course, some value in other forms of training, but the majority must be performed on the bicycle. Actions from the activity should also be replicated during training	Be sure to train the: • relevant muscles • energy systems • relevant fibre types • fitness components. Use appropriate technique
Overload	If training is to have the required effect, then the performer must find the training taxing. The level of training must be pitched at a level greater than the demands regularly encountered by the player. The old adage 'no pain, no gain' can be applied here!	• Use heart rate to gauge how hard you are working • Work at an appropriate percentage of max heart rate or 1RM • Increase the duration of the activity if needed
Progression	As the body becomes better with coping with the training over time, greater demands must be made if improvement is to continue. This is often linked to overload and known as 'progressive overload'	Increase: • percentage HR max • percentage 1RM • duration • frequency of training
Reversibility	Use it or lose it! If the training load decreases or if training stops altogether, then the benefits of the prior training can be lost	Unless injured, training should continue
Moderation (adequate recovery)	Sufficient recovery time must be built into the training programme to prevent over-training. Rest allows the body to overcompensate and adapt to the training, leading to improved performance. Overtraining is characterized by muscular fatigue, illness and injury	Heavy training sessions should be followed by lighter sessions or even rest days. The ratio of 3:1 is often used to express the number of hard sessions to easy sessions within a week's training cycle
FITT	F (frequency) = how often we train I (intensity) = how hard we train T (time) = how long we train for T (type) = what type of training we use	• Train 3–6 days/week • Percentage HR max or percentage 1RM • 30 minutes to 2 hours session • Use the principle of specificity!

given below for low, moderate and high intensity exercise:

• low intensity = 30–49% of HR max
• moderate intensity = 50–69% of HR max
• high intensity = 70–85% HR max.

Assuming you wanted to work at moderate intensity, your target heart rate should therefore lie between 50 per cent and 69 per cent of your HR max. This should equate to a target heart rate zone of between 102bpm and 141bpm:

$$0.5 \times 204 = 102\text{bpm}$$

and

$$0.69 \times 204 = 141\text{bpm}$$

The closer to 141bpm, the harder you will be working. The great part about this is that you now have some objective data to ensure training is going to be effective.

This formula has been criticized, however, for being too simplistic as it treats all people of the same age as the same and does not really take into account current fitness levels. Karvonen therefore developed a more appropriate formula, which takes account of individual levels of fitness, as resting heart rates are required to work out an individual's training heart rate zone.

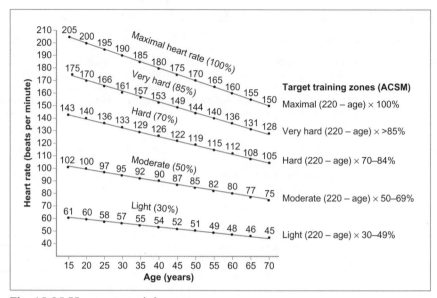

Fig. 15.05 Heart rate training zones

To calculate the heart rate training zones in this instance, you must first find your maximum heart rate reserve. This can be calculated by subtracting your resting heart rate from your maximum heart rate:

$$\text{maximum heart rate reserve} = \text{HR max} - \text{HR rest}$$
$$= 204 - 70$$
$$= 134\text{bpm}$$

For training to be effective, Karvonen suggested a training intensity of between 60 and 75 per cent of maximum heart rate reserve, which in this case is between 150 and 171bpm:

lower training threshold $= 0.6$ (max heart rate reserve) + HR rest
$$= (0.6 \times 134) + 70$$
$$= 150\text{bpm}$$

higher training threshold $= 0.75$ (max heart rate reserve) + HR rest
$$= (0.75 \times 134) + 70$$
$$= 171\text{bpm}$$

How can I make sure that I am training at the correct intensity when I am performing strength training?

First of all you must decide upon the type of strength that you wish to improve. Remember, there are three different types of strength: maximum, elastic (power) and strength endurance. The intensity at which you train will also depend upon you finding out your one repetition maximum (1RM). Once you have discovered this, you will have the tools necessary to calculate an appropriate training intensity or load. The examples in Table 15.04 gives you a good guideline to follow for each type of strength.

Table 15.04 Strength training guidelines

Maximum strength	High load, low reps 5 sets × 6 reps × 85% 1RM
Elastic strength (power)	Moderate to high load (must be rapid contractions) 3 sets × 12 reps × 75% 1RM
Strength endurance (muscular endurance)	Light load/high reps 3 sets × 20 reps × 50% 1RM

Performing the programme

Section 5: Completion of exercise/technique in safe/efficient manner

- *Has a warm up and cool down been completed for each session as outlined in the planning section?*
- *Have all safety checks been completed to ensure the facilities and equipment are fit for use?*
- *Have the selected training method and selected exercises been completed correctly as outlined in the planning section?*

Advice
- The member of staff will assess your ability to complete all the safety aspects correctly as outlined in the planning section. To achieve the highest marks, they will need to observe you completing the training sessions correctly independently.
- If you complete the warm up, cool down and training method correctly but do not explain each fully in the first section, you cannot access all the marks.

Section 6: Implementation of planned programme

- *Have the training sessions been completed as planned?*
- *Have the details of exercises and workload intensities been included?*
- *Have clear outlines of each session been kept with relevant modifications?*

Advice
- Keep clear and accurate records of all the sessions completed. For each, outline the intended aims including any changes made based on previous evaluation.
- Include details of workloads, repetitions, sets, target zones and so on.
- Ensure you complete at least two sessions per week for the duration of the PEP.

Section 7: Attitude/motivation towards improving personal training/fitness/skill level

- *Have all the sessions been completed as planned?*
- *Have other training sessions and competitive performances been completed?*
- *Have you gained a good understanding of training methodology and are you able to explain why the PEP has been structured in a particular way and justify those reasons?*

Advice
- Complete as many training sessions as possible and provide evidence of additional activities that have been undertaken. Extra sessions do not have to be evaluated.
- To gain the higher marks, if questioned, you must demonstrate a good level of theoretical understanding of all aspects of your PEP.

Evaluating the programme

Section 8: Ongoing and personal evaluation of level of training/fitness and of improvement in level of skill

- *Has an evaluation been completed for each training session?*
- *Is the evaluation logical and structured?*
- *Was the session completed as planned and did it meet its stated aims?*
- *Were the workload intensities correct?*
- *What was the recovery period (if applicable)?*

Advice

- Complete a detailed evaluation after each session and include reference to the aims. Discuss the appropriateness of workload intensities and comment on the need to make alterations based on the principles of training.

- *Were the exercises completed safely including the warm up and cool down?*
- *What modifications are needed for the next session?*
- *Has the fitness training to date made any impact on performance levels and skills?*

Advice

- Comment on the appropriateness of the exercises and outline any alterations that may be needed. For example, more emphasis may need to be placed on the upper body during the warm up or certain exercises in a circuit may need to be made easier/harder.
- Reference could also be made to the effect the training may be having on your sporting performance, either in a positive or negative manner. There may well not be a noticeable difference.

Section 9: Summative evaluation of programme in terms of aims, performance, the improvement of skill and outcomes

- *Did the PEP meet its stated aims?*
- *Did the PEP affect your fitness, skills and performance level?*

Advice

- Discuss the overall effectiveness of the PEP with clear reference to the fitness and skill targets.
- Comment on any changes that may/may not have taken place.
- If there has been no improvement, outline possible reasons for the lack of development.

- *What were the results of the retests?*
- *Were the fitness tests appropriate – if not, how would they change in the future?*

Advice

- Analyse any changes in the various components of fitness. Remember, only the tests for the specific aspects of fitness targeted need to be completed.
- Discuss the effectiveness of the tests and modifications for future use. Outline the reasons why some tests may have been of limited use.

- *Was the selected training activity suitable to achieve the stated aims?*
- *Were the selected exercises suitable?*
- *What changes would be made if the PEP were to be repeated or used as a basis for further training?*

Advice

- Discuss the effectiveness of the training method and exercises used. Explain either why they were appropriate or the limitations their selection caused. For example, the stated aim may have been to develop stamina and circuit training used. Could any gains have been increased by used continuous training?
- Outline specific alterations in the training activity or exercises; try not to give vague descriptions.

Section 10: Appraisal of programme in terms of a discussion/explanation/justification through synthesis of theory

- *Were the principles of training applied correctly?*
- *Were the workload intensities suitable to achieve to stated aims?*
- *What changes would be made if the PEP were to be repeated or used as a basis for further training?*

Advice

- Using specific examples from the performance section, discuss whether or not the principles of training were used effectively. Explain in detail each principle and how, if appropriate, it may be applied differently during future training. For example, the overload may have been too quick or the exercises not sufficiently specific to the activity or stated aim.

Key points to remember

- There are no marks for improvement.
- Do not set unrealistic targets.
- Only one method of training needs to be used.
- Do not just copy theory from the textbook – it must be applied to you as a performer.
- Justify the reasons for applying theoretical aspects in a particular manner.

Chapter 16: Practical coursework

Introduction

The practical coursework is your opportunity to demonstrate your skills in your chosen activity. You have the opportunity to dictate how well you do because you know exactly the areas in which you will be assessed.

The chapter will outline advice on assessment and preparation for the moderation, the roles you are expected to master and details of how to analyse your performance. Many of you will relish the opportunity to master the skills previously developed through physical education lessons, the GCSE course and extra-curricular activities. However, the requirements of the course at AS level demand a technical competence via demonstration and execution through conditioned practices rather than playing in a competitive situation. Both of these require practise and concentration to achieve high marks.

The aim of the practical coursework component is to assess not only the physical skills and application of strategies and tactics, but to bring together all the various theoretical components allowing the optimization of performance. The task facing students is to use their knowledge and understanding of the theoretical aspects of the course to identify weaknesses in their performance, possible causes and use the acquired knowledge to address the faults.

Table 16.01 outlines the examination board requirement for AS and A2 levels of study. It is useful to have some understanding of the A2 course because if you develop a clear understanding of the correct technique during the first year of study, it will make your studies easier the following year.

Table 16.01 Requirements for AS and A2 levels of study

Exam board	AS level	A2 level
AQA	• One practical activity selected from choice of groups • Personal Exercise Programme	• One practical activity, which may be the same as that offered at AS level or different • Written/verbal observation and analysis of performance compared to an elite performer • Synoptic assignment

Assignment 1
Obtain a copy of the practical specification and make notes on the exact requirements.
Visit the AQA website. Go to www.heinemann.co.uk/hotlinks, insert express code 9300P and click on this topic.

Structure of the course and preparation advice

This element of the course aims to develop many skills and prepare students to fulfil a number of roles. Figure 16.01 outlines such roles.

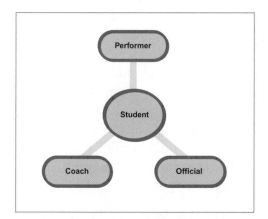

Fig. 16.01 Roles that students will fulfil

In order to complete each of these roles successfully, time must be devoted to practice and development of knowledge about the rules, scoring systems, tactics, strategies, technical skills, specific terminology, physical preparation, psychological requirements and any other areas that may hinder or promote performance.

It may be easier to view this section of the course as progressive, with the foundation skills and knowledge being laid during the AS year and the refining and optimizing of performance occurring during the A2 year. Many of the skills developed via practices at AS level will be examined in more detail during full competitive situations at A2 level.

Many students often neglect the practical element of the course and tend to focus on the theoretical aspects. However, a large percentage of the final marks are allocated to this section, up to 30 per cent. Therefore time should be devoted to developing the skills required from the onset of the course and not left until close to the final assessment or moderation.

To fully understand the nature of performance and how to facilitate improvement, links should be made with the theoretical components as frequently as possible. Individual strengths and weaknesses should be identified and, as the course progresses, possible causes and corrective measures can be implemented.

The selection of activities must be carefully considered, as there may be restrictions. In addition to your own experience, other factors may include the time available to complete extra training, the opportunity for extra-curricular activities, the accessibility of facilities and resources plus the expertise of teachers and coaches.

The nature of assessment requires the demonstration of named core skills related to a specific activity, the difficulty of which gradually increase due to the requirement of executing effectively in more pressurized or demanding situations.

Assignment 2
1 List possible activities that may be selected based on your experience and strengths.
2 Outline the opportunities that will allow skills and performance to develop outside normal lesson time.
3 Select the activity to be assessed and highlight the core skills to be assessed.

The marking of the practical activities is conducted by continual assessment. This allows for ongoing development of performance and caters for students who may have an 'off day' during a moderator's visit. There are several key terms that need to be outlined in order to fully understand the assessment procedure:
- *skills in isolation* – the demonstration of specific core skills, which will be compared to a correct technical model (see later for full explanation)
- *conditioned practice* – the demonstration of core skills and some tactical awareness in a more pressured practice situation, but not a full game or equivalent competitive situation
- *competitive situation* – demonstration of core skills, strategies and tactics, the application of the psychological and physiological qualities needed within a fully competitive environment or appropriate alternative. This is not actually assessed until the A2 year of the course.

To facilitate development, the various skills need to be analysed to identify personal strengths and personal weaknesses. More detailed advice to complete this process is outlined in the next section.

Each activity is different in terms of core skills; examples from different categories are shown below in Figures 16.02–16.05, which illustrate the diverse nature of each activity.

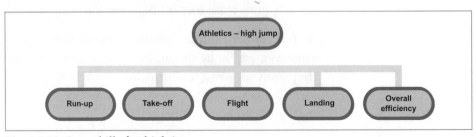

Fig. 16.02 Core skills for high jump

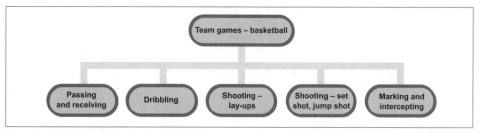

Fig. 16.03 Core skills for basketball

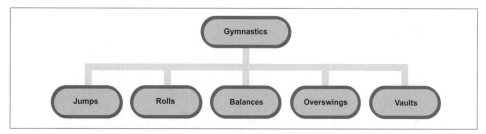

Fig. 16.04 Core skills for gymnastics

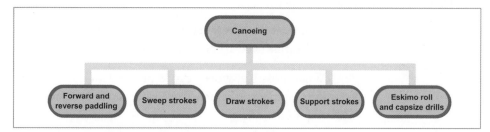

Fig. 16.05 Core skills for canoeing

Assignment 3
1 Identify the core skills and their subroutines for your chosen activity.
2 List your strongest and weakest skills.
3 Outline any specific requirements for your conditioned practices.

Once this process has been completed for all the core skills, time should be devoted to rectify faults. The assessment is based on competence of performance when compared to a correct technical model (see next section for further details) and marks are awarded to subroutines of the skill as well as end result. For example, the subroutines for a squash stroke may be the grip, footwork and preparation, shot positioning and timing, follow-through and recovery, and finally effectiveness.

To develop the necessary skills and tactical awareness required, time must be given to practice. It is of no use simply reading books or watching videos informing you how to complete the skills correctly. They may be useful as a reference resource but there is no substitute for actually performing the skills.

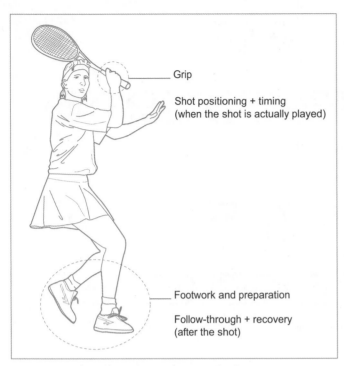

Grip

Shot positioning + timing
(when the shot is actually played)

Footwork and preparation

Follow-through + recovery
(after the shot)

Fig. 16.06 The subroutines of a squash player

Training sessions are always easier with others not just because it is more sociable but they can actually help to improve your performance by observing and coaching. If the practice takes place with another student who has limited knowledge of the activity, outline the identified weaknesses of the skills and prepare a sheet of the correct techniques and coaching points required.

However, if time can be spent with a teacher or another student who is experienced and is able to identify your weaknesses, this may be of greater benefit. Allocated time for development may be available either during lessons or extra-curricular activities.

Further time for development may take place at a local club and the expertise of their coaches may be utilized. If this is the case, it may be advisable to inform them of the specification criteria so that they are aware of your aims and the specific skills that need to be developed.

When possible, video record any practice sessions and analyse your development. Evaluate any progress and restructure your training schedule as required.

To develop the effective application of your skills in a competitive situation, set targets for each game or event and ask someone to evaluate your performance. Do not set too many each time, possibly two or three, but try to concentrate on these, and do not get over-concerned with other areas of weakness – they can be targets next time.

When developing skills, do not try to change everything at once or expect a huge improvement in performance overnight. The process may take months or years to complete. Many elite performers strive to make minor modifications to their technique in order to achieve the optimum performance. The aim of the AS/A2 course is not to make you compete at this level but to be competent performers. Try to remember that when developing your practical performance.

Assessment procedures

The school/college will be assigned an external moderator to ensure the marking criteria are applied correctly by the teachers when compared to recommended national standards. The moderation may involve either:

- one school/college
- a group of schools/college
- video evidence.

The moderator may not see all the activities being offered by the school/college due to time restrictions, availability of facilities or numbers involved. However, the assumption must be made that they will observe any possible combination of activities and as a consequence you should be fully prepared. This may involve not only the actual practical performance but also any analysis of performance requirements. The best way to prepare for the moderation is to start practising the core skills as early in the course as possible and give yourself the opportunity to experience as many conditioned situations as possible to develop your skills.

The moderation usually involves both AS and A2 students. Consequently, it may be easy to lose focus and concentration. Many students assume the moderator is not watching them because they are at the other end of the sports hall or far side of the playing field. They may be assessing you at any time.

A common error during the moderation visit involves a lack of concentration during the demonstrations of the core skills. Many students appear to not apply themselves fully and produce weaker demonstrations compared to their actual ability. This may be due to the misconception that they are easy, do not require much attention and are less intense compared to the conditioned practice or competitive situation.

It also helps to make the effort to dress appropriately and 'look the part'. This will at least give the moderator the impression that some preparation and thought have been given to the assessment rather than simply turning up on the day.

The nature of physical activity inevitably involves mistakes being made during performance; it is almost unavoidable. Even performers at the highest level make errors of judgement or are influenced by the environment, occasion and opponents. If mistakes are made, do not worry about them, redirect your attention and concentrate on the task ahead. The moderator will look at the overall performance, not just one small part.

If the selected activity is a team game or one that involves other performers, do not try to be the centre of attention all the time. The assessment is based on your ability to fulfil a role within a specific position. Marks may be lost because of the inability to implement certain tactics, strategies and systems of play.

The moderator may require the analysis of your own performance and a comparison with another student. If this does happen, further advice is outlined in the next section covering all aspects of preparation for this assessment.

Analysis of skills and performance

As the course progresses, there will be a requirement to analyse the performance of yourself and others in greater detail. In order to successfully achieve this, a coaching cycle should be used ensuring a consistent approach; an example is shown in Figure 16.07.

Fig. 16.07 A coaching cycle

Understanding each element is crucial if the coaching process is to be effective and actually develop skills and their application.

- *Performance* – the actions of the performer either in isolation, practice or competitive situation.
- *Observation* – the actions of the performer are watched either by another person or video recorded.
- *Analysis* – the actions of the performer are assessed. Notes should be taken when possible to highlight key strengths and weaknesses.
- *Evaluation* – the actions of the performer are compared to a correct technical model, competent performer or past performances.
- *Planning* – possible causes of weaknesses are identified and corrective measures devised to eradicate the problems. These may be in the form of physical practices, physiological adaptations or psychological preparation. It is also important at this stage not to neglect the strengths of the performer but to maintain a level of training to ensure they do not decline at the expense of improving the weaknesses.
- *Feedback* – the identified training adaptations are discussed with the performer and implemented during the forthcoming performances.

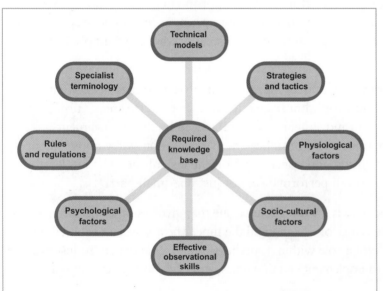

Fig. 16.08 Knowledge required to complete the coaching cycle

When the coaching and analysis process occurs, there are many factors that may need to be considered and knowledge of each must be established if the outcome is to be successful. Many students can identify basic faults in technique and performance but not expand their responses with the use of detailed technical information or appropriate terminology. Figure 16.08 highlights some of the knowledge that may be required to successfully complete the coaching cycle.

As you can see, the knowledge base required to be an effective coach who is able to observe and analyse performance is wide ranging and varied. During the course of your studies, you should aim to improve each of them.

Assignment 4
For your selected activity, place in rank order the types of knowledge on Figure 16.08 and assess your own strengths and weaknesses as a coach.

Technical models

Often reference will be made to your performance compared to a 'correct technical model'. This term refers to the performance of a skill that is considered to be of a very high standard. There may actually be several variations of a skill and different performers may have their own individual peculiarities but still be highly successful. Similarly, as many activities become exposed to scientific and technological support, alterations in techniques are becoming more common as actions and techniques are refined.

As a consequence, it is advisable to base your comparisons on the most recent information or a performer who is generally accepted as being close to the norm. The technique of many international competitors may be considered unique and inadvisable to coach to developing athletes. For example, the technique of the South African bowler Paul Adams and the running style of 400 metre sprinter Michael Johnson are unlikely to be actively encouraged amongst younger performers but are highly effective for them personally.

There are many resources for appropriate technical models, often published by the national governing bodies. Suitable sources any include:
- coaching manuals
- photographs
- instructional videos
- CD-ROMs
- the Internet
- television recorded performances with expert commentary
- live events.

When studying and developing an awareness of each skill, refer back to the specific subroutines identified previously. A thorough knowledge and understanding of each phase of the skill is vital if the observation and analysis process is to be effective. For each skill, make diagrams and notes of the key points for each subroutine. Initially, concentrate on the major technical points, including the correct terminology, but later, once these are well learnt and easily recognized, develop an awareness of the more advanced technical points.

Assignment 5
Research and find relevant resources to identify the key technical points for each of the core skills.

A useful aid to developing this understanding is a chart containing all the basic information for each subroutine of the specific skill. Often an A3 piece of paper divided as shown in Table 16.02 can be easily constructed and contain all the information required.

Table 16.02

Subroutine 1	Subroutine 2	Subroutine 3	Subroutine 4	Subroutine 5
Diagram or photographs of this phase				
Correct technique *Include two or three points*				
Common faults *Include two or three points*				
Corrective practices *Include one per fault*				

Assignment 6
Complete a chart for each core skill using the resources identified above.

Observation advice

When observing any performance, the various viewing angles may provide different information about the effectiveness of performance. Imagine when watching a sporting event on television the numerous camera angles employed by the editor and the different impression and information that is produced by each. It is now common practice in many high level sporting events to use such technology to aid referees in their final decision. This approach should be employed to aid your observation and analysis.

Different views give very different perspectives and the aim of the observation should be identified clearly. The actual execution of skills may require a position as close to the action as possible from the side, front and rear, while the observation of tactical awareness and effective implementation may require a location further away. However, a view from behind the field of play may provide different information compared to one from the side or elevated in a stand. It may be advisable to vary your position to maximize the information upon which to base your judgements.

When observing, either live or from video evidence, make notes to remind you of specific instances or actions. Divide the observation sheet into sections covering the areas required. For example, when observing a game, the sheet may consist of sections for attacking skills, defensive skills, tactics and set plays.

Analysis of personal performance

Before any personal development of skill and technique can occur, your own performance must be analysed and evaluated. This can be achieved in a number of ways:
- teacher/coach observing performance and providing feedback
- another student observing performance and providing feedback
- video recording of performance and personal analysis.

If possible, the third is in many ways the most useful as you can see the faults (via visual guidance) and develop a better understanding of the exact modifications needed. Video footage is also useful as a means of stopping the action and making specific comparisons to the technical model, which may be more difficult during live or full speed actions.

Once the actual skill has been analysed, the next stage in the process involves the evaluation of the effectiveness of its application either during conditioned practices or competitive situations. For game activities, these are often split into the following sections:

- effectiveness of attacking skills
- effectiveness of defensive skills
- effective implementation of strategies and tactics
- effective implementation of physiological and psychological factors that affect performance.

Other activities have alternative categories which are more appropriate, for example swimming and athletics may require the comments to be based on two events and gymnastic events on agilities and twists. Detailed requirements need to be obtained from the specification criteria.

Assignment 7
Observe and analyse your personal performance in the various core skills and conditioned practices.

Once this process has been completed, a structured training programme should be followed to develop the identified weaknesses in the skills. Frequently assess your development either via a teacher/coach or by video recording again. Do not just assume because practice is taking place an improvement will occur – you may be practising the wrong technique!

Key points to remember

The following points should be applied from the start of the course.

- Start preparation for the final assessment at the beginning of the course – do not leave it until the last few weeks.
- Learn the correct techniques for the chosen activities.
- Take time to analyse your strengths and weaknesses.
- Set realistic targets for performance development.
- Evaluate progress regularly and revise targets.
- Look for the links between the theoretical aspects of the course and personal practical performance.
- Keep notes updated regularly and use them as a revision resource.
- Enjoy it – the practical aspect of the course is supposed to be fun!

Chapter 17: Written investigation

Learning outcomes

By the end of this chapter you should be able to:
- have necessary details for completing the project option of the AS coursework
- have ideas you could adapt for your own original piece of work
- understand the method of assessment
- understand the assessment criteria.

Introduction

You have decided to opt for the project option for your coursework. There may be various reasons for this choice. It may be the only option offered at your centre, you may be injured and unable to complete any practical work, or you may feel confident in your ability to produce a sound piece of coursework, therefore achieving a high grade.

Whichever of these is the case, the positive aspect to consider is that *you* can control the process. You will know the assessment criteria beforehand and, if completed well, should ensure a sound grade before you sit the actual examination papers. However, the biggest mistake students make is thinking an 'A' grade will appear without too much effort. Generally speaking, 'what you put in to it will be what you get out of it'.

Individual qualities required for producing an effective project include the following:
- well motivated
- interested and focused on the task
- prepared to spend time on the project
- prepared to research relevant information
- reasonable IT skills (these skills can also be developed during the process).

Is this you? It is very important to thoroughly understand what is required. So what does this option involve?

Overview

- It is worth 18 per cent of the AS grade.
- It needs to be no more than 1500 words in length.
- It should be based on the observation and analysis of a sporting performance.

What should you do in the initial stages?
- Familiarize yourself with the coursework process (there is no substitute

for knowing the specification – ask your teacher for details or, alternatively, visit the AQA website (go to <u>heinemann.co.uk/hotlinks</u>, enter express code 9300P and click on this topic). You also need to know the assessment details, that is, how your work will be marked – see Table 17.01, page 295).

- Choose a sport and performer that you feel confident with (see the list of categories on page 296). Factors that may affect your choice of sport would be your own knowledge and expertise, any limitations/restrictions that may be imposed by your centre, the facilities and resources available to you, the availability of a reliable performer.
- Devise a timetable that will help you keep focused throughout the process (see Table 17.02, page 297).
- Devise observation sheets for the five core skills of your chosen sport (see Table 17.03, page 297).
- Preferably video record five core skills. These core skills should be performed by the same performer.
- Complete your observation sheets based on the evidence.
- Analyse the performance – you need to suggest major strengths or weaknesses of the performances.
- Evaluate the strengths and weaknesses by identifying the greatest weakness for development.
- Complete a bibliography (list of books). It is important to record from the very start every piece of research material you use to help you develop your project. This includes textbooks, reference books, sport magazines, videos, websites and so on. The information should include the author, the year of publication, the name of the publishing centre and so on. In the case of a website, the correct address should be provided (see Table 17.08, page 301).
- Make sure you source all the information you use otherwise your project could be considered to have been plagiarized.
- Label all sections according to the exam board criteria and in criteria order (for example, A1, B1, B2 and so on).
- Submit the coursework to the deadline given by your teacher.

Format for the project at AS level:
- Contents
- Planning
- Observation and analysis of five core skills
- Evaluation
- Bibliography
- Communication
- Appendices (optional).

Planning

You will be awarded marks for providing evidence of your planning throughout the development of your project, similar to the Personal Exercise

Programme. You will need to provide a timetable (see Table 17.02) and your teacher will also want to be confident that you are taking this aspect seriously. Any weaknesses at this stage will often be reflected later on in the main body of the project. The planning will also involve the compilation of data collection sheets to use for the observation of the performance.

Observation and analysis

Before you can observe and analyse any performance, you first need to make an informed decision about the sport and the performer you will focus on.

- The activity: ideally the activity should be one you enjoy and have some knowledge and expertise in. Do you play the sport at club level or school level? Do you have any coaching experience? Do not worry if you have not, but this is something you can consider. You will need to be able to access coaching manuals in order to help you with the perfect models and evaluation of strengths and weaknesses.
- The performer: the performer could be yourself or anyone else. Consider the implications of observing and analysing yourself. The performance would have to be videoed and it may be more difficult to be objective. On the other hand, you would be working for yourself and therefore be reliable. You could choose a club member, a family member or a member of your peer group. The person you choose must perform all five core skills.
- The facility: which facilities do you have access to? This must also be taken into account. For example, access to a swimming pool can be a problem.

Once you have decided who and what to observe, you need to plan when to carry out the observation session. You need to accurately record your observation and make appropriate analysis of the performer's strengths or weaknesses.

Evaluation

You need to summarize the observed performance and suggest some factors that may be the cause of the strengths and weaknesses. Consider physiological, psychological and sociological factors as well as resources you would need.

Bibliography

This section should record the number and type of resources used to help you complete the project. The Harvard method is required for this project.

For a textbook (alphabetically): Author/s (year), title, where published: publisher

For a journal: Author/s (year), title of article, journal, volume number, pages

For a website: The full website address

It is important that you do not just make a list of resources if you have not used them. Your teachers will require you to know about these materials. The purpose of a bibliography is that the reader should be able to obtain the referenced material from the information you have given.

Communication

Examiners/moderators need to be able to read and cross-reference the project easily. In order to do this, the piece of coursework should be neat and well organized. Any diagrams, pictures, charts and so on should be a valuable part of the project and should not just be included to make it look as if you have done more work than you actually have.

Table 17.01 AS marking rationale, example: 'Football'

A	Timetable	
Marks		
3	A1	• 1 mark – detailed breaking down – specific dates for observation of the performer • 1 mark – reference to all five core skills • 1 mark – covers all areas of the project
Total = 3 marks		
B	**Observation**	
3	B1	Detailed observation of core skill 1 – for example passing • 1 mark – attempted • 1 mark – splitting skill into component parts • 1 mark – for relating it to ideal model
3	B2	Detailed observation of core skill 2 – for example dribbling (marks divided as B1)
3	B3	Detailed observation of core skill 3 – for example shooting (marks divided as B1)
3	B4	Detailed observation of core skill 4 – for example heading (marks divided as B1)
3	B5	Detailed observation of core skill 5 – for example tackling (marks divided as B1) (B1–B5 – technical model details should be supplemented by well-labelled diagrams)
3	B6	Identification of all five core skills Use of camcorder to allow repeated viewing • 1 mark – identified all five core skills • 1 mark – observations done on each one • 1 mark – use of video/knowledge that several observations made
3	B7	Detailed qualitative observation • 1 mark – qualitative observations on each • 1 mark – split skill down in all sheets (core skills) • 1 mark – specific/appropriate detail in each component part of each skill
3	B8	Basic raw data Averages calculated Explanation for choice of analysis • 1 mark – record of quantitative data for at least two skills • 1 mark – for average, mean, mode or percentage calculated (show working) • 1 mark – calculation justified in terms of type of data calculated (for example ordinal/interval and so on). Brief description of what the data means
Total = 24 marks		
C	**Analysis (Need only strengths *or* weaknesses, but need weaknesses for D, Evaluation, below)**	
Must relate to comments on observation sheets, use headings. • 1 mark – minimum of two observations identified • 1 mark – at least one analysed/justified in terms of effect on skill • 1 mark – analysis/justification of at least two observations		
3	C1	• More than two strengths/weaknesses identified for core skill 1 • More than two justified
3	C2	• More than two strengths/weaknesses identified for core skill 2 • More than two justified

3	C3	• More than two strengths/weaknesses identified for core skill 3 • More than two justified
3	C4	• More than two strengths/weaknesses identified for core skill 4 • More than two justified
3	C5	• More than two strengths/weaknesses identified for core skill 5 • More than two justified

Total = 15 marks

D	**Evaluation**	
3	D1	• 1 mark – identify an appropriate weakness to focus on (must be relevant to performance observed) • 1 mark – consideration of resources needed to improve the weakness • 1 mark – is weakness logical, compare focus to others
3	D2	• 1 mark – justify your main weakness (similar to D1) • 1 mark – justify in terms of resources available to use (best suited, what is available and so on) • 1 mark – discussion of the performance benefits to improving weakness

Total = 6 marks

E	**Bibliography**	
3	E1	More than two items of two different types Use of Harvard system in listing of texts • 1 mark – any two items • 1 mark – two different sources (for example book/web) • 1 mark – more than two items from two sources

Total = 3 marks

F	**Communication**	
3	F1	• 1 mark – neat • 1 mark – easy to follow, for example headings/follow project order • 1 mark – criteria assessment order/every section accounted for
3	F2	Spelling/punctuation/grammar correct throughout project
3	F3	Tables/photographs Well labelled • 1 mark – table/illustration • 1 mark – table and illustration • 1 mark – correctly labelled

Total = 9 marks

Overall total = 60 marks

If you follow these simple rules/steps, you should produce a very creditable project.

The sports categories you can choose from are:
1 Artistic/aesthetic activities: dance (contemporary/creative/ballet), gymnastics, trampolining, diving
2 Athletics, cycling
3 Swimming
4 Outdoor and adventurous activities: canoeing, mountain activities, climbing, sailing, horse riding, skiing
5 Individual activities: tennis, badminton, golf, judo, rowing, table tennis, squash, fencing, horse riding and karate
6 Team games: basketball, cricket, Gaelic football, goalball, handball, hockey, lacrosse, netball, Rugby Union/League, soccer, softball/baseball/rounders, volleyball, water polo

The assessment criteria in detail

A1 Planning (Total 3 marks)

There are three marks available for this section, and they are marks you should not lose. Three marks of the planning section are allocated to a timetable. These three marks are easy to obtain if you follow the guidelines below:

- include all aspects of the project. This is where you need to refer carefully to the assessment criteria
- set realistic deadlines.

Your timetable should start immediately, as the timetable should be forward planning and looking ahead rather than adopting a retrospective viewpoint. By this, you should not write, 'on 3 October I observed my performer'; rather, it should state, 'I intend to observe my performer this week.' Notice the timetable is clearly labelled 'A1'.

Table 17.02 A1 Timetable

Date (should be broken down into weeks)	Intention
Example: Week beginning 1 September	
Week beginning 8 September	
Week beginning 15 September	
Week beginning 22 September	

B1–B8 Observation (Total 24 marks)

Before you design your observation/data collection sheets, it is important that you understand what you are trying to discover. You need to find out:
- what the performer can do
- what the performer struggles to achieve.

Find out your five core skills from each of your chosen activities. Refer to the current specification or ask your teacher for details. Decide how to break your skill down into its component parts – this makes the observation process much simpler. Put this breakdown onto an observation sheet (see Table 17.03). A suggestion would be to have four columns, (see Table 17.03).

Table 17.03 Suggested component parts for observation

Skill breakdown	Perfect model	Strengths of performance	Weaknesses of performance

HOT TIPS

A quick check with the assessment criteria should indicate you need to label this section 'B6'.

Fill in the 'perfect model' column using books, possibly videos, coaching manuals and so on (remember to record these in your bibliography). You should also include diagrams, not forgetting to label your diagrams if you have photocopied them from a book.

Suggested skill breakdown

The exam board has given a useful system of breaking a skill down into easily identifiable parts. You are perfectly at liberty to use your own ideas. Table 17.04 is an example for athletics.

Table 17.04 Suggestions for skill breakdown in athletics

Athletics	Track event: Start, posture, head carriage, arm action, leg action, finish
	Throwing event: Grip, preparation, travel/trunk action, release, overall efficiency
	Jumps: Approach/run-up, take-off, flight and landing

The core skills

You need to devise an observation sheet for each of the core skills B1–5 for your chosen sport. The example given in Table 17.05 is for golf.

Table 17.05 Observation breakdown for golf

Golf	**Driving** Mid irons Approach shots (pitching and chipping) **Putting** Bunker play

Observations of performance (Total 15 marks)

These are your completed observation sheets and should be an accurate record of the performance you observed. Remember to look specifically at each point on your perfect model and compare your performer to that point. If your performer is doing what the perfect model suggests, then put it in the strengths column: if they are not, put it as a weakness.

Remember: to achieve full marks, the reader should not have to ask any questions. Everything should be fully explained. Remember to complete one for each core skill!

HOT TIPS

Check the assessment criteria code now and accurately label each part of the observation process.

Table 17.06 Example of a data collection sheet for netball – Skill: shooting

Skill breakdown	Perfect model	Strengths of performance	Weaknesses of performance
Preparation			
Execution			
Follow through/ recovery			
Result			

B6–8 Observation technique (Total 9 marks)

These marks are based upon the variety of techniques you have used when carrying out your observations.

In order to achieve the full three marks for B6, you should have:
- referred repeatedly to the video evidence you collected
- created and used effective observation sheets with an appropriately broken-down skill and a detailed perfect model.

To achieve full marks for B7, your observations for B1–5 should be very detailed, for example 'Arm movement in preparation for the smash was good' would achieve virtually no marks for B7, whereas a thorough description of the arm movement would gain three marks.

Full marks for B8 can be achieved by using quantitative data. This may be a time/distance for each athletic event, a number of how many shots were scored in hockey shooting (make sure that you record out of how many shots they scored, for example one out of seven attempts were successful). The way in which you present this data is up to you, but do try to record some numerical data for each of the core skills that you observe. Any sheets that you include containing quantitative data, label B8.

In order to achieve the three full marks, you will need to provide a simple statement explaining your choice of analysis. This will be dependent on the type of data collected, but consider the percentage, mean, mode, median and ordinal or nominal data. For example, if you use percentages, you need to give a simple statement such as, 'Percent changes are useful to help understand changes in a value over a period of time.' Below is an example of how you might present your quantitative data. Now consider your five core skills and the different quantitative analysis possible.

Table 17.07 B8 – Quantitative data for observation of netball performance

Core skill	Description of quantitative assessment	Tally	Total	Percentage of successful shots
Passing (chest)	The number of passes caught by receiver at chest height (out of 10)	⊣⊣⊣⊣ II	7	70% *You should show the workings out for the percentage
	The number of times the performer transferred her weight during the pass (out of 10)	IIII	4	40%
Shooting	The number of goals scored (out of 10)	⊣⊣⊣⊣ I	6	60%
	Of the shots that were missed, how many hit the rim?	II	2	20%
Footwork	Number of times the footwork rule was successfully followed during the drill	⊣⊣⊣⊣ ⊣⊣⊣⊣	10	100%
Moving free	Number of times the performer was able to lose her marker to receive the pass	⊣⊣⊣⊣	5	50%
Marking	Number of times the performer was able to prevent the attacker from receiving the pass	II	2	20%
	Number of times the performer positioned themselves for a rebound	⊣⊣⊣⊣ II	7	70%

C1–5 Analysis (Total 15 marks)

In this section, you are required to go back to your observation sheets and select various strengths or weaknesses of your performer. These should be the ones that you consider to be the most important aspects of the performance you observed.

You need to select a minimum of two for each sport/activity, but a total of four to six strengths/weaknesses will make your analysis more thorough (a total of four to six strengths or weaknesses for each skill). Your strengths and weaknesses must relate to factors that you have written on your observation sheet – do not include new observations here.

Once you have selected your strengths or weaknesses, you need to analyse each one. You need to justify why it is a strength or weakness.

Example of an analysis for a strength:

'The performer's hands formed a "W" shape behind the ball (observation). This meant that they covered more surface area of the ball, which allowed more power to be transferred to the pass (analysis).'

Critical analysis: state the observation that you consider to be a strength or weakness, for example 'The netball player followed through with the chest pass,' then use one of the following phrases to analyse that strength/weakness:

- which meant that …
- this resulted in …
- which had the effect that …
- meaning that …

Example of an analysis for a weakness:

'The performer rarely jumped to intercept the shot (observation). This meant that they were unable to achieve the same amount of height to block the shot (analysis).'

Criteria order: keep sections C1–5 in the correct order, for example
C1 = major strengths or weaknesses from core skill 1, should be followed by
C2 = major strengths or weaknesses for core skill 2 and so on.

D1–2 Evaluation (Total 6 marks)

D1 – Focus on an area of weakness (Total 3 marks)

Having analysed your performer's strengths and weaknesses in sections C1–5, you are now required to consider the weakness that you consider to be the most important to improve. This weakness can be improving a skill as a whole or just a particular aspect of a skill.

Before making your final choice of one skill/aspect of a skill to improve, to get full marks in this section you need to suggest two to three weaknesses that are possible areas. Write a little about the importance of improving each weakness before you decide on your final area. Suggest how improving each weakness would improve their game/performance overall.

You need to mention the resources you would need to improve each weakness.

Conclude this section by stating which weakness you are going to improve.

D2 – Justification of choice of weakness (Total 3 marks)

Now you need to state say why you have decided to choose the weakness that has just been selected in the previous section. The justification should involve:
- why you have chosen that weakness
- what effect it currently has on the performance
- how performance would improve if you were to correct this weakness
- why you did not choose the others.

E1 – Bibliography (Total 3 marks)

A bibliography is a record of the books/magazines/Internet sites that you have used/referred to in your project. **All** sources of reference need to go in your bibliography. The bibliography is worth three easy marks. To gain any marks for the bibliography, you must follow the format in Table 17.08. To gain all three marks, you must use more than two resources of at least two different types.

Any source that you use should be recorded on your bibliography table straight away rather than at the end of your project.

Useful points:
- In a book, the information can usually be found inside the front cover.
- For a website, put the name of the website in the 'author' section. For example UK Athletics, and put the full web address in the 'title' section, also put the date you accessed the website in the date column.
- For a magazine, include the author if possible and the title as normal. The publisher should be available and the date/issue number.

Table 17.08 Organizing a bibliography

Author	Title	Publisher	Date

F1–3 Communication (Total 9 marks)

F1 – Neat and well-organized report (Total 3 marks)

To achieve the three marks for this section, you need to have presented a neat, well-organized and well-presented report. You should make sure that all sections follow the criteria order and that each section is clearly labelled, for example 'A1' heads up the section for the timetable.

You also need to make sure that the project is neat. It should be word processed or very neatly handwritten and maintain the same style and size font. A suggestion is for the project to:

- be spaced at 1.5 line spacing
- have a reasonable sized font (point 12, Times New Roman).

F2 – Communicate clearly in writing (Total 3 marks)

Make sure that you run a spell check on all of your work before the final print. Also get someone else to spell check and proofread. Having someone else to proofread your project is useful, as you may have become so involved in it that you read what you expect to see. There is no excuse these days to lose these three marks!

F3 – Use clear, labelled illustrations (Total 3 marks)

You need to make sure that you have used a range of illustrations within your project, for example photographs, diagrams, tables.

Refer to these diagrams as figures and number each one throughout the project, for example Figure 1, Figure 2 and so on. This makes for easy referencing, for example in your text you can say, 'See Figure 1 for a diagram of the tennis serve grip.'

Under the diagram you should have written Figure 1 and clearly labelled what Figure 1 one is showing, for example, 'The grip for a tennis serve.' If the diagram has been photocopied from a book/magazine or taken from the Internet, you must label the source from where you took the picture.

What happens to my project on completion?

- Present it to your teacher by the stated deadline.
- Your teacher will mark the piece of work.
- It may then be sent on for moderation purposes to an external examiner.

Index